also by Glen Klinkhart

A Cybercop's Guide to Internet Child Safety

Author, Glen Klinkhart

Glen Klinkhart was born and raised in Anchorage, Alaska and graduated from Linfield College in 1988. He was a police detective for over seventeen years and has worked hundreds of murder cases. One of the most successful and decorated detectives in the state of Alaska, he has been featured on such television shows as ABC's 20/20, CNN/TIME magazine and Dateline NBC. He is an experienced lecturer and trainer on such topics as overcoming adversity, Internet safety, personal safety and homicide investigations. He has given talks to local, statewide and national audiences. He is also recognized as an expert in the fields of Internet crime and computer forensics. Besides writing a number of short stories, his first book, a well received non-fiction book entitled, "A CyberCop's Guide to Internet Child Safety," is available on Amazon.com, iTunes, Kindle and the Nook ebook readers. Visit his web page at www.glenklinkhart.com.

To ANDREW,

ALL THE BEST!.!

Finding Bethany

By Glen Klinkhart

To Andrew,
ALL THE BEST !!

Dedication

To Dawn, for beginning my search.

To Bethany, for helping to find me.

Acknowledgements

This true crime memoir is based upon a story, my story. Some of the names have been changed and some of the characters have been combined for the sake of brevity. The crime scene re-creations in this narrative are based upon my years of training, experience, the physical evidence and my interviews with the witnesses and suspects. There were far too many people who assisted me along this path to single each and every one out by name. Suffice it to say I thank all of the hundreds of people who took their time to help find Bethany.

I must acknowledge a few people without whom this book would have never become a reality. To my son Evan, thank you for teaching me what it means to be a dad and what unconditional love is. To my oldest and dearest friend, Sabrina, thank you for believing in me and in *Finding Bethany*. Linda and Billy Correira, thank you for trusting me with your hopes and with your daughter. To my editor, David Holthouse, thank you for being willing to take a chance on this project and for pushing me beyond what even I believed was possible.

And to everyone reading this, may each of us find our own Bethany.

- *Glen Klinkhart*

Table of Contents

Chapter I   The Day

You don't have to have a murdered sister to be a good homicide detective, but it helps. Only now do I realize just how much it helps.

When I was a teenager I thought turning sixteen and getting my driver's license was going to be the most exciting time in my life. I had been saving for months and finally was ready to go shopping. Having a car meant everything to me. With a car I could get a job after school, see my friends and enjoy more than just a life of being sandwiched between a baby brother and older sister.

My sister Dawn was seventeen, the first born and favorite in the family. She was tall and thin. Her forward style and strong personality coupled with her blonde hair and deep blue eyes made her stand out in school. To Dawn school was a social activity, simply a place to meet and socialize with her friends.

Dawn was dedicated to finishing high school early. It wasn't that she was smarter than anyone else. She just wanted to finish school so she could finally be treated like a real adult. Dawn wanted to be a hairdresser and someday own her own salon. Anything she could do to speed up that process was fine by her.

My brother was four years younger than me and still in grade school. He was in every way the baby of the family. He too was gifted with blond hair and blue eyes. The genetic lottery saw fit to give me brown hair and green eyes. I was a quiet child and I worked hard for what I wanted. I worked odd jobs until I was finally able to get work fishing on a boat. Commercial fishing was the hardest job I ever had. By the end of the first summer I had already begun to develop arthritis in my young hands. The work was tough but the money meant I was going to be able to buy a car.

"Can we go look this weekend?" I asked my father.

"No," my dad told me. "It's Easter and we're going to Kenai to see

I

your Grandma and Grandpa. When we get back we can go look."

My father was a smart man. He was a biologist and had come to Alaska right out of college to study Alaska's various marine mammals, including whales and sea otters. In Alaska he met my mom, a stewardess for Cordova Airlines. They fell in love and stayed in Alaska to raise their family.

At sixteen years old I never truly appreciated the wonders of living in a place like Alaska. It seemed normal that the Chugach mountain range was behind our house. It was normal to me that the sun was up all day during the summer months. I could stay out late riding bikes or going fishing. Wearing sunglasses at midnight was not just a fashion statement but sometimes a necessity.

As the Easter weekend approached I learned that not all of us would be making the trip.

"Have a good time in Kenai," Dawn teased me. "I get to stay home."

I wasn't sure what made me angrier, the fact I had to put off my car shopping, or the fact that she got to stay home.

"Why do you get to stay?" I asked.

"Because I have a job and I have to work this weekend," she said in a syrupy tone.

I stormed off to confront my parents.

"That sucks. Why can't I stay home, too?"

My parents made it very clear that Dawn indeed had to work and the rest of the family was going to spend Easter with our grandparents. No matter how hard I tried, my parents would not budge. That only seemed to make my sister even more pleased. Later, as I was carrying my gear to the car I passed Dawn as I was going down the stairway.

"Are you going to have friends over?" I asked.

"Just a couple," she replied with a smile, prancing up the stairs.

That was pretty typical of my sister. She would often have people over when my parents were gone. My sister and her friends would sneak beers into the house and smoke cigarettes. Dawn's parties were never a large affair, but by the end of the night there was usually quite a series of small messes that needed to be cleaned up. It was I who often ended up making sure everything was safely put away before Mom and Dad got home. I would make sure my sister was safely in bed too. If Mom and Dad ever suspected anything, they never mentioned it.

After hearing Dawn's comment I again proposed to my parents that I not go to Kenai. I wasn't going to dime out my sister, no matter how shitty she was acting, but I was unable to come up with a good reason to tell my parents why I should stay. Their answer was a direct and stern "No."

By the afternoon the family car was packed. I was still too mad at Dawn to tell her goodbye so I just looked at her and scowled. She smiled and waved nonchalantly as the car pulled away.

I settled down in the back seat with my brother for the two-hour drive south. By the time we reached my grandparents' house I had all but forgotten about my sister. My grandparents had been living along the coast near the Kenai River for many years. It's famous for its world-class fishing. The largest king salmon ever caught was taken from the Kenai River and weighed nearly 100 pounds.

My brother and I played on the beach and searched the gritty sand dunes for buried treasures in the form of small, colorful rocks and shells. That evening we made a fire down on the beach where we cooked hotdogs and roasted marshmallows until it was time for bed.

The next morning brought a knock at my grandparents' door. I didn't hear the knock. I just remember being told by my father to gather up our things because we were heading back home immediately. My dad was standing at the bottom of the stairs. He didn't look like my dad. His face was sullen and his eyes were glassy. He seemed calm. But he didn't seem right.

"Did you hear what happened?" he asked.

I hadn't, but I opened my mouth and said the first thing that popped into my head.

"Yes," I replied.

"Okay, then get down here and get your bags in the car," he said.

We piled into the car. I moved to the back and sat by myself. For the next several hours nobody said a word. I didn't know what happened. I didn't know what to think. I didn't know what to do. Nobody was saying anything. I just sat in the back quietly and stared out the window.

As we got closer to Anchorage I reached into my bag and grabbed my portable radio. For a while I was able to lose myself in the music. Soon the music ended and the news came on and then came that moment I'll never forget:

In other news, a fire today has claimed the life of a girl in a residence in the Upper O'Malley area of Anchorage. Firefighters and police are on the scene of the blaze on Snowline Drive. The girl, whose name has not been released pending notification of next-of-kin, appeared to be home alone at the time of the fire.

I reached over and turned off the radio. I wanted to cry but for some reason I could not. I just sat there and wanted to get home as fast as I could.

When we arrived on the street along Snowline Drive, my dad had a difficult time finding a place to park. There were fire trucks and police everywhere. My dad settled on a parking spot way at the end of our street. We got out of the car and began walking towards our house. My father was just ahead of me as we reached the bottom of our driveway. I stopped as I felt something moving around my feet. I looked down and watched a stream of water

4

rushing down the road and around my shoes. It looked like a river had opened up at the top of our driveway. I realized the water was coming from inside our house.

Our home was on the side of the hill. It was a brown colored, three-story A-framed house. My father had bought the land several years earlier. A contractor built the outer structure but my father finished it himself. He still likes to tell the story of how he climbed a tree on the lot just so he could decide exactly where and how high to build the house. It worked. The view from our home overlooked the entire city of Anchorage and the waters of Cook Inlet. On a clear day you could see the highest mountain in North America, Mount McKinley, a hundred and fifty miles away from our front deck.

As the water rushed around my shoes I looked up and saw a large man in a bright blue uniform walking quickly in our direction. I recognized the police uniform and the round hat of an Alaska State Trooper. He stopped in front of my father.

"We don't like what's going on here. We're not happy about it at all!" he shouted at us.

My father said nothing and waved at me to stay put. He followed the Trooper up the river that was once my driveway.

The Trooper doesn't like what is going on here?

He is not happy?

What the hell does that mean?

I was confused.

I walked back to our car and waited with my mom and my brother. All I could think about was that Trooper.

Why is he being rude?

My sister's dead and he doesn't like what's going on?

He's not happy? What about us? Do we look like we're happy?

What the hell is wrong with him?

A few minutes later my father returned. He said something to my mother and we drove away to spend the next several nights at a friend's house. I couldn't rest as my younger brother kept me up each night with his incessant crying. I begged my mother to please make him stop but there was nothing she could do. I didn't cry. I just wanted to sleep.

I learned the next morning that there was more to my sister's death than simply a fire. My parents told my brother and me that there had been some sort of party at our house. They said someone had killed Dawn and set our house on fire. The police were still looking for the person responsible.

Someone killed her?

They set the house on fire?

Who would do that?

Why?

A few days later my father said that the police were done with whatever it was they were doing in our house. He asked me if I wanted to go back with him. I did in the worst way. I grabbed my jacket and jumped into the front seat of our car.

Soon I was standing in front of our house. I didn't see much out of the ordinary at first, just a huge black hole in the top of the roof, but I sure could smell it. The odor was not like anything I had smelled before. The overpowering stench was that of burned wood, charred household items and wet sheetrock. It was everywhere.

I followed my dad as he walked into the house. Everything was covered in ash and soot. The carpet squished with water. In the downstairs family room I saw scattered plastic cups, glasses and beer bottles. On the floor was a silver beer keg. It appeared Dawn had had more than a few friends over this time.

Why wasn't I here?

I should have been here.

I walked up the stairs, turned to my left and into my bedroom. Wet, broken sheet rock and large chunks of ceiling tiles covered the floor. All four walls were covered in black charred soot. The floor had standing pools of water where carpet should have been. I stepped into this terrible place that was once my bedroom. There was a huge hole in the ceiling. I looked up and into the charred blackness of what was once my sister's upstairs bedroom.

I wanted to cry but I didn't. I had seen enough. As I was about to turn and leave I noticed something on the floor near my foot. I bent over to get a closer look. In amongst the black debris, a necklace with a small gold crucifix attached was barely visible. It was Dawn's. It must have fallen through the hole from upstairs. I reached over and pulled the necklace out of the debris. I stood up and put the necklace in my pocket then walked out. The toxic smell lingered in my nose even after I left.

Our local newspaper reported the story:

Anchorage Daily News: Homicide Suspected in Fire Death

Alaska State Troopers say the Easter Sunday death of a 17-year-old Anchorage girl in a one-room fire may have been a homicide. Firefighters discovered the body of Dawn Marie Klinkhart after they had extinguished a fire at the Klinkhart residence on Snowline Drive near O'Malley Road. Capt. Lowell Parker of the Troopers said an autopsy would be conducted today to determine the cause of death. But he said suspicious circumstances surrounding the fire have made law officials believe the blaze was not an accident.

Each night at bedtime the scene repeated itself. My brother would cry and my mother would hold and comfort him until he finally fell asleep from exhaustion. Only then would I be able to sleep.

7

On the third night I lay in my unfamiliar bed and listened to my brother's crying. This night his sobs were accompanied by the sound of heavy rain beating against the window. My brother was finally asleep when I heard the doorbell. Trying not to wake him I rolled out of bed and put on a pair of pants and a sweatshirt before sneaking into the hallway. I pressed myself up against the wall so no one would see me. I watched as my father answered the front door.

In the light of the open doorway I could see rain coming down. Two dark figures stood in the entrance. As my eyes adjusted I could see the two men were soaking wet despite their raincoats. My father showed them into the small living room where they all sat down.

"Thanks for seeing us," one of the men said as he took off his hat. The other man turned to my mother and spoke, "Ma'am, I'm Assistant District Attorney Steve Branchflower and this is Detective Chuck Miller."

My mother nodded her head.

"We hate to bother you so late but we wanted to tell you folks first," the man said. "Tonight we arrested someone for Dawn's murder."

My father held my mother as she began to cry.

"His name is Alan Chase Jr. He was one of the guests at the party. He wasn't a friend of your daughter's. We believe that he was there with someone else."

"Did he rape her?" my father asked bluntly.

"We believe that he did, sir," said the detective.

My teeth clenched as I heard the detective's words. My father held my mother even tighter.

"We believe that he entered the house. He attacked your daughter as she slept. She managed to fight him. During the fight we believe she bit him. When we tracked him down he had a bite mark that appears to match Dawn's teeth impressions. When confronted, Chase admitted to the murder."

Who was this man Chase?

Why was he there?

I could have stopped him.

Branchflower continued: "Chase said that he strangled Dawn. He started the fire and he ran out of the house. We're charging him with murder in the first degree, sexual assault, kidnapping and arson."

My mother again began to cry. My father rocked her back and forth.

Why did I have to go to Kenai?

Why couldn't I have stayed home?

I should have been there.

Both men thanked my parents for their time and stood up to leave. Branchflower glanced down the hallway where I was hiding. For a moment our eyes met. He nodded at me. I quickly hid behind the corner as the men left.

Quietly I crept back into my room. I drew the covers up close to me. I rolled over and stared out the window. I watched as the drops of rain repeatedly, almost rhythmically, struck the glass. The rain danced on the window as I closed my eyes and tried to sleep.

Dawn Marie Klinkhart, age 17.

The author, Glen Edward Klinkhart, age 15.

Chapter 2   Good Night Becky

"Good night, Becky," Dawn said as she hugged her friend.

"Great party!" Becky replied.

"Well, I'll see you on Monday," Dawn yelled as Becky and the other girls drove away from the house. Dawn shut the door and started upstairs. She paused for a moment as she noticed the cups and bottles strewn about the downstairs family room. "I'll pick it up tomorrow," she thought. Her head was cloudy and ringing from all of the beer. She had to use the handrail to steady herself as she went up the stairs to her bedroom. Reaching the third floor of the house, Dawn entered her room and prepared to go to sleep. Her clothes smelled of beer and cigarettes. She disrobed, leaving her clothes on the floor and changed into her nightgown. She lifted up the covers on her bed and slid onto her mattress.

Dawn closed her eyes for a moment and then remembered she had to be up by noon. She reached over and set her alarm clock. "Ahhhh, sleep at last," she thought.

Outside the house, a small brown sedan drove up the long driveway. A man got out of the passenger side door. He turned and said to the driver, "Don't worry I'll get a ride back later." He shut the car door. The vehicle backed up and drove away.

Alan Chase Jr. approached the front door and tried the knob. It was unlocked. He eased the door open and stepped inside. . .

Chapter 3   Rain, Rain, Go Away

The rain was falling in buckets. It doesn't rain much in Anchorage but when it does it can really come down. I switched off the windshield wipers and peered through the rain-spattered windshield of my unmarked police car.

This looks like the right address.

After avoiding the inevitable soaking for as long as I could, I half-ran to the door of the residence and pressed the doorbell. I held my breath as I waited for an answer.

The door swung open. The woman before me was in her mid-forties and blonde like her sister. And like her sister, this woman too looked like she had not had an easy life.

"Terry Payne?" I asked.

"Yes. Who are you?" she said, holding the door in front of her like a shield.

"I'm Detective Glen Klinkhart, Anchorage Police Department." I held up my badge.

"How can I help you?"

"I would like to talk to you about your sister, Denise," I said.

Nervously, she pushed the door aside and allowed me into the apartment. Toys, papers and other items strewn about the tiny home. As I walked towards the kitchen I recognized the distinct odor of a cat, possibly more than one. Terry motioned for me to sit down across from her at the kitchen table. I brushed away the rain from the back of my neck.

"Would you like something to drink?" she offered.

"No thanks" I replied. "I hate to bother you this late but I wanted

13

to tell you first. Earlier tonight I arrested a man for your sister's murder."

Terry looked down at her hands folded in front of her. She paused, looked up and then spoke, "Thank you. I thought everyone had forgotten about my sister."

"I didn't. She didn't deserve to die like that. She had family who cared about her," I said.

She replied: "I know that Denise wasn't always a good person. But she wasn't always like that. It was the drugs that put her on the street."

Her sister was right. Denise wasn't a bad person. She was a beautiful, tall blonde with long legs and an incredible smile. Her friends and family told me she was once a fashion model who traveled around the country doing photo shoots. That was before she became hooked on drugs. After years of addiction and bad relationships she fell into prostitution. At the time of Denise's murder she was working as an escort for the Bunny Club, one of Anchorage's more notorious fronts for prostitution.

It had only been a few years earlier when I was working as a rookie detective in the downtown district for the Anchorage Police Department that I first became interested in learning more about homicide investigations. One day I got up enough courage to approach the head of the Homicide unit, Sergeant Spadafora. I asked him if there were any cold case files I could read. "Spad," as we called him affectionately, directed me to a large cardboard box underneath his desk.

"Here ya go!" he said handing me the box. "Knock yourself out."

In the box were a series of case files referencing an eight-year old murder of a local prostitute named Denise Payne. The files included reports, transcripts, photos and videotapes. They were a mess. I spent the next three days poring over the contents. I put the loose and torn reports into binders and separated them by topic. Narratives written by the investigators went in one section, the interviews in another and the evidence lists went in still another section.

The case fascinated me. I began spending all my free time on it. The basic facts were that a client known only as "Frank" had called Denise at the Bunny Club to arrange an escort for the night. A taxi driver dropped her off late at night at an office building in the Fairview area of Anchorage. During the day the business was an office and gathering place for people with mental health issues. At night the building was supposed to be locked up. The cab driver recalled dropping Denise off and seeing a white adult male open the door to let her inside. The cab driver was the last person to see Denise alive.

The next morning, the building's office manager noticed the door to the upstairs office had been forced open. He went upstairs and found Denise dead in the middle of the hallway. She had been beaten multiple times about the head and face with a hammer. A blanket had been placed over her head. A red, checkered shirt was underneath her body.

According to the cold case file, investigators had interviewed dozens of people and seized hundreds of items as evidence. Many of the individuals associated with the building were clients of the mental health facility and their accounts had proven difficult for detectives to check out.

I continued to read and re-read the Denise Payne files in between my normal police duties. I pulled the physical evidence and examined each of the items from the crime scene. I questioned the forensic lab personnel. I met with other officers and detectives who had been at the scene and had worked the case. I watched the crime scene video over and over again, hoping to find anything that would help me figure out who killed Denise.

I didn't have a great deal to work with. The clues were sparse. There was the unidentified adult white male who answered the door. There was a box of office equipment found outside the building near a window. I often wondered if the items in the box were part of an actual burglary or put there as a ruse.

In the shirt found underneath Denise's body there was a bogus printed check made out to the Bunny Club in the amount of $500. I was able to determine that an office computer in the building was used to print the check on the night of the murder. Investigators had previously located a book of stamps in the shirt pocket. The stamps contained a single fingerprint. Every so often I asked our internal fingerprint lab to run the unknown print through the statewide and national fingerprint databases looking for a hit. Each time I had no luck. I pulled the shirt from evidence and personally examined it for clues. Using a cotton applicator I swabbed the area around the collar of the shirt for any possible DNA that might identify a suspect.

I sent the swab to the State of Alaska Scientific Crime Detection Laboratory for DNA analysis. After several months I received word the swab from the shirt yielded a suitable DNA profile for comparison. Unfortunately, however, the DNA profile did not match anyone in the known DNA database.

For the better part of two years I worked Denise's case as best I could. I came up with a good suspect, the computer administrator at the mental health office. He had set up the office computer network and was responsible for the accounting software that printed the fake Bunny Club check.

I looked closely into the suspect's background and discovered that besides his own mental health issues he had a history of picking up prostitutes and occasionally getting into a few physical altercations with them. One witness I interviewed explained how he had pushed a prostitute's head into the dashboard of his car when she demanded payment for her services. When questioned by the original detectives in Denise's case, the suspect was unable to provide a good alibi for the night of the murder. He told investigators he went to the movies alone that night. The movie theatre he named was easily within walking distance of the murder scene.

I interviewed my prime suspect on several occasions. He continued to deny having anything to do with Denise's death. There were two pieces of evidence that supported his story: it wasn't his fingerprint on the stamp book, nor was it his DNA on the shirt collar. Other detectives encouraged me to arrest him despite the physical evidence, but I couldn't bring myself to do it. It was a stalemate.

It had been over three years since I first looked into Denise's cold case. One day I was at the police station when one of the senior homicide detectives, Joe Hoffbeck, caught me in the hallway. Detective Hoffbeck had over 30 years of experience as a law enforcement officer. Not only was Hoffbeck one of the most experienced investigators we had, he was well liked by everyone, including me.

"Glen, have you got a minute?" Joe asked.

"Sure Joe, what ya got?"

"There's a guy at the front counter who says he killed a lady a few years ago. I don't know what he is talking about," Joe said. "The only case that I can recall that's even remotely close is your lady at that mental clubhouse."

We walked to the front counter together and there stood a short, stocky and unkempt young man. His hair was greasy and the shirt he wore indicated that he worked at a local fast food restaurant. The nametag on his lapel read "ALEX." He didn't look like a clever murderer. He looked more like an underachiever barely out of high school.

I introduced myself and we walked to a private interview room. The soft-spoken young man told me his name was Alexander Eckhardt. As I listened to his words, his inflections and his difficulty in searching for cohesive thoughts, it became apparent he likely had mental health issues.

"Great," I thought. "I don't have time for this. I'm going to get stuck for hours listening to someone confess to something he didn't do."

I turned on a tape recorder and asked Alex to tell me about himself. Alex spoke about growing up in Alaska. He said he'd worked as a fast food cook for the past several years. When I asked Alex to explain why he was at the police station, he said that several years ago he'd broken into an office building in the Fairview neighborhood and that he killed a lady there.

"Did you steal anything from the business?"

"I stole a box of office supplies but I left them outside," he replied.

"What did you use to kill the lady?"

His voice never wavered and continued in a stoic tone, "I found a hammer in one of the rooms."

"Okay, Alex, how many times did you hit her with the hammer?" I asked.

"I dunno, maybe four or five times," he replied. "She tried to get away by running down the hall."

I listened carefully but didn't hear anything from him that hadn't already been reported by local newspapers and TV stations.

It was only when I asked Alex to describe how he got into the upstairs portion of the office, did the hair on the back of my neck stand up.

"I kicked the door with my foot, but it wouldn't open, so I found a shovel and pried the door open," Alex admitted.

"What did you do with the shovel?" I asked.

"I think I left it upstairs," he replied. "I don't remember for sure."

After initially poring over this case my theory was the killer had kicked in the door in order to access the upstairs part of the business. The door had indeed been forced open and a very good shoe impression had been found on the door panel. It wasn't until I looked at the crime scene video years afterward that I spied on the tape a brief image of a shovel in the corner of an upstairs closet. I thought a shovel in an empty closet was unusual, but it did not seem significant to me at the time. I, like other investigators, assumed the footprint on the door meant it was kicked open. The presence of the shovel had not been reported in the media. The investigators at the time didn't even feel it was important enough to photograph. Its existence was only documented on a few incidental frames of video tape.

I asked Alex if he would consent to giving me his fingerprints and a DNA swab. He agreed. While he and I were still in the interview room our fingerprint lab technicians compared his prints with the impressions on the book of stamps from the shirt found underneath Denise's body. They matched. Later testing showed the DNA on the shirt also matched his.

This short, unassuming man who had difficulty keeping his thoughts together was confessing to a murder he had in fact committed. I had been looking at the wrong person all along. In another place or time I might have even arrested the wrong man. Alexander Eckhardt had indeed killed Denise Payne. It wasn't my talent or skills that found him. It was his own conscience that brought him in that day. I simply sat and listened.

"And so, Ms. Payne, I am convinced Mr. Eckhardt is responsible for your sister's murder," I told her. "He has been charged with murder in the first degree and his bail had been set at $200,000, cash only."

"Will he get out on bail" she asked.

"No, Ms. Payne. I am quite certain he is going to stay in jail."

I gave her my business card. She led me from the kitchen to the front door.

"Detective Klinkhart, I can't thank you enough for not forgetting about my sister." Terry reached over and hugged me.

"There are some people you should never forget," I whispered to her. "Your sister was one of them."

I stood outside as the apartment door shut. I paused for a moment as the rain continued to fall. I made a dash for the car. Getting into my seat I brushed the water from my face and started the car. It roared to life. Instead of putting the car into gear, I turned the key and shut off the engine.

I just sat there, staring out the window, listening to the rain pound the car and watching the water run down the glass in sheets. For the next few minutes I simply sat in my car and tried my best to remember my sister.

Chapter 4   Look What You Made Me Do

"Hi, baby," the voice whispered in her ear.

Dawn's eyes flashed open. A man was climbing on top of her. His eyes were bloodshot and his breath smelled of stale beer. He was completely nude.

"Ready for some fun?" he said.

"What the hell are you doing?" she screamed. "Get the fuck off of me!"

Dawn rolled over and tried to get up. Alan Chase Jr. grabbed my sister's hair and pulled her back down onto the bed.

"The party's not over, bitch!"

As Chase began to yank Dawn's gown up with his right hand she instinctively reached over and bit down on his left forearm as hard as she could.

"Fuck!" Chase screamed in pain. He released his grip on her gown and began to punch her repeatedly in the head. Finally Dawn released her grip on Chase's arm. Enraged he continued to strike Dawn repeatedly. She tried to protect herself by raising her arms but he was too big and the blows came too fast. Dawn began to lose consciousness.

"Fucking bitch!" Chase yelled and ripped Dawn's nightgown. Chase lowered himself and forced himself into her. Dawn came to, cried out in pain and tried to push him away.

"Stop fuckin' moving!" Chase demanded.

"Fuck you!" Dawn screamed. She managed to reach an empty bottle on her nightstand. She swung the bottle as hard as she could. It struck Chase on the side of the head with a dull thud. Chase stopped and held the side of his face with his hands.

Chase's eyes widened and his teeth clenched.

"You fucking cunt!" he yelled as he pounded her skull against the headboard. Dawn quit moving and fell into unconsciousness. Chase reached over and grabbed the bottle.

"You like this bottle so much, bitch? You can have it!"

He shoved the bottle repeatedly between her legs.

When he finished Chase stood over her. He was covered in sweat and blood.

"Why the fuck did you make me do that?" He said to the body on the bed. "Look what you made me do."

Chase gathered up his clothes, but forgot his green baseball cap on the floor. He dressed and headed downstairs to the garage. There he found containers of gasoline and starter fluid. He gathered up the bottles and quickly took them upstairs. He re-entered Dawn's bedroom and poured the contents around the floor, the bed and onto her half naked, motionless body.

Chase struck a match and threw it at her. Dawn was still breathing as the flames exploded. Chase ran down the stairs and out the front door.

A few minutes later a third story window of the house exploded and clouds of black smoke billowed out. Neighbors noticed the commotion and called 911.

Chapter 5   The A Street Bridge

It was just another workday when I arrived at the office. The Anchorage Police Department homicide unit was a large, open expanse of desks and chairs. My desk was located in the back of the office. There was a large white dry erase board on a nearby wall. I glanced at the prominent "Murder Board." It displayed each of the various murders for the year. Each row on the board designated a murder along with its case number, the crime date, the victim, the suspect and the detective assigned to the case. Black ink meant the case was solved and a suspect was in custody. If the case was written in red marker then the case was still unsolved. Black was good. Red was bad.

It had been another good year for the APD homicide unit. It was March and we had five homicides thus far. Four of them were in black ink. The previous year we'd investigated twenty homicides and we solved every one. Our unit has a 94 percent average solve rate. The national average is a pitiful 64 percent.

I grabbed a black marker and wrote:

APD Case 53092
D. Payne/A. Eckhardt
Det. Klinkhart
Case: Closed

I placed the marker back in the tray and continued walking over to my office. I walked past the sergeant seated at his desk.

Sarge, as we called him, looked as if he had just stepped out of some old police television show. He was a large-framed man with a foul, imposing disposition. Sarge's hair was always meticulously cut in clean, short, military style and was colored so dark I often suspected there was a liberal application of hair dye. Sarge was brash, loud and always had something to say about you and your case. His answer to everything was to shout. If that didn't work his next logical step was to shout even louder. Sarge's interviewing techniques consisted entirely of getting in the suspect's face and yelling at the top of his lungs. That might look good on TV, but it never works in the real world. When he wasn't yelling at us, Sarge could typically be found surfing the Internet for guns or Marine collectables. He often took time to remind me he had been in the military while I had not. I went to college.

Next to the Sarge was the desk of my partner, Detective Mark Huelskoetter. Huelskoetter was the brainiac of the Homicide Unit. He could recite witnesses' Social Security and telephone numbers from memory. Detective Huelskoetter's desk was also the most cluttered in the unit. No one else could ever find anything on it.

The rest of the homicide detectives had their desks lined neatly in rows, one after the other. I was one of the newer detectives, so my desk was way back in the corner. It was metal and tan in color with a fake wood veneer top. I called our office furniture "government plain."

I dropped my briefcase on the side of the desk and threw my coat over the chair. I began searching through the many piles of papers on my desk. After a few minutes I located a single brown file folder. I opened the folder and pulled out a driver's license photo. It showed an attractive, blonde, blue-eyed woman in her twenties. Denise Payne. I grabbed a pushpin from my desk drawer and pinned Denise's photo on the wall next to my desk. Denise's picture was not alone.

Next to her was a black and white photograph of Shawna Evon, a nine-year-old girl found dead in an alley behind a bar called The Monkey Wharf. Her murder was still unsolved. Next to Shawna's photo was a picture of Cynthia Henry. I didn't have a good photo of Cynthia to put up on the wall, so I had to use one of her old driver's license photographs.

Cindy Henry was a person who did what she had to do to survive living on the streets of downtown Anchorage, even if that meant committing petty theft or prostituting herself. Cindy was one of the first homeless people that I met as a young rookie patrol officer. Growing up in Anchorage I had no idea that people like

Cindy even existed. Other than the occasional sighting of a homeless person begging for money on a street corner, I never really gave them much of a thought. But as a rookie officer I spent a lot of time working the downtown area and as such I had the opportunity to get to know many of the homeless, including Cindy.

She was a short, Alaska Native woman. Although she was usually unkempt and wore whatever clothes she could get her hands on, Cindy was almost always smiling. Whether she was drunk, sober or in handcuffs for some minor offense, Cynthia's big smile and large rosy cheeks greeted me each time I saw her.

Except for the last time I saw Cynthia Henry, she was not smiling and neither was I. That particular day was a cold, wet, fall morning. A 911 dispatcher telephoned and pointed me to the A Street Bridge in downtown Anchorage. A citizen had reported seeing a body on top of one of the concrete support buttresses under the bridge. The A Street Bridge is the thoroughfare that connects downtown traffic to the Government Hill suburb and the military base north of Anchorage. I knew the area well. I used to take my young son, Evan, sledding when he was a toddler on the nearby hills during the Fur Rendezvous Winter Carnival. After sledding we would drink hot chocolate and watch the colorful carnival fireworks explode high over the A Street Bridge.

This time I was standing underneath the bridge's massive steel supports in a cold drizzle. The ground under the bridge was littered with cigarette butts, discarded beer cans and used condoms. An old wooden pallet was pushed up against the cement foundation wall. I surmised that homeless individuals used the pallet as a makeshift ladder to reach the landing on top of the wall. There wasn't much room between the landing and the beams supporting the road above it. The homeless would often seek refuge in the space to sleep, drink or both.

As I looked up at the top of the large concrete wall I could see the outline of her body. Cynthia Henry was lying face down on top of the ledge. She was completely naked except for her jeans, which were pulled down around her feet. A trail of blood dripped from underneath her body. A dried waterfall of crimson worked its way down the side of the wall and onto the ground. On the wall next to the drips of blood I noticed some old spray-painted graffiti that read, "Native Pride."

Our evidence team had set up a ladder next to the wall. I climbed up to get a better look. The roar of the cars and trucks on the highway above me shook the bridge as they passed only a few feet above my head. From this vantage point I could see that the blood trail originated from Cindy's back. There were at least four large stab wounds. Each appeared to have been made by large, single-edged knife. The blood pooled and then dripped onto her cardboard bed. Eventually the cardboard became saturated, allowing the blood to drip over the edge of the wall. Cindy's head was turned away from me and was facing the wall of the alcove. Based upon her body positioning and cramped area I surmised that there was only one assailant. Cindy was likely asleep when she was attacked. She probably never even saw her killer.

Looking along her body I saw a vodka bottle. The neck of the bottle had been shoved in the space between Cindy's nude butt cheeks. It was a cheap brand of vodka. Five dollar rotgut.

This guy wanted to do more than just kill her.

He wanted to humiliate her.

He wanted us to see this.

I found a few other items in Cindy's makeshift concrete and cardboard bedroom. Trash, including some old newspapers and empty food wrappers, littered the tight confines of the urine and alcohol-soaked space.

I climbed down the ladder and asked the crime scene team to make sure to photograph and seize the liquor bottle.

I spent the rest of the fall working in and out of the homeless camps and bars around the downtown area, looking for leads on Cindy's killer. I personally spent so much of my time going into and out of the downtown bars looking for witnesses that I became accustomed to the stench of stale beer and cigarette smoke. Even the bartenders knew me by name in downtown dives like the Panhandle and the Avenue Bar. Everyone there had known Cindy and they all said the same thing: Cynthia Henry may have been homeless but she didn't have any enemies. I heard time and time again how Cindy would share what she had, no matter how little it was, with anyone who asked. She, like many homeless women, spent her life living in fear of being a victim.

Meanwhile the vodka bottle provided me with more questions than answers. The bottle itself did not even contain vodka. In fact there was no alcohol in it whatsoever. The clear liquid inside was simply water. Examining the bottle in the laboratory revealed no fingerprints. It was only after I accidentally tipped it over I noticed on the very bottom of the bottle, in the concave portion of the base, there appeared to be some sort of faint impression. Spraying that portion of the bottle with Luminol, a chemical that reacts with blood, revealed a perfectly preserved partial palm print. The negative image of the print also told me that whoever left the print had blood on his hand prior to leaving the impression.

I surmised that whoever killed Cindy had stabbed her, causing her to bleed out from her multiple wounds. Only then did her attacker insert the neck of the bottle into Cindy's anus, leaving the bloody impression on the base of the bottle as he applied pressure with his blood-soaked hands.

The problem with this clue was that in the normal course of business we in law enforcement don't often take people's palm prints, so there was no large database like that of fingerprints I could use to find a match.

Cynthia's case remained stagnant for several years until one night one of our patrol officers arrested a man for a drunk driving offense. Like many streetwise criminals, he wanted to make a deal by exchanging information for leniency. He told the officer that he had information about a murder. He said that his old roommate years earlier had come home one night with blood all over him and said that he was attacked while in downtown Anchorage. The roommate claimed that he stabbed the guy who attacked him. The next morning the roommate became very nervous when the media reported that a body was found under the A Street Bridge. The snitch told the officer that his roommate had even insisted on driving downtown where they saw the Anchorage Police Department crime scene van parked next to the bridge. The officer wrote down the information and forwarded it to my office. I found the report on my chair the next morning.

As I drank my coffee, I painstakingly read the report. The suspect's name was Roger Wade McKinley.

McKinley was not a homeless person. Rather he was a man with a troubled past who frequented downtown bars, drinking and getting into trouble. I pulled up his criminal history. The 30-year-old McKinley had logged over 25 documented criminal charges, beginning when he was still a minor. They included multiple alcohol offenses, burglary, resisting arrest, forgery and several assault charges. I pulled his case files and found that he had been charged with assaulting several people and had once threatened a girlfriend with a knife.

I picked up my phone and called the dispatch center.

"Hi, this is Klinkhart," I said. "I need to put out a Stop and Hold in the computer system for a murder suspect."

It didn't take long to find Roger Wade McKinley. Patrol officers found him later that night downtown in the Gaslight Bar. One hour later he was at the police station.

I opened the door and entered the interview room.

"Mr. McKinley?" I asked as I reached out my hand to him.

A tall, muscular, Alaska Native man stood up. The various jail tattoos, his handle bar mustache and his muscular frame led me to believe I'd been smart to have a couple of officers stand guard just outside the door. If McKinley went sideways on me I was going to have a tough fight on my hands.

I smiled while simultaneously trying not to give away my own nervousness. McKinley looked at me. He was clearly sizing me up. He paused, smirked and then shook my hand. I noticed one of the tattoos on his forearm, a native art design done in red and black ink. It looked like a whale or a fish of some kind.

"Is that a native ink?" I asked, pointing to the tattoo.

He smiled. "Yes, I am a warrior. This is my symbol, the shark."

"So were you born in Southeast Alaska?" I asked.

"Yeah, I grew up in Juneau, I'm Tlingit." he said.

I knew he was Tlingit Indian before I walked into the room. I asked about his tattoo because I hoped that talking about his connection with his own tribal history might get him to talk to me or at the very least keep him from beating the crap out of me in the confined interview room.

"Roger, I asked that you be brought down here so you and I can have a chat," I said. "And by the way, you are not under arrest."

McKinley simply stared at me. He looked as if he was ready to pounce over the table at any moment.

"I just have some questions to ask you and I certainly don't want to insult your intelligence, but I have to read you your Miranda rights because you are here in a police station and it's important that you know those rights. Okay?"

I waited. This was where McKinley was either going to tell me to fuck off or where he was going to say something useful.

He stared at me without blinking and said, "I wanna hear what you got to say."

I pulled out my Miranda card and read each of his rights to him, including his right to remain silent. At the end of each right I asked him if he understood what I had just read to him.

McKinley replied with a simple "yes" to each of the rights. He had clearly heard them before. Just as clearly, he wanted to know what I knew.

When I was finished, I put the card back in my pocket. I then gave McKinley my opening speech. Having an opening speech to sell to a suspect gives you the opportunity to tell him what it is you want to talk about and it sets the stage for the entire interview. In this case I wanted McKinley to believe that his trip to the police station was no big deal and that I was going to eliminate him as I had much more important things to do with my time.

"Roger, you are only here because your name came up in an investigation."

McKinley sat up straight.

"It did huh?"

"Well, it's likely bullshit," I said. "But I wouldn't be doing my job if I didn't at least give you the courtesy of asking you about it in person. It's just a formality and you likely have nothing to do with it. Listen, it's three o'clock in the morning. I don't want to be here anymore than you do. I just want to ask you about this case and when you tell me that you had nothing to do with it, then we both can go home."

I looked at him for a reaction.

Defensively, he folded his arms in front of him. "Ask your questions," he said.

I pulled out a driver's license photo of Cindy Henry and slid it across the desk. His eyes glanced down at it for a moment and then came back to meet my gaze.

"Do you know Cindy Henry?"

"Nope."

"Did you hear about her murder?"

"Nope."

"Have you ever been down underneath the A Street Bridge?"

"Nope."

"So you have never been underneath there or up on top of the buttress of the cement wall?"

"I've never been there," he said.

"Okay, good," I said. "Then you and I are just about done."

"Do you have a knife, with a six-inch, single edge blade?" I asked.

"Nope" he said.

"Did you kill Cindy Henry underneath the A Street Bridge?"

"Nope," he said and then added. "Like I told you, I am a warrior and warriors don't hurt women."

From reviewing his case file, I knew that was a lie but I kept going.

"Good... that's what I thought too," I said. "That's about it... oh, one more thing, would you be willing to give me a set of palm prints before you go?"

"Sure" he said.

The next time I saw Roger Wade McKinley was only a few days later. He was back in the interview room, except this time I had him brought in handcuffed and under arrest for murder.

"Hi Roger," I said as I sat down in a chair in front of him. "Roger, I understand that you are under arrest for the murder of Cindy Henry underneath the A Street Bridge."

"That's bullshit!" he screamed as he started to get up. "I told you I was never fucking there!"

"Yes, yes you did, now sit down..."

I put up my hand and he sat back.

"...and that is why I wanted to ask you a couple more questions about it... perhaps between the two of us, we can clear this whole thing up... I just need to read you your Miranda rights again."

Although McKinley was clearly pissed off at being in custody, I figured that he might believe that with my help, he might be able to talk his way out of this. If he believed that, then my plan might work.

He again agreed to waive his rights. I asked him a series of preplanned questions. The exact wording of the questions and the order in which I asked them were going to be my key to gaining a confession.

"Roger, you told me last time that you had never been under the A Street Bridge. Correct?"

"That's right, I've never been there." His hands moved slightly forward towards me. He heard the rattle of the cuffs and stopped moving.

"Well, I'm sorry Roger but it turns out that wasn't completely true was it?" I said, trying to portray myself like a concerned guidance counselor talking to one of his students.

"It doesn't mean that you killed Cindy, but you were there... your prints were found under the A Street Bridge."

Roger's dark eyes stared at me.

"Well, yeah maybe I was there a long time ago," he explained. "Maybe that's it."

McKinley was clearly an experienced criminal. He knew that fingerprints can't be dated and that it was possible that his prints could have been left there years before.

"You are right Roger, but that is why I wanted to talk to you myself," I said. "See, when you and I talked last, you told me you are a warrior and warriors don't hurt women, which is why I was so confused by all of this."

He leaned forward.

"Roger, I don't necessarily think that you meant to hurt Cindy, in fact you strike me as the kind of guy that may have been up there checking on her... isn't that what your warrior spirit would do?"

McKinley's hands began shaking. I couldn't tell if that was because he was nervous or because he was thinking about strangling me.

"Look Roger, I know that you were up there with Cindy that night. Your prints were found up there."

I waited. I was going to let the silence speak in McKinley's ears for a while. I waited. He waited. Neither of us spoke.

Then suddenly McKinley did it. He put himself there.

"You're right" he said. "I was there. But she was fine when I was there."

"Okay, Good." I said. "So she was fine huh? Laughing, talking, drinking?"

"Yeah, we drank some booze and I left. She was alive when I took off."

"I guess I am still confused," I said. "That's a good story but it can't be right. You say that you were never there, then when I mention that your print was found up near her you say that you were there, but that Cindy was fine."

McKinley nodded.

"Except she wasn't fine was she? What I forgot to tell you was that we found your print in Cindy's blood. That's how I know you were there around the time that Cindy was killed. Did you check on her and find her bleeding? Is that how it happened?"

"Yeah, that's right," he said. "I went up there and she was hurt bad. Lots of blood. I only checked her pulse. That's when I got her blood on me. That's all I did. I only touched her for a pulse."

"Okay," I assured him. "That would explain how your bloody print was found there, right?"

"Yeah," he said.

"Did you touch her in anyway?" I asked.

"What the hell do you mean did I touch her?" McKinley said angrily.

I paused, "Sexually I mean. Did you touch her sexually, in any way, vaginally or anally?"

"No fucking way!" he answered.

Time to end this Roger.

"You know what Roger... I think I may have forgotten to tell you where exactly we found your palm print," I said.

I pulled out a crime scene photograph of the vodka bottle still inserted in Cindy's body. I held it up.

"Roger, tell me about this bottle, you picked up the vodka bottle, didn't you? You took a swig thinking it was alcohol. You were pissed when there wasn't any booze in it... it was only water... that made you mad didn't it?"

Roger's hands were again shaking. This time the rattling of the cuffs didn't stop.

"Cindy didn't even put up a fight, did she? She never even saw your face?" I said. "You were so pissed at her that after you stabbed her you shoved that bottle up her ass and left her to bleed to death didn't you?"

"You can't prove it. You can't prove anything," Roger said.

I kept talking.

"Roger, I can prove it. I know about the knife you would always carry with you. I interviewed your other friends. They told me that you showed up later with her blood on you. You told them that you had made a big mistake. You told them that you killed someone who attacked you that night. You even asked your friends to help you burn your bloody clothes, didn't you?"

Roger again said nothing.

"You told them that you were attacked by a guy but you weren't in a fight, were you?" I leaned closer to Cindy's killer.

"You attacked her. Her blood was on your hands and your print got on that bottle when you shoved it up her ass."

I was so close to McKinley I could smell the stale alcohol on his breath and his rancid body odor.

"You killed her," I said, "You are no warrior. You are a coward."

I put the photo of the bottle back into my case file and I stood up. I walked out of the interview room leaving Roger Wade McKinley to be escorted to the Anchorage Jail.

I went back to my desk. This time I took Cindy Henry's driver's license photo out of my file and pinned it up on my wall next to the photograph of Patrick Ramones. Patrick was gunned down in a hotel parking lot just before Christmas. One of the friends Patrick was out with that night had a new girlfriend, unfortunately for Patrick, the girl's ex-boyfriend was following her. He showed up as Patrick and his friends were walking across the hotel parking lot. The ex-boyfriend started shooting. Patrick was hit three times. He died at the scene.

On my wall next to Patrick's image was a family photo that included 16-year-old Nancy Brower. Nancy was sexually assaulted and beaten to death by her cousin as she slept in her grandparents' mobile home.

Cindy, Patrick, Nancy, Denise and all the rest are there. Every case I was assigned meant another photo added to my wall. Each photograph represented a life that ended too soon. Each of their faces staring back at me reminded me of why I was there and who I worked for... the victims.

Detective Klinkhart under the A Street Bridge in downtown Anchorage, Alaska. The body of Cindy Henry was discovered up on top of the cement buttress (right) and between the steel girders of the bridge.

Chapter 6   Welcome to the Police Academy

"Good morning, recruits!" Sergeant Rob Heun said. "I am here to welcome you to the new Anchorage Police Academy."

Heun was the training sergeant for the entire police academy. His pose and exacting demeanor showed off his West Point education as well as his ten years in the U.S. Army.

I sat in the classroom along with 27 other new police recruits. I listened to every word. I had been trying for over a year to get accepted into the police academy. The Anchorage Police Department had a lengthy and difficult recruitment process. For the past twelve months I had been subjected to written tests oral examinations, physical agility tests, polygraphs and even psychological exams. The day I got the phone call from the police department saying I was accepted in the police academy was an incredible moment in my life. Just being accepted, however, wasn't going to be enough. Many police academy recruits fail the course and even more drop out before making it to the rank of patrol officer. I was determined not to be one of them.

I had already gone to college and earned my degree in business. After college I tried my hand at several different jobs including working as a computer programmer and a commercial artist. I even worked for a local Anchorage newspaper as a young marketer, but none of those jobs ever seemed to hold my attention for very long.

"For the next sixteen weeks you will be instructed in every aspect of police action, policy and procedure. You will learn to rely on yourselves and on each other," Sgt. Heun began.

He turned and looked right at me. "We will teach you how to act and look like police officers, including how to get a haircut."

Embarrassed, I looked down at the tabletop. That night I went straight to the barbershop.

It wasn't just my hair that made me feel out of place. At the age of 29 I was the oldest recruit in my academy. The rest of my peers were in their early twenties. Most were fitter and faster and many had prior police experience. I had none. All I could do was continue to listen, watch and learn.

Having never even fired a handgun in my life, I was trained in the art of the Glock 21, a .45 caliber handgun. The first time I fired the weapon, the noise, the flash and the kick of the weapon shocked the hell out of me. The firearms instructor standing nearby noticed and shouted, "The recoil from a Glock 21 will not hurt you!" I was again feeling out of place.

We learned report writing, first aid and how to perform field sobriety tests. I listened and I read and I studied. The academic portions seemed easy to me. It was the physical challenges I struggled with. Despite working out and training for months prior to the academy, I struggled to do as many pull-ups or to run as far or as fast as the rest of the group. I did however have a knack for communicating and for organizing so I traded my study guides to other recruits in return for help with defensive tactics and firearms.

One day Sgt. Heun gathered us up for physical training or "PTs" as they are called. We lined up in our gray colored sweats and waited for the inevitable physical torture we all knew was coming. It began slowly, first with stretching followed by jumping jacks. Next came push-ups followed by standing and running in place. The pace became faster and the workout harder as we went along. The sergeant began a vocal cadence with "One, Two, Three... pick it up. Let's see what you can do." Faster and faster we began running in place. Every so often Sgt. Heun would shout "Down!" and we would hit the floor and switch to push-ups. A few moments later he would shout "Up!" and we would jump up and begin running again. My arms felt like they weighed a ton. My legs felt like rubber. I could hardly breathe.

Others in my group began to falter and stop. "Keep Going!" Heun would shout.

I'm not going to make it.

38

At that moment I could see all my hard work was going to be for nothing.

If I fail it won't be because I didn't try.

I started running faster. It hurt, but I kept going. Faster and faster I went. A few moments later I was running faster than even the sergeant. It hurt so much I wanted to scream. Just then Sergeant Heun looked over at me. "Keep it up Klinkhart!" he yelled. Only a few recruits remained running in place. "Faster!" I yelled back at him. Sure enough he matched my pace.

I'm going to throw up.

Right here, right now, in front of everyone.

Just as I was about to pass out, Heun yelled, "Stop!" I put my head down and rested my arms on my hips. My chest burned. The room spun.

Whatever you do, don't pass out.

Just stay standing.

I knew if I sat down I wasn't going to get back up.

"Take a break, drink some water," Heun ordered. The class dispersed. Sergeant Heun grabbed his towel and walked by me. I made sure to look straight ahead. As he passed me he spoke.

"Good job today, Klinkhart."

"Thanks," was all I could get out without throwing up on the man's shoes.

It was then I began to believe I might just make it. All I had to do was tough it out.

Each class brought me into a whole new world. The lectures on investigation were by far my favorites. The crime scene class was taught by two of the most decorated homicide investigators in Anchorage Police Department history, Lieutenant Bill Gifford and Detective Steve Edwards.

"The first 24 hours of the investigation is the most critical," Gifford explained. "Evidence gets removed or destroyed, people change their stories and memories fade."

"The sooner we get in and gather up as much information as possible, the better," Edwards added.

The investigators lectured about trace evidence such as DNA, hairs and fibers.

"Locard's Exchange Principle states that whenever two objects come into contact with each other, a transfer of material will occur," said Edwards.

Dr. Edmond Locard, the "Sherlock Holmes of France," was a forensic science pioneer in the early 20th century. His principle dictates that items such as hair, fiber and DNA can be collected and used to associate people to a scene or show that someone was connected to an object. These items can be compared microscopically to determine a match.

As the lecture continued, I realized for the first time in the academy, I hadn't written down a single word. I was too enthralled to do anything but watch and listen. Gifford and Edwards continued to instruct us in every aspect of crime scene techniques and the procedures they employ at a death scene.

Finally, Gifford put up a slide showing a bite mark on a man's arm.

"These are the teeth impressions made by a murder victim," Gifford lectured. "We took these photographs of the suspect's arm at the time of questioning."

The goal, he said, was to compare the teeth of the victim to a bite mark found on the suspect.

I froze in my chair. Suddenly I wasn't interested in the lecture anymore.

Dawn bit him right before he killed her.

They aren't talking about my sister are they?

"We later created dental stone castings of the entire mouth of the victim."

Gifford held up a model cast of a complete set of human teeth. He handed the model to the front row of students and asked that they pass the teeth around. Each student carefully examined the molded cast with great interest. A couple of the more witty students opened up the jaws of the model and pretended to bite each other with them. Laughter filled the lecture hall.

By now I was fairly sure I was going to be sick. There was nowhere to go. No place to hide.

Breathe, just breathe.

My heart began to pound so loudly I was sure everyone could hear. My hands began to sweat. One of the students asked the instructors, "What case was this from?"

"This was a case where a 59 year old woman bit her husband who was stabbing her with a kitchen knife," Gifford said. He continued to describe the case to the class in great detail, but I wasn't listening. A wave of relief had passed through me. The cast was not Dawn's teeth. When the plaster of Paris model was passed to me I examined it intently.

"A piece of a puzzle, just a piece of a puzzle," I said out loud to no one in particular.

After a minute or two I handed the teeth to the student next to me and refocused my attention on the two instructors.

"The crime scene investigators work with the detectives," Gifford continued. "Communication is the key."

As Lieutenant Gifford spoke I noticed standing behind our group was a tall, well-dressed man. He had entered through a side door of the classroom. The man took off his overcoat and sat down in a chair at the back of the room. In his finely tailored suit the man looked more like a successful businessman than a cop.

"The third component in a successful homicide investigation is the partnership between the detectives on the street and the District Attorney's office." Gifford said.

"When a homicide occurs, while the crime scene team is out doing their thing, the detectives work with a lawyer from the DA's Office. The attorney is an important team member. They are there to assist as legal counsel, be a confidant and to help legally obtain search warrants."

Gifford continued, "If you are working on a case and you need a DA to help, you should consider yourself lucky if our next speaker is on the scene."

Gifford directed our attention to the man seated in the back of the classroom. As I turned to get a good look the man stood up and nodded to the class. It was then that I recognized him. He was older and better dressed than when I last saw him, but there was no mistaking his strong jaw line, the neatly combed hair and that distinctive nod, the same nod he'd given me when I was a young boy, hiding in the hallway.

"Class, talking next about the role of the DA's office, is the District Attorney for the State of Alaska, Mr. Steve Branchflower," Gifford said.

Branchflower walked to the front of the lecture hall and spoke for nearly two hours. I hung on every word. After the lecture I watched as many of my fellow recruits walked up to talk to Branchflower and the two detectives. The recruits wanted to know more about the gory details of some of their more infamous investigations. Some were clearly just sucking up to the teachers.

I walked directly out of the classroom and into the hallway to wait. A few minutes later, Branchflower walked out of the room followed by Gifford and Edwards. As they stopped to turn and leave I walked up to Branchflower.

"Mr. Branchflower." I said nervously, "Do you have a moment, sir?"

Branchflower looked at me. His eyes moved down to the nameplate on my police recruit uniform. It said "G. KLINKHART". As he read my name, I could see his eyes widen.

"My name is Glen Klinkhart, Sir," I said. "You probably don't remember me, but you prosecuted the man who murdered my sister, Dawn."

Branchflower looked at me. I couldn't tell what he was thinking, so I simply continued speaking, "I just wanted to take a minute of your time and say thank you. My family appreciates what you did for us."

"I remember you, Glen," Branchflower said, "I'll never forget your sister's case."

He paused, "You're a little older now.... how old were you at the time?"

"I was sixteen, sir."

Branchflower turned to the other detectives, "His sister's case was one of my very first homicide trials. It was also the first time in the state's history we used dental impressions to convict."

He turned back to me. "She bit him didn't she?"

"That's right, sir," I said nervously.

"So you've decided to join the police department, huh?" he asked.

"Yes, sir, I still have three more weeks of training."

"Well, Glen it was nice to see you again. Good luck with the rest of your academy and if you are ever in the DA's office, stop by and say hello."

Branchflower shook my hand and nodded before walking away.

I nodded back and turned towards the locker room to change out of my recruit uniform.

Chief of Police Kevin O'Leary and rookie Officer Klinkhart
at police academy graduation.

Chapter 7   The Johnson Brothers

I picked up the phone. "Homicide Unit, Klinkhart," I said.

"Detective Klinkhart, This is Donna upstairs in dispatch."

"Ya Donna, what's up?"

"Has anyone briefed you about the missing boys?" she asked.

"What missing boys?"

"Last night we had a 911 call about two boys who went missing near their house. We've had patrol and our search teams out all night. So far there has been no sign of them. It doesn't sound good and the Chief wanted you guys to know what's going on."

"Thanks, Donna we'll get right on it," I said as I hung up the phone.

Soon the entire homicide unit met in our conference room, which we fondly called the Homicide Lounge. Sarge gave us the briefing.

He informed us that the night before, at approximately 7:45 P.M., two boys, Malcolm Johnson, age 8 and his brother, Isaiah Johnson, age 5, were reported missing by their mother. She said the boys were outside their house on Doil Drive around 5 P.M. They were last seen in the area by friends around 6:30 P.M. The boys never returned home.

"Patrol officers conducted the initial search of the area," Sarge said. "By 10 P.M. a larger search of the area was done by the search teams and by helicopter."

He explained that a search and rescue plane from Elmendorf Air Force Base equipped with heat seeking equipment had flown over the neighborhood and surrounding area and that several ponds nearby had been checked, all to no avail.

"How about the neighborhood canvass?" Detective Huelskoetter asked. "Anything?"

"No," Sarge answered, "No one in the area reported seeing them after 6:30."

"Did we check the hospitals?" someone asked.

"Yep. Hospitals, the airports, the cab companies and every other law enforcement agency in the state has been notified. So far, nobody has seen anything."

"What's the description of the boys?" I inquired.

"Malcolm and Isaiah are both black male juveniles," Sarge stated. "Malcolm was last seen wearing light blue-colored jeans, a black-colored fleece jacket, a green sweater and black and red-colored tennis shoes. Isaiah was wearing dark colored blue jeans, a maroon coat and white tennis shoes."

The boys weren't dressed very well for Alaska in March. Spring was still at least a month away. The nighttime temperatures were below zero. If they had been outside overnight they were almost certainly dead.

An officer walked into the briefing carrying a stack of missing person flyers. He handed them to Sarge who in turn passed them around the table. I looked at the photographs of the two boys. They both looked like babies as they smiled and posed for their elementary school pictures. Isaiah looked barely old enough to be in kindergarten. My own son Evan, like Isaiah, was only 5 years old.

Their family must be out of their minds with worry.

"Klinkhart," Sarge said looking at me. "You're the case officer on this one."

"Yes, sir," I responded.

That was how it all began. The search for the Johnson brothers became the largest investigation in the history of the Anchorage Police Department. I was responsible for coordinating it. Luckily I didn't have to tell my fellow homicide detectives what to do. Everyone took to working on some portion of the search or investigation. We began looking into the background of the boys, their mother, Angel and their estranged father who lived out of state.

As there was no direct information that a stranger had kidnapped the boys, we needed to look at the family and their friends first, if only to rule them out as suspects.

Detective Mark Huelskoetter interviewed the mother. Angel Brown was a single mom with four kids. Malcolm and Isaiah were her middle children. Malcolm often took the role of father over his brother, Isaiah. According to their mother, the two of them were inseparable.

I watched Angel Brown's interview on one of the APD interview room cameras. She appeared to me to be forthcoming, but at times I noticed that she did not seem as emotional as I thought was natural for the mother of two missing children. Over the course of the next several days, the boys' mother continued to answer questions put to her by investigators, but she still appeared to be emotionally detached.

Meanwhile other detectives looked into the boys' father, who lived in Ohio and was not a part of the boys' lives. There did not appear to be a custody issue regarding the Johnson brothers and their father was quickly ruled out as a suspect.

Police officers that weren't handling emergency calls were mustered up to set roadblocks into and out of the boys' neighborhood. By the afternoon I had contacted the local offices of the Federal Bureau of Investigation. The FBI had experience in dealing with missing children and child abductions and I was willing to take any help I could get. In addition to providing special agents to assist in the search, within days the FBI provided us with computers and software designed to take in leads and to organize incoming investigative information.

Within the first 24 hours, the FBI had flown up two of their top agents, Special Agents O'Brien and Macon, from their Behavioral Sciences Unit in Quantico, Virginia. I had learned about Behavioral Science while still in police academy nearly ten years ago. The first thing I learned was they don't like being called "profilers." They are Behavioral Scientists. O'Brien brought with him over twenty-five years of experience in child abduction investigations and Macon had nearly ten years of field experience. They did everything they could to help me learn and to understand the complexity of these cases.

"It's all about the timeline," Special Agent O'Brien said. "You have got to develop the timeline as to where the boys were and when."

Special Agent Macon added, "Once you know where they were, then we can work on who they are and their behavioral patterns."

With the help of the FBI we began to piece together a rough timeline of the boys' whereabouts on the day they vanished. On the afternoon of their disappearance Malcolm and Isaiah rode the bus from Tudor Elementary School to their home in midtown Anchorage. The boys both stayed at home playing video games until around 5 P.M. when they went outside to play. According to their family and friends, on evenings when they wandered the neighborhood they typically stuck together and usually returned home for dinner by 7:30 P.M.

A witness reported seeing the boys about four blocks south of their house at about 6 P.M. on the night in question. A schoolmate of theirs said they stopped by his house around that time and asked if he could come out and play but he could not join them as it was his family's dinner time. Malcolm reportedly told the friend that he wanted to go "somewhere else" before going home for dinner. The time was approximately 6:15 P.M.

The last potential sighting of the boys was approximately 7 P.M. by a neighbor who reported seeing Malcolm and Isaiah six blocks north of their house, close to a construction site for new housing.

Knowing how boys can easily gravitate toward big machines and large piles of dirt, I personally contacted the construction company. They informed me that they had recently filled in some large areas at the site with earth moving equipment. Once I explained the situation to the owner of the company he quickly ordered his crews to stop everything and they spent the entire day and several thousands of dollars carefully removing every square inch of dirt that had been laid down the day before. Unfortunately no signs of the boys were found anywhere in the construction zone.

I had so much to do I didn't sleep for the first 72 hours of the investigation. I had worked hard before on cases, but this case was different. I was responsible for these two little boys who needed to come home. I would sometimes think about my son, Evan and what I would do if he were missing. Finding Malcolm and Isaiah became all I thought about. The more we searched the longer and the harder I worked.

On the third day, I began hearing from several different investigators and police brass asking repeatedly about the ponds south of the boys' home. Several other officers and supervisors had assured me the ponds had been searched. I had even been over to the area myself the day after their disappearance. Both of the ponds were completely frozen over. There had been a recent cold spell in the area and the temperatures had been in the low to mid-teens. As the day wore on I began thinking more and more about those ponds and the boys. As I was walking down the hall to another meeting to coordinate the search efforts, I spotted another detective and former academy mate, Jennifer Hill.

"Hey, Jen, you got a sec?" I asked.

"Sure, what's up Glen?

"I've been told the pond near the Johnson boys' house has been searched, but I want someone to take the Anchorage Fire Department and their dive team over there," I said. "I just need someone I trust to come back and tell me they aren't in there. Then I can get all these people asking me about the pond off my back. Would you be willing to do that for me, please?"

"Sure thing."

Later that afternoon I got a call from Jennifer. The fire department had assured her that the boys weren't in the pond. With that I turned the investigative efforts towards more sinister possibilities.

The boys' mother, Angel, was still cooperative, although her lack of outward emotion continued to bother me and other investigators. We eventually put detectives in unmarked cars on her to follow her every move.

I continued to work at a feverish pace. I only went home to get an hour or two of sleep and a quick shower. I was the first one back at the office and the last one to leave.

As the search wore on into its seventh day, Special Agents O'Brien and Macon had to return to Quantico. "You'll do fine Glen," Agent O'Brien told me. "Keep working on the timeline and keep your people talking with each other. Keep everyone involved and together you will find them."

I could only hope he was right. We didn't know where the boys were but it wasn't from lack of trying. Meanwhile, the case still dominated local headlines and led the evening newscasts each night.

On the morning of day eight, Sarge strutted over to my desk. "The command staff is making a change," he said. "They want us to start a task force which will be dedicated only to this case."

"Isn't that what we are doing now?" I asked.

"They want this to be a separate group. This group will answer directly to a supervisor who will then report directly to the police commanders. We'll be housed in another room and will have our own support staff and investigators. I, of course, will be the supervisor."

I didn't understand the reason for the change and was about to say as much when Sarge cut me off.

"You will still be the case officer, Klinkhart, but the commanders and the Mayor's office want a task force."

Ah, the Mayor's office. Now I understood. The mayoral election was only three weeks away. I had seen the mayor on the television a lot lately. He had already held several press conferences with the boys' mother, Angel, at his side.

"What if I don't want to be on this Task Force?" I asked.

"You don't have a choice," Sarge said and then added, "It's a direct order from the Chief's office."

"When do we start?"

"Right now."

The task force members met in a cramped conference room on the first floor of the detective wing. We were each assigned specific responsibilities and duties. As the second week wore on we began to hit more and more dead ends. Leads in the case dwindled as I began to notice changes around the task force office. Instead of allowing me to make decisions about the case on which I was supposedly still the case officer, certain police commanders, many of whom had never solved a homicide in their life, were deciding what was best for the investigation.

I would often return from working on something to find the other detectives had been told to work on something completely different or even counter to what I said needed to be done. I found several detectives redoing work that had already been done by other investigators.

"Why are people going out and re-doing this interview?" I asked Sarge. "This is ridiculous!"

"You are out of line Klinkhart," Sarge yelled.

"This is bullshit! I'm not being told anything. You and the rest of the commanders have people running in every fucking direction. That's stupid!"

Sarge's face turned red and he balled up his fist. "You're being insubordinate and you need to be careful or you'll be writing parking tickets for the rest of your career!"

I backed off. The next morning during the daily briefing Sarge informed all task force members we were no longer allowed to talk with anyone outside the task force about the case, including fellow officers and detectives. The Chief and City Hall were worried about leaks. Everything was to be kept within the task force. Failure to do so would result in serious disciplinary action.

"You got to be kidding me!" I complained. "How the hell do we do our job if we can't talk to other cops? They might be the ones who break this case wide open for us!"

"That's the way it's going to be Klinkhart, so watch your attitude," Sarge warned.

It had been over two weeks since the boys had gone missing. I was averaging less than three hours of sleep a night. I was beyond exhausted. I bit my lip and put my head down.

Faster, smarter, faster, smarter.

I can get through this.

I can do this.

Detectives watching the boys' mother found that some of the people she was hanging out with were involved in low-level drug dealing, mostly marijuana. This information seemed to light a fire under people higher up in the chain of command because the next thing I knew the task force was spending every waking hour looking into the mother's friends and their connections with drugs. Someone higher up in the police department had developed a wild theory that Malcolm and Isaiah must have been grabbed by dope dealers and were being held over a drug debt owed by Angel or someone connected with her. There was no proof of this but it didn't seem to matter what I thought. The task force was now given the mission to look into any and all drug dealing and find out where the boys were being kept. It was no longer my decision to make. It was clear I was the case officer in name only.

I went home that night but could not sleep. No matter how hard I tried every time I closed my eyes all I saw were those two little boys. I saw their faces in my head and I wondered and worried about where they might be. I thought about where we had looked and where we hadn't. I dwelled on what I could have missed. When exhaustion finally overcame me I woke up an hour later in a pool of sweat. After a couple more hours of tossing and turning, I gave up and went back to work. It was the end of the third week and I still had not found the boys.

That afternoon the members of the task force met again. We had little or no new information to share. We had been constantly looking into the boys' mother, her friends and associates and we were coming up with nothing. Some of these people weren't the most upstanding citizens but I again began to question what my supervisors were doing. As I went through the case files it seemed to me that none of the mother's small-time pot dealing associates seemed to have the skills, the resources or the time needed to construct such an elaborate kidnapping of these boys. The more I thought about it the more I thought that my bosses were out of their minds. They had no idea who did this. Nobody knew who was behind this or if anyone really was behind it. I had never been a drug cop, but even I felt that this just didn't seem like some sort of drug deal or drug retribution. I simply didn't have the experience in these things to be able to make my case.

"We are going to begin 24-hour-a-day surveillance on Angel Brown," Sarge announced. "I need volunteers to take 12 hour shifts." There was a sigh from the entire group. After each of us grudgingly signed up for a shift, I left the conference room and went back to my desk. I thumbed through my contact list and found the number I needed. I dialed it. As the phone rang I began to wonder if I was doing the right thing. I also wondered how much trouble I'd be in if anyone found out.

"Detective Koch," the voice answered.

"Dave, it's me, Klinkhart," I said.

"How's the search going Klink?"

"That's what I want to talk with you about. Can you meet me after work?" I asked. "Say, 7 P.M. at your office? And please don't tell anyone I'm talking to you, okay?"

"Sure thing, Klink," Koch said inquisitively. "I'll see you at seven."

As it got closer and closer to 7 o'clock I looked around the office just to make sure no one would see me leave. Once everyone was gone I headed up stairs to the police department's Metro/Drug Enforcement Unit. If anyone knew something about drugs and drug dealers it was Detective Dave Koch.

Detective Koch was well known for his twenty years of drug enforcement experience. He had arrested more people for drug dealing and had taken down more drug operations than anyone else in the Anchorage Police Department. I first met him while still in the police academy. Koch was the one who taught us about drug enforcement and investigation.

I entered his office and shut the door quietly behind me. Koch was at his desk, leaning back in his chair. His feet, wearing his signature cowboy boots, were up on his desk.

"Why the cloak and dagger shit, Klink?" Koch asked as he took his feet off of the desk. He leaned forward in his chair.

I sat down and shook my head. "If anyone knew I was talking to you, I'd be in deep shit and probably fired," I explained.

"Well, yours won't be the first career I've helped tank, so what can I do to help you?" Koch joked. I smiled and nodded my head. Koch was also known for doing things his way whether or not the police administration approved it.

"It's the Johnson brothers. There are a lot of people here at APD who are convinced they were kidnapped because of drugs or drug dealing. I can't seem to understand that. We are spending a lot of time and resources trying to prove this theory. I want to hear your opinion on it."

"Okay, Klink, tell me everything you know about these supposed drug dealers, who are they, where they live, what they move... everything."

I spent the next two hours going over every detail I knew about the investigation, especially the drug kidnapping theory. After I finished answering every question, Koch sat back in his chair, put his hands behind his head and spoke in his southern drawl.

"This ain't about drugs. This isn't Medellin, Colombia and these people aren't top level drug dealers Klink." Koch said. "Look at the risk they are taking and for what? You've looked at the mother's finances, right?"

"You bet we did. She has got nothing," I said.

"Even if she owed someone money, it wouldn't add up to the risk that these people are taking by grabbing two kids. Kidnapping is serious jail time. These characters you are looking at are strictly penny ante users or small time dope dealers. They don't have the intellect or the balls to be able to do what your supervisors are saying they did. It's bullshit."

"That's what I thought, too. I just wanted another opinion. Thanks."

I stood up to leave.

"What are you going to do, Klink?" he asked.

"I don't know. I just want to find Malcolm and Isaiah, but nobody is letting me. I've told them what you're telling me. Nobody will listen."

As I opened the door to leave I heard Koch say, "Legally do what you got to do Klink. I've been in trouble at this department lots of times. It's not that bad..." Koch paused, smiled and added, "as long as you don't get caught."

That night all I could do was lie in bed and stare at the ceiling. I could feel the anger, the frustration and the pain welling up inside of me. My left eyebrow began twitching, a new stress tic.

Was this why I wanted to be a cop?

It wasn't supposed to be like this.

What the hell am I doing?

I don't have a clue.

Just then I heard my wife stir.

"Could you please stop it?" she said under her breath. My tossing and turning had obviously disturbed her sleep again.

I hadn't seen much of my wife in the past three weeks. We weren't two ships passing in the night; it was more like two vessels on different sides of the earth. I hadn't given her or Evan, any attention since the Johnson boys had gone missing. Not that it mattered. When I did give her my attention it was always the same thing. Everything had to be the same. She wanted no ups and no downs. No emotion. No anger. No sadness. No passion. It was difficult for me to feel anything when we were together as she wanted everything to remain without emotion. The problem was I wanted to feel something, anything. I needed to feel. I wanted to feel.

"Okay," I said to her. I got up and headed to the bathroom. I closed the door and I sat down on the floor.

I held my hands up to my face. I closed my eyes. All I could see was Malcolm and Isaiah's faces.

"They won't let me find them," I said aloud as I began to shake. Tears ran down my face. My eyebrow kept twitching.

Nobody is listening to me.

I can't do this anymore.

I should just quit.

I had been thinking about leaving the department ever since I was ordered to be on the task force. The only reason I hadn't quit was I didn't want to fail the boys. I wanted to find them. I needed to find them. I rolled over and laid my head on the cold linoleum floor. I closed my eyes and for the first time in days, I fell asleep.

Chapter 8   Day 23

It had been twenty-three days since the boys had gone missing. We had amassed enough leads, narratives and analysis reports to fill two entire filing cabinets. I kept myself busy each day by going over the day's lead sheets. Patsy, our full time police clerk, entered data into the computers provided by the FBI. The laptops were designed to help track, monitor and classify leads in large cases. Although I appreciate technology, I still insisted on going through each lead sheet by hand. Not everything always got entered into the computers and every once in a while I would catch something that failed to make it into the system.

"Any more lead sheets?" I asked.

"Nope, that's all I have for now," she answered.

"Do you want me to get you a sandwich?" I asked. "Ham and cheese again?"

"Yes, please and a Diet Coke."

Patsy looked down next to her at a pad of yellow note paper. "Klink, on your way out you might want to check with dispatch about a shoe someone found," she said.

I spun around. "Shoe? What shoe?"

"Dispatch took a call earlier today about a tennis shoe found near one of the ponds. We sent an officer over to check it out. I don't see any notes for any follow-up so it didn't look like anything."

Patsy ripped the sheet of paper from the pad and handed it to me. According to the dispatcher, approximately two hours earlier a citizen called into APD and reported seeing a single tennis shoe near the pond. The report had no description of the shoe and no information as to where exactly the shoe was found in relationship to the pond. I asked Patsy which officer was sent to the call.

59

"Officer Washington. He went out about 9 A.M."

Thirty minutes and two requests later my phone rang as I was driving to pick up lunch.

"Klinkhart," I answered.

"Hello, sir, this is Officer Washington."

Rookie officers were always polite and formal, especially when they had to call a detective. I laughed to myself. I was only thirty-six years old for God's sake.

"Washington, please call me Glen," I asked.

"Yes, sir," he replied. I smiled to myself and got right to the point, "Washington, you went out on a call a few hours ago that referenced a found tennis shoe near the pond. What can you tell me about the call?"

"Well, sir, I responded to the area," he said. "I located a single child's tennis shoe. I collected it and I wrote a report."

"Where exactly did you find the shoe? I couldn't tell by your report. Along the trail? By the sidewalk? It's important that I know exactly where you found that shoe."

"Actually sir, it was under water, near the edge. I had to use a stick to reach it and pull it out."

I hesitated for a moment. "What color was this tennis shoe?"

"Red and black, sir," he replied.

Instantly I hit the brake pedal. My car screeched to a halt. I slammed the car into reverse and spun around.

"Where is the shoe now?" I asked.

"I brought it to the station and I hung it up in the drying room. Did I do something wrong, sir?" the young officer asked.

"No, Washington, you did exactly what you were supposed to do. Thanks." Without saying goodbye I hung up the phone. I floored the gas pedal. The car lurched forward as the transmission kicked into a higher gear.

"They are in the fucking pond!" I screamed out loud.

The Anchorage Fire Department dive team was already in the water by the time I arrived at the pond. Onlookers gathered to watch. As I got out of my car I asked the other police officers on scene to please keep people back. I already knew what was about to happen.

The surface area of the pond was not that large. You could easily throw a rock from one side to the other. Though it was only a few feet deep at its edges, the pond itself was ten-to-fifteen feet deep at its center.

The divers were moving through the pond going from side to side. Bubbles rising to the surface gave away their underwater positions. Each diver would come up every so often and give a thumb down signal, indicating they'd found nothing. Yet. Each of them would then move forward a yard or two and the process began anew. I watched for a few minutes until the sergeant arrived. He scrambled out of his car, his clothes askew, looking hurried and disheveled.

"Find anything yet?" he growled.

"Not yet, but we will," I said.

"Are you sure?" he asked with one eyebrow raised.

I looked back at him with all the bitterness I could muster and said, "Abso-fucking-lutely."

Another five minutes passed before one of the divers again came up to the surface. This time he gave a "thumbs up" signal.

All heads turned towards me. I didn't blink. I just stared at the pond. It was all I could do to keep from completely losing it. The diver went back under the surface of the water. A few minutes later he came back up. This time I could see that he had a hold of something. He held it just above the surface of the water. It was the top portion of one of the legs. The foot had no shoe on it, just a gray sock.

A few minutes later the other diver indicated he had also found a body under the surface of the pond.

"I knew it," I muttered under my breath, "I fucking knew it."

Sarge heard me and shot me a glassy stare. I turned and started to walk away.

"Where the hell are you going?" he shouted.

Malcolm and Isaiah's mother needed to hear the news from me first and not from the media. I tossed back, "I'm going to notify the mother."

"Too late," Sarge said as he pointed to the parking lot. "Looks like she knows already."

I turned and saw Angel being escorted from a car and towards the police perimeter. The media surrounded her with cameras and microphones all pointed right at her. Her attorney, Rex Butler, was at her side, holding her arm.

I felt sick. I felt defeated and I felt angry. I started to walk back to my car.

"Klinkhart!" The sergeant yelled. "Get over here."

I stood my ground. I'd had enough.

Sarge stomped over to me. He leaned over and spoke closely but loudly into my ear, "You'll be personally escorting the bodies to the coroner's office."

I nodded and stood there waiting and watching as they brought the boys over, each in his own body bag. Two firemen and two police officers easily lifted each of bright orange nylon bags into the back of the ambulance. Body bags are designed to fit adults; with the boys in them they simply drooped in the middle.

I walked over to the ambulance and stepped up and into the back of the vehicle. The sergeant followed. I turned and looked at him. I expected yelling. Instead, he looked at me and for the first time that I could recall, he had nothing to say.

Without a word we each began to prepare to examine the bodies. Instinctively we both donned rubber gloves. Sarge took one body bag and I took the other. Without thinking I quickly stuffed my tie into my front shirt pocket so it wouldn't touch the corpse or any bodily fluid.

Senior Detective Joe Hoffbeck taught me the trick. His advice had saved me from having to throw away many a good necktie over the years.

As I undid the zipper of the body bag I looked down. The face staring back at me was the very same one that I had seen in the photograph on my desk for the past 23 days. It was the face I had seen every night when I closed my eyes. It was the face of a five-year old boy named Isaiah Johnson. He wore a maroon jacket and blue jeans. Just as I knew he would.

The cold March temperatures had preserved Isaiah well. The only evidence that he had been in the water for three weeks was some discoloration and wrinkling of the skin, especially around the fingers and hands. I looked at his body for any signs of external trauma. There were no bullet holes, no knife wounds and no blunt force trauma to his small head or other extremities. Each article of clothing was exactly as it had been described to me by his mother on the day he and his brother went missing. I searched his pockets and found nothing. As I grabbed the top of the zipper I took a moment to look at Isaiah's face one last time. It was a face I would never ever forget. This was the boy that I had been looking for. And now here he was lying in the back of an ambulance.

He was cold, he was wet and he was dead.

"Find anything?" asked Sarge.

"Nope. No trauma, no signs of foul play," I said, "It appears they've been in the pond ever since the night they disappeared."

"You're not the expert," Sarge said. "We'll let the medical examiner determine that."

As he spoke Sarge stepped out of the ambulance. He gave me a look like I was some kind of disobedient dog that was being told to "stay." He reached over and closed the doors to the back of the ambulance, leaving me in the dark. The sergeant pounded his fist twice on the rear of the ambulance and it lurched forward.

I could do nothing else except sit in the darkness with two dead boys to keep me company and wonder what the hell I was going to do next.

Malcolm and Isaiah Johnson's grave sites at the
Anchorage Memorial Park Cemetery in Anchorage, Alaska.

Chapter 9   A Fire On M Street

Sunday mornings the APD 911 dispatch center is usually very quiet. Most citizens are still asleep and those who were out late the night before are not in any hurry or condition to make or report much trouble. The night shift patrol officers are heading back to the station and the day-shifters are just getting their briefing prior to hitting the streets. Anchorage Police Call-Taker Elizabeth Baker was seated at her desk and was getting ready to end her day when the board lit up with a 911 call on line four. She reached for the connect button and pressed the switch.

Just as she had said a thousand times before Elizabeth recited, "911, what is your emergency?"

A female voice answered. "Um, there's a fire... I'm a newspaper carrier... and there's a fire at... umm 622 M Street."

The woman's voice was hurried, but not frantic.

"622 M Street... is that a house or an apartment?" Elizabeth asked the caller.

"It's a house and it's on fire," the caller answered, "There's smoke billowing out the windows... it just started."

"Do you know if anyone is inside?" Elizabeth asked.

"I don't think so, there's no car in the driveway."

"Okay and you can see flames?"

"Ya, there's smoke pouring out the upstairs window... it's definitely on fire.

"Okay, we're on our way. Thank you."

"Bye."

Elizabeth logged the call, the caller's ID and the time. She confirmed the fire department trucks were en route and she looked at the clock. The time was 6:45 A.M.

Anchorage Fire Department Crews arrive at the scene of the fire on M Street. *Photo courtesy of the Anchorage Police Department.*

Six hours later in another section of the Anchorage Police Department, a call came into police clerk Betsy Forester.

"Anchorage Police Report Taking," Betsy answered.

"Who?" the voice asked.

"Anchorage Police Report Taking," Betsy repeated.

The female voice on the other end stuttered and tried to speak. "I um... I want to report a missing person."

"Who would that be?" Betsy asked.

The woman on the other end tried to get the words out. "My daughter."

The caller started to cry.

Betsy pulled up the Missing Person's report subsystem on her computer and began to take notes.

"What is your daughter's first name?" she asked.

"Bethany," the mother replied.

"And her last name?"

"Correira... C O R R E I R A."

"How long has she lived in Alaska?" Betsy asked.

"All of her life... she's 21."

Reading from the missing person form, Betsy continued, "Does Bethany have a history of drinking alcohol?"

The caller tried her best to answer the question through her tears. "Very little... and no drugs at all."

"Has Bethany ever been treated for depression or any other mental health issues?"

"Never."

"Does she take any medications prescribed by a doctor?"

"No," the mother said.

"Does she have any scars, marks or tattoos?"

"She does," the voice said. "She has a tattoo on her lower back, just above her bottom. It looks like a sea turtle."

"Anything else?"

"She has one earring in one ear and three earrings in the other ear, I think. Her sister would know better than me, but her sister is in South Africa right now."

"Does she wear glasses?" Betsy inquired.

"She wears contacts. And I know she has them on because her glasses are sitting by the sink in the bathroom."

"What color are her eyes?"

"Her eyes are brownish green and her hair is brown."

"How long is her hair?"

"It's shoulder length."

"Any idea what she was wearing last?"

"No, I have no idea 'cause I live in Talkeetna."

"Who was the last person to talk to her?"

"I'm thinking it was her boyfriend," the mother answered.

"Have you checked with her boyfriend?" Betsy inquired.

"Her boyfriend lives in Nome. His name is Ray. I don't know his last name. Bethany just left Nome three weeks ago and she moved to Anchorage only a week ago."

The voice continued, "I talked to her apartment manager who said he talked to her about 8 or 8:30 A.M. yesterday. I think her boyfriend talked to her too yesterday."

"What is your name, hon?"

"Linda."

"Same last name?"

"Yes," replied Linda Correira.

Linda explained to Betsy that Bethany's apartment door was unlocked when she arrived and Bethany's driver's license, keys and the cell phone were all inside of her apartment. Linda described Bethany as a bit of a homebody who didn't like to go out at night. Betsy had been with the Anchorage Police Department long enough to know that most missing people are missing because they don't want to be found or they simply don't care to stay in touch with other people. Betsy knew from experience that most adults who are reported missing return home or are found within a few days of the report being taken. But for Betsy, this girl and her mother didn't seem to fit into any of the normal categories. This mother did not appear to be a flake, at least not of any sort of flake she had ever encountered.

Betsy provided Linda with the police case number of 23775. "I am going to file this report and put her name into the statewide database as well as the national database," Betsy informed the distressed mother. "Should an officer come into contact with Bethany, she will come up in the computer as a missing person."

"What about the fire?" Linda asked.

"What fire?"

"Yes, there was a fire sometime today at the building next door to Bethany's. I don't know what time, but the firemen were still here when I arrived at 10 A.M. to pick up Beth," Linda said.

Betsy paused.

"Hold on Linda, I'm going to transfer you up to dispatch."

Betsy put Linda on hold and dialed the dispatch center.

"Anchorage Police dispatch," the supervisor answered.

"Hi, this is Betsy in Report Taking. I just took a missing person report from a woman and it's real suspicious. I've got mom under the button. She would really like to talk to an officer. The missing girl lives in the apartment next to where the fire was this morning on M Street. This girl appears to have just disappeared off the face of the earth. The address is 612 M Street apartment number three."

"Okay, we will send someone to contact her at the apartment on M Street as soon as an officer is available," the dispatcher answered.

Betsy thanked the dispatcher and said, "Great, I'll tell her mom to wait right where she is."

Chapter 10   Will Be Back Very Soon

It was Sunday, May 4[th and] I finally had a day off from Homicide. My son Evan and I were outside playing catch when the call came.

"Glen! Phone for you!" my wife shouted from the back door.

"Be back in a second, Buddy," I told Evan.

I tossed him the ball one last time. He managed to catch it but it was difficult, as his glove was much too big for his little five-year-old hand. I set my glove down and walked into the house. The caller ID said it all.

"Hi, Sarge," I said without hiding my disappointment.

"We've got a missing girl down at Bootleggers Cove."

"It's my day off. Who else you got?"

"It's either you or Ratcliff" he said.

I really did not want to go, not even a little bit, but Detective Ratcliff had joined the homicide unit only a few weeks earlier.

"How about Ratcliff and I both go? It would be good experience for her and to have someone else to be with her," I suggested.

"No. I said I'm only sending one. You want it or not?"

I could almost see the vein in his forehead bulging out by now, which made me smile.

"I'll go. What's the address?"

"612 M Street. Oh and there was some sort of fire next door, too," my sergeant yelled. The phone went dead.

"A fire?" I said out loud to no one in particular. I turned to go upstairs to change.

"You have to go?" my wife asked.

"Yeah, some girl is missing down by Bootleggers Cove."

"Can't someone else go?" she asked as I began to put on my tie. Another day off ruined. The look on her face said it all. I was frustrated too, not just because another day off was ruined, but because I knew I couldn't keep this up much longer. The Johnson brothers had been too hard on me.

I pulled my handgun from the safe in the closet. It felt heavier than usual. I rocked the slide of the Glock back and did a quick look and feel in the chamber with my finger. The .45 caliber round was ready to go.

"She is probably just out with friends," I said hopefully.

I kissed my wife on the cheek as she coldly turned her head away. She said nothing. I took a deep breath and headed out the door.

As I drove towards the downtown area of Anchorage, I spent my travel time going through all the steps in my mind of what I needed to do when I arrived. First I needed to find the on-scene patrol supervisor and get a good briefing. I also wanted to speak with the first officer on scene. The initial officer on the call asks the very first questions and gets those immediate reactions from people. Those reactions can be important to see and to hear. I remember my very first day in homicide when I was partnered with Detective Joe Hoffbeck. Very few people had Joe's experience, nor did they have his special way with people. Joe was a man who never minced his words and could be blunt at times, however he was compassionate and thoughtful to those he chose to let inside his inner circle.

On that first day I could not believe I got to be partnered with a legend like Joe Hoffbeck. I was eager to learn everything I could from him. Joe smiled and told me to come with him. I grabbed my notebook. What an opportunity I thought as we walked across the police parking lot.

"Detective Hoffbeck," I asked as I followed close behind, "If you had one piece of advice for a new homicide Detective what would it be?"

I wondered if I was being too eager or too pushy. Joe stopped and turned to me. He paused for a moment and thought.

"When you interview a homicide suspect..." he said. I hung on his every word. I should be writing this down I thought but I was too excited to do anything but listen.

"Ask a question," he said, "and then shut the fuck up."

My drive to Bootleggers Cove wasn't a long one. This area of town sits along the coastline where downtown Anchorage meets the waters of Cook Inlet. It is near a popular recreational spot known as Westchester Lagoon. Legend had it, back in the early 20s, Westchester Creek, which was used to form the lagoon, also provided water and byways for illegal moonshiners.

Back in those days Anchorage was awash with railroad employees working on the new railway designed to reach into the wilds of Alaska. The railroad company banned all liquor and underworld characters with names like "The Lucky Swede" were more than happy to provide the workers with booze. Legend has it moonshine was loaded onto small boats which were then rowed up the Cook Inlet shoreline to the waiting railroad workers. Today, Bootleggers Cove is coveted for its close proximity to downtown shops and offices. Some of the older buildings have been torn down and rebuilt to meet the high demand for luxury homes, but many of the older houses are still standing.

I turned my vehicle onto M Street. As I approached I noticed dozens of people milling about. Several parked Anchorage Police Department patrol cars blocked the street. I found a spot off the road and parked. As I exited my vehicle I smelled it. The odor.

It was as if a switch inside my head had been thrown. The smells in my nose took me back to my house, my bedroom and to Dawn.

I could see the dark hole above me as I stared through it and up into what was once Dawn's bedroom. The smoke, the soot and the cold wet pieces of my house all flashed before me.

Not here. Not now.

I don't have time for this.

I immediately came back to what I was here to do.

There were three buildings on the east side of the street. The first, a white triplex, was on the corner of 6ᵗʰ Avenue and M Street. It was old and in a terrible state of disrepair. The unkempt yard indicated that it had not been lived in for some time. Next to the triplex was the address I had come to see, 612 M Street. It was a fourplex apartment building with a blue cosmetic paint job. A large sign in the yard displayed that some of these buildings were destined to be torn down to make room for a new complex. The sign read "Park West Condominiums" and it promoted the soon-to-be condos as "Luxury Living Space."

I turned my attention to the burned out building next door, the duplex. This was definitely where the smell was coming from. The two-story building stood approximately twenty yards next door to the missing girl's apartment. The duplex was almost completely destroyed by a fire. The outer walls were still standing but the windows were either blown out from the explosion of the fire or blackened on the inside from the flames and smoke. It looked like the old wood frame construction had burned up pretty fast. The first floor of the duplex was already boarded up and caution tape hung across the front door and the garage.

I walked over to one of the police vehicles where a couple of officers and a supervisor were standing. They were poised over a map laid out on the hood of the car and were talking with a man in an orange safety vest. I recognized the gentleman as a member of the Anchorage Police Department Auxiliary Search Team.

The Search Team was made up of citizen volunteers who are trained in various aspects of search and rescue. They use coordinated search groups as well as dogs to assist law enforcement in locating missing people. They also sometimes help search larger crime scene areas for potential evidence.

"Hello, Sergeant Hatch," I said.

"Hi, Klink," Sergeant Hatch responded. He turned and said something to the Search Coordinator. The man took the map and headed off, speaking into a mobile radio.

Sergeant Matt Hatch was one of my favorite police officers. He had over twenty years of law enforcement experience and yet the job to him always seemed new and exciting. His presence alone gave me some peace of mind.

"What we got?" I asked.

The sergeant pulled out his notebook and checked his notes.

"The call came in about six hours ago from the missing girl's mother, Linda Correira. Apparently the mother was supposed to pick up her daughter, Bethany, today to go to garage sales. When the mother arrived this morning her daughter was not at the apartment."

The sergeant pointed to the blue fourplex.

"Bethany lives upstairs, there, in apartment number 3."

I went through my plan again in my head. It's all about the timeline. That's what the behavioral scientists had taught me. Keep going back to the timeline: When did they disappear? Who saw them last? What did they do in the last 12 hours prior to the disappearance? Who had contact with them? How did it fit into the timeline?

I had a million questions for the sergeant, but I tried to keep things in order and my mind on track. Sergeant Hatch was able to tell me that the missing girl was Bethany Rose Correira. He read me her date of birth.

"Okay she's 21," I thought, doing the math quickly in my head.

"Did we do a bar check?" I asked.

The sergeant responded that the initial officers took the missing girl's mother at face value and had begun a coordinated search, including checking all of the usual bars, clubs, hospitals and even the jail.

Hatch further reported that he'd contacted the cab companies inquiring about any pickups in the area. He'd also sent an officer to a nearby Kinko's store to have copies of flyers made with Bethany Correira's photo and information on them. A boat was dispatched by Sergeant Hatch to check the nearby coastline. The local news stations were also contacted about the missing girl.

Over the next few minutes I learned from the sergeant that Bethany Correira had recently moved here from her hometown in Talkeetna, Alaska, a small rural community 115 miles north of Anchorage. Bethany had only recently rented her one-bedroom space in the fourplex apartment.

"Does she live alone?" I asked.

"Yes, but she has boyfriend, a Ray Betner. He's in Nome. Sergeant Parker spoke with him earlier."

"One more question Matt..."

I turned and faced the burned out building next door.

"What the hell is up with the fire next door?"

"The Fire Department says it's electrical, accidental." Sgt. Hatch continued: "The fire was reported this morning. According to our accounts Correira disappeared before that. The two don't seem connected."

"Good. I hate fire scenes," I said. "Who spoke with Bethany last?"

"That would be her mother, Linda Correira," he replied. Sergeant Hatch turned and pointed to a small, thin, woman in the driveway of Bethany's apartment complex. She held a cell phone up to her ear.

Linda Correira looked tired. She was a small-framed, thin, demure woman with shoulder length brown hair. I placed Linda at about 50 years old. She paced back and forth while talking on her cell phone. I could hear an accent in her voice, but couldn't quite place it. It wasn't until I walked over that I recognized the distinct sound of a thick Boston accent coming from this little woman. Linda Correira hung up her phone as I approached.

"Ms. Correira?" I asked. "I'm Detective Klinkhart with the Anchorage Police Department." I didn't mention to her that I was with the homicide unit. Linda Correira looked up at me and into my eyes.

"Can I ask you a few questions?" I said.

She nodded her head yes.

We walked along the street and talked. I wanted to spend a few minutes with Linda Correira alone. I needed to get a feel for her and to try and gauge how truthful and honest she was. I've had cases where the parents have done harm to their own children, so no one is above suspicion. As we talked I learned Bethany was the second of four children born to Linda and Billy Correira. All of the children grew up in a log cabin Linda and Billy built with their own hands in the homestead area of Talkeetna, Alaska. Each of the Correira children was raised without running water or central heat. The children took turns carrying wood for the stove and water for the family.

As Linda spoke about her children and especially her oldest daughter, Bethany, I could sense this small woman with the big accent was likely not going to be my main suspect. She spoke with passion; her voice at times strong and direct, in stark contrast to her frail stature.

Linda Correira told me that Bethany had recently moved from Nome and had only been in Talkeetna for a few months before she decided to move to Anchorage for the summer. Bethany hoped to attend fall classes at a college in Anchorage. She'd been looking for a place in town and fell in love with the small apartment in Bootleggers Cove. It was an inexpensive short-term summer rental for her as the buildings were expected to be demolished in the fall. Bethany told her mother the apartment was perfect as it was close to running trails and downtown. Bethany enjoyed running, hiking and biking. In fact, she liked anything having to do with the outdoors. Her mother said that Bethany had only moved into the apartment on M Street five days earlier, but already had part-time employment doing odd jobs around the apartment for the building management company.

I asked Linda about the last time she spoke to Bethany. Linda informed me that she'd talked with Bethany two days prior, on Friday night. Linda said that the plan was for her to drive down from Talkeetna on Sunday and take Bethany to some garage sales. Linda stated she drove the two-hour route from Talkeetna to Anchorage and arrived at Beth's apartment around 10 A.M. There was no answer when Linda knocked at the door. In fact it was unlocked, yet Bethany was not home. Thinking her daughter would be back shortly, Linda left Bethany a note. She noticed the burned out building next door. Neighbors said it was unoccupied. To kill some time, Linda went to a few local garage sales, but she could not stop thinking about Bethany and soon she returned to the apartment. Nothing inside appeared to be disturbed. Bethany's keys were on the table as was her cell phone. It was then that Linda decided to call the police.

Linda Correira stopped telling me her story and looked up at me. It was the first time during our conversation that I saw her appear vulnerable. I could see in this mother's face she was scared. I did my best to assure Linda Correira that we were going to do everything we could to find her daughter. I tell every parent that. It's my way of trying to reassure them. I know that most people reported as missing people show back up within the first 24 to 72 hours. I asked Linda Correira for her phone number so that I could contact her if anything important came up overnight. Without thinking, I gave her my personal cell phone number. For some reason it seemed appropriate. Linda Correira also agreed to my request for her and her family to come to the police station in the morning for an update and formal interviews. I thanked her and told her we would be in touch.

I turned away from Linda Correira and immediately saw the friendly face of Officer Chris Ritala over by the burned out duplex. Patrol Officer Ritala and I had been in the police academy together. Chris grew up in the Matanuska Valley, just an hour north of Anchorage. Chris had become known on patrol as quite a bulldog for being tough, tenacious and always getting his nose into something. Such work had earned him respect from his fellow officers and sometimes concern from police administrators for his lack of regard for proper protocol. Chris was exactly the person I wanted to see here.

"So what do you think Chris?" I asked.

"This doesn't seem right," He responded with concern.

"What do you mean?" I said.

"What I mean is that this fire doesn't feel like it's accidental," Chris said. "I was a volunteer fireman in Palmer and I can't say what, but it sure doesn't seem like it's electrical."

"How so?" I asked.

"Well the fire inspector showed me the electrical panel he said was the origin of the fire. He seemed pretty certain the fire started in an electrical box inside one of the walls. I'm no expert, but it just doesn't look right to me."

"Well, they are experts," I said.

"Maybe so," Chris responded.

I told Chris I had just spoken with the mother of the missing girl and that she seemed to be above board. Chris agreed and pointed to a blue-gray colored Toyota sedan, Alaska plate number CJN308, parked in the driveway of the apartment building. He indicated it was Bethany's car. He had looked through the car and found little other than some workout clothes and a pair of running shoes. He was thinking about moving it, but the battery was dead. I decided we needed to have the car towed to the police impound lot and to hold it securely until we could search it for hairs, fibers and fingerprints.

"Have you been in the apartment yet?" I asked. Chris shook his head no. We walked around the blue fourplex and up the stairs to the second floor. At the top of the stairs was another Anchorage Police officer standing guard at the front door of apartment number three. I pulled out a couple of rubber gloves from my coat pocket and snapped them onto my hands. I always hate having to wear rubber gloves. My hands sweat so much that rubber gloves become hot and uncomfortable in no time. As I walked into the apartment I saw a small kitchen to my left. The early 1970s-style wooden cabinets had been painted over so many times they looked as if they might not be able to handle the weight of one more coat. On the countertop were some keys. I pulled out my digital camera and photographed the keys before placing them in my pocket.

On the other side of the counter were two disposable cameras. I took both cameras and placed them into a plastic evidence bag. I told myself I needed to remember to drop them off at our photo lab for development in the morning. I looked around the rest of the kitchen. Taped to the door of the refrigerator was a business card for someone named Michael Lawson with a company called Branch Associates. On the back of the card was a hand written note that said, "Beth, please call me," along with a cell phone number. I noted the address on the front of the card.

Behind the kitchen was a hallway closet. The closet door was open. I observed a small green fabric purse hanging on a hook. I opened the purse and found a driver's license with the name "Bethany Rose Correira." I looked at the photo. Bethany appeared bright-eyed, hopeful and young, more like a teenager than a 21-year-old woman. "She looks like a kid," I said to Chris as I put the ID back into the purse. Also inside the purse were several dollar bills and a couple of credit cards.

"Well it's not a robbery and if she ran away, she did it without her driver's license and her money," I said to no one in particular. Chris and I continued looking around Bethany's apartment.

In the living room there was only a simple single chair, a television and a glass coffee table. A newspaper was on the floor. I bent down to look at it. The date on the paper was Friday, May 2nd. The page was open to the Help Wanted ads. I stood back up. The living room was tidy or at least as tidy as a room with little or no furnishings could be. On the coffee table was a white pad of paper. As Linda Correira had said, there was the note she had left for her daughter.

Beth,
Where are you? Was here at 10:15 A.M. Waited until 10:45.
Will be back very soon.
Love, Mom.

The single bedroom in the rear of the apartment was nearly as sparse as the living room. A box spring and mattress sat on the floor. A crate once used to hold milk cartons had become a makeshift nightstand. It held a clock and a single lamp. The bed was unmade. A book lay open, face-up, on the covers. It was Ernest Hemingway's *The Sun Also Rises*. A receipt in the pages indicated Bethany had purchased the book on April 28th at a local store, Title Wave Books.

There were a few items of clothing in the closet, mostly jeans, T-shirts and sweatshirts. I mentally noted that Bethany was clearly not a big collector of clothes which might make it easier to figure out what she was wearing when she disappeared.

The only other item of interest in the bedroom was a gray North Face backpack on the floor near the foot of her bed. It was adorned with a multitude of patches from foreign locales including New Zealand, Nepal, Norfolk Island and Australia.

She is well traveled for a 21-year-old.

Inside the pack there were notebooks, a day planner, check books and a passport.

"Well, she didn't leave the country," said Chris as he looked over my shoulder.

"It's like she walked out for a minute and just never came back," I said.

Something wasn't right. I was not sure what it was, but I could not afford to take any chances. I made my decision as I zipped up the backpack. "Lock the place up. I'm calling out the crime scene team."

I snapped off my rubber gloves and felt the sweat dripping off my palms. I told the officer at the top of the stairs to stay put until the crime scene team arrived. I walked outside to my car to call Sarge.

"Nope. Sorry, no crime, no crime scene," he barked in my ear.

"What? Are you kidding me? I just told you, things aren't right here. I can't put my finger on it, but this girl did not just up and walk away from her apartment."

"Any signs of forced entry?" he asked.

"No, but..." I said as I was cut off.

"And the fire was ruled accidental."

"Yes, but... my gut is telling me..." I said.

"No buts, Klinkhart, no crime scene. That's final." He continued, "We are not spending overtime money on this, period."

"Damn it, Sarge! What if she ends up dead? I need to have her apartment properly processed."

"Then do it yourself."

"Not a problem, Sergeant."

I turned my phone off and threw it across the front seat of my car.

"I'll fucking do it myself!"

I started my car and rolled down the window. I yelled to Chris, "Officer Ritala, you're with me. The searchers will call if they find anything. We have to go to south Anchorage."

Ritala got into the car as I slammed the gearshift into drive. I accelerated and spun the car's tires throwing up a cloud of dust as we left the area of M Street. We turned off 9th Avenue and took the freeway heading south.

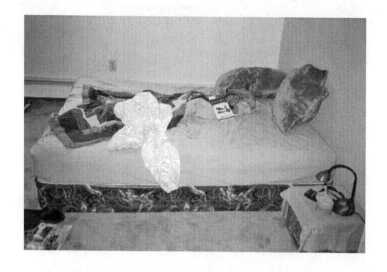

Bethany Correira's master bedroom inside of her M Street apartment. *Photo courtesy of the Anchorage Police Department.*

Bethany Correira's backpack as police found it in her bedroom.
Photo courtesy of the Anchorage Police Department

Chapter 11   Creepy

The home of Michael Lawson was in south Anchorage, on Hancock Drive just off Oceanview Drive. I knew the area well. In high school I spent a great deal of time with my friends in the middle-class neighborhood of Oceanview. I had driven by this particular residence on many occasions as a young man, either seeing my high school friends in the neighborhood or picking up my girlfriend at the time, who lived just down the street.

The Lawson residence was a two-story home set slightly off the main road. As we pulled up to the front driveway it was already getting dark. Chris and I got out and approached the residence. A white pickup truck was in the driveway. I noted the plate on the vehicle. Chris turned on a tape recorder nestled in his ballistic vest as we approached the front door. A sign next to the door read, "Welcome to the Lawsons." I rang the doorbell and instinctively stepped back. I had been trained as a young officer that not everyone likes the police. No one knows who or what might come through a front door and it was safer to be standing to the side of the door when it opens.

The knob turned and a man opened the door. I smiled. It's amazing what a smile will do for you, especially when you are the police.

"Hi, Mike Lawson?" I asked.

"Yep," the man answered.

"Hello, I'm Detective Glen Klinkhart, APD," I said as I showed him my badge.

Michael Lawson was a large man in his mid-50s with a booming voice. He was clean-shaven, with a round face and slicked-back hair that was unnaturally dark, almost black, clearly the result of a bad dye job. Lawson looked like he was trying to portray himself as an Italian mobster. I asked if we could step inside and talk to him. He waved his arm and I stepped inside followed by

Officer Ritala. Lawson escorted us into the living room. I noticed framed NASCAR posters hanging on the wall and racecar memorabilia located in various places around the room. Mike Lawson noticed me looking.

"Are you a NASCAR fan, Detective?" he asked.

"Nope. I know little or nothing about it," I replied.

Lawson motioned for us to sit down. Normally I would have stood, but I wanted this man to feel comfortable talking with me. People are more willing to open up when they don't feel like they are on the spot. As I sat down, I noticed another man seated in the room.

"Oh, this is my brother, Bob," Lawson stated.

"Hi, Bob," I said smiling in his direction.

Bob nodded but said nothing. Bob was smaller than his brother. He was thinner and nearly a foot shorter. He had a thick mustache and was wearing a black baseball cap. Unlike his brother, Bob did not appear to be much of a talker. I observed that Bob's hands were worn and tough looking.

He looks like a hard working guy.

I carefully observed both men. Neither of the brothers appeared to have any visible signs of injuries.

"Mr. Lawson, I hope this won't take long," I explained. "I saw your business card on the refrigerator of a girl named Bethany Correira. She is missing."

I looked at Mike Lawson for any reaction and I asked, "Did you hear about her going missing today?"

"Yes," he said calmly. "Her mother called me. I rented her the apartment. I work for Branch Construction. I'm their project manager."

Lawson told me that he had no idea where Bethany Correira was and that he'd last spoken with her the day before. According to Lawson, Correira had been hired to do some cleaning in some apartment buildings that Branch Construction owned, including the one where Bethany lived. Lawson said that Bethany had called him to report a problem with some keys to one of the buildings and then called him again the next day to report that she'd gotten into the building all right. Lawson claimed he had neither seen nor heard from her since then and didn't realize anything was wrong until he got a call from Bethany's mom that morning wanting to know if he had heard from her daughter. Lawson said he gave Linda Correira the exact same information he'd just given me.

I asked Lawson what he thought of Bethany. He paused, then looked me in the eye and said, "Well, I met her parents. They are good people. God bless her, she is trying to go to college. Please let her parents know if there is anything we can do, to let us know."

"I will pass that on to the Correiras," I said, "I do need to know where both of you were this weekend. It's standard procedure."

Lawson shifted his gaze from me to look directly at his brother before answering, "Well... On Saturday I was sleeping until 10 A.M. Then I went to the To-Go mart and bought some cigarettes. Other than that we were both here watching NASCAR all day." Lawson stared at his brother again. Bob said nothing. Lawson continued, "Last night we went out at the bars and got home late. In fact, I was too sick today to go to M Street to board up the duplex so Bob went."

Lawson explained that the company he worked for owned all three of the buildings in Bootleggers Cove, the triplex, the fourplex and the duplex. He said all of the buildings were going to be leveled at the end of the summer to make way for new condominiums. As he spoke, Bob seemed like he was about to say something until his brother shot him a reproachful look. Bob closed his mouth and sat back in his chair.

I kept questioning Lawson. He said he regularly drove a white

Mercedes SUV. I wrote down its license plate number as well as a list of bars Lawson said he and Bob had visited the night before. Both men sat quietly while I scribbled notes. Out of the corner of my eye I noticed that Bob was glancing at his brother while Lawson stared directly at me.

After getting their phone numbers, addresses and work schedules I gave them one of my business cards. "Thank you for your time and may I call you if I have any follow up questions?"

"Yeah, good luck. I hope she shows up, Glen," Lawson answered.

So we are on a first name basis now huh?

"Thank you Mr. Lawson. You guys have a great evening," I said. Chris and I stepped out of the house and into the dark evening.

Making sure not to turn around and look, I could hear the front door close behind us.

Chris reached over and turned off his tape recorder.

"That was creepy," he said as we got to the car.

"That's one way to put it my friend."

Although I did not know it at the time, a figure was standing in the living room watching as we drove away from the house.

Chapter 12   After The Fire

The next morning I was up early, anxious to find out if the missing girl had turned up overnight. I slipped out of the house before sunrise and called dispatch. They informed me Bethany Correira was still missing.

I was still pissed off about the Sarge refusing to call out the Crime Scene Team as I gathered up the items from my office that I would need to process Correira's apartment. I grabbed a camera, flashlights, finger print powder, tags, bags and tape and stuffed them into a search kit. I had everything ready to go when the first detective, Phil Brown, walked into the office. I didn't even wait for the other detectives to arrive, I told Brown to follow me and we headed out the door. I was happy to get out before Sarge arrived.

The search of Bethany Correira's apartment was uneventful. Her bike was present. Her running shoes were in her car. I seized her hairbrush and her tooth brush for possible DNA. We took photos. I lay on my stomach and slowly crawled across the entire floor of the apartment. I looked for blood or any signs of a struggle. We checked the garbage cans. We combed every square inch of the apartment for anything of use. There was nothing.

Afterward, I released the patrol officer who was still guarding her door and took down the crime scene tape. Frustrated, I took the wadded-up tape and threw it into the back seat of my car. As Detective Brown and I drove out and along M Street I could not help but look over at the burned-out building next door. I stopped the car in front of the duplex. I rolled down the window. I could still smell the odor of ash particulates in the air. I turned to Detective Brown.

"I need to know something, Phil," I said.

"What's that, Klink?"

"I need to know for sure that she's not in there."

"Are you going in yourself?"

I thought for a moment. I hadn't been in a burned-out building in over 21 years and I sure the hell wasn't about to go in that one. Not when there could be another dead girl inside.

"No, but the fire department is," I said. "This time I'll make damn sure they search the *entire pond*."

Detective Brown gave me an inquisitive look as I put the car in drive and headed back to the police station. When we returned Sarge was at his desk. I tried to walk by without making eye contact, but it didn't help.

"Find anything?" he growled.

I wanted to say, "No, thanks to you," but all I could get out was "nada."

"The Captain wants a briefing," he said.

This was good news. The only thing Sarge disliked more than dealing with me was dealing with the administration. I thought perhaps I could turn his disdain to my advantage.

"The captain wants to see you now," Sarge said, smirking like it was punishment to go see the top brass.

I acted as if I was upset for being interrupted as I headed upstairs to the captain's office. Captain Audie Holloway was a good cop and a good commander. He had been in charge of the Metro Drug Unit for years. He knew how cases worked and how to put bad guys in jail. Even as an administrator he would occasionally come down to our unit and join our case discussions in the Homicide Lounge. He went out of his way to be helpful and made suggestions without sounding like a know-it-all. I liked him.

I knocked on his door. "Hi Cap, you wanted to see me?"

Captain Holloway looked up from his desk.

"Hey, Klink. Yeah, sit down and tell me about this missing girl."

I briefed him about what I knew. I told him just how little we had but how very suspicious I found her vanishing. I didn't tell him about the lack of a crime scene team. I figured any waves I made now would get back to Sarge. Holloway seemed pleased with the work I had done so far. When I finished I asked him for a favor.

"Captain, I know this may seem overly cautious and I hate to bring it up, but about the fire next door..." I began.

Holloway smiled. "You want the fire department to search the place again? Make sure that she's not still in there?"

"Yes, sir," I said as I looked down at my feet. "I need them to be sure this time." The Johnson brothers still stung.

"Consider it done. I'll call the Fire Chief... anything else?"

"No, sir. Thank you, sir." I turned and left his office.

I returned to the Homicide Unit and briefed the rest of the detectives. Everyone agreed that from what we knew of Bethany Correira her disappearance was, at a minimum, suspicious. Sarge didn't say much. He just sat there with his arms crossed while I discussed what we should do next.

Shortly after the meeting I was sitting at my desk when I received a call from the Anchorage Fire Department Chief Investigator Bob King.

"Hey, Klink! How you doing?" King asked.

"Busy, Bob. What's up with you?"

"Well, I'm working on that M Street fire. So you have the case of the missing girl next door, huh?"

"Ya, that's me... the missing person guy. What can you tell me about this fire?"

"I still think it's electrical, but we were asked to go back in and make sure there were no bodies or body parts in there."

I responded, "Well if you don't mind, I want to be able to tell the family with absolute certainty that she isn't in that burned out building."

"I understand," King said. "And we just came back from there. I went over myself with the engine company. We looked everywhere, including the chimney. We even opened up walls to be sure. No signs of a body, no bones, nothing."

He hesitated then added, "Klink, I went through the place like I was looking for my own daughter."

"Thanks I appreciate it," I said.

"Anything else we can do to help you Klink?" King asked.

"Not right now. We will be in touch. Thanks."

I hung up the phone, stood up and yelled to any of the other investigators working in homicide unit.

"Who else besides the fire department does arson investigation?" I asked.

The room was silent.

Chapter 13   The Correira Family

While other detectives interviewed Linda Correira and her husband, Billy, I took a crack at Bethany Correira's boyfriend, Ray Betner.

Ray had flown into Anchorage the night before after hearing about his girlfriend's disappearance. He was a commercial pilot based in Nome. Located northwest of Anchorage, the small arctic town of Nome has a population of less than 4,000 people. A town on the edge of the Bering Sea, it's known for its historical gold rush of the early 1900s and for being the finish line to the world famous 1,049 mile Iditarod Sled Dog Race.

As Bethany's boyfriend, Ray Betner needed to be looked at closely as a suspect or a potential witness. I just didn't know which one he was yet.

The Anchorage Police Department interview rooms are designed for discomfort. When interviewing a difficult suspect, sometimes your only option is to simply wear them out. I have had some interrogations last over seven hours. Being in a small, confined room with only a single table and two chairs makes most people uncomfortable enough to give an interviewer a slight edge. A one-way see through mirror hangs on the wall and completes the room's décor.

I checked on Ray from the back viewing area. Through the mirror I could see he was seated at the table, his hands clasped together. He was wearing jeans and a white collared shirt. Ray was a thin man with blond hair. He looked to me to be about 35 years old. I scanned his background file.

"According to his date of birth that would make him 37 years old, dating a 21 year old... Not too bad," I said to the other detectives in the room. "And according to one of the family interviews, Ray is still married."

The other detectives looked at me. I smiled.

"Let's go see what he has to say about his missing girlfriend."

I'm the sort of interviewer who likes to take his time. I don't get easily upset nor do I play the role of a "bad cop". Ranting and raging at suspects may look good on television, but good interrogators are friendly and only confrontational when absolutely necessary. Interrogations are part theatrics and part chess game.

Ray looked up as I walked into the room. I extended my hand and introduced myself. Ray rose and reached his arm out. As he shook my hand I asked him to please sit down. I sat down and turned on an audio recorder.

The interview began with my explaining to Ray he was likely the closest person to Bethany Correira. I told him I believed he could provide information that might be beneficial in helping us find her. That seemed to put Ray at ease. Putting the suspect at ease is important. To find a lie I look for changes in a person's demeanor. The more comfortable a suspect is with me, the easier it is to ask a question and to see and sense his reactions, especially when he jumps from comfort to nervousness after I pose a particular question.

I asked Ray to go back to the time he first met Bethany. He paused and then explained that he'd first met Bethany Correira about eight months earlier. They both worked for Bering Air in Nome, he as a pilot and she at the front counter. They'd met in August, but didn't start dating until three months later.

As Ray spoke I watched for signs of deception. Was he making eye contact? Was he making too much eye contact? Was he repeating my questions back to me? Was he being evasive? I asked him specific questions designed to give me some clue as to whether or not he was deceitful. I wasn't seeing anything yet that hinted he was lying, but I had been fooled before and this was too important to make any assumptions.

It was only when Ray told me about still being married that he became visibly nervous. When I asked him to explain further, Ray looked down at his feet. He said that he and his wife split a couple of months before he met Bethany. According to Ray, his marriage was effectively over well before he and Bethany got together. Ray defended Bethany by saying that she would not date him until he convinced her things were finished between him and his wife, Lacy. I got Ray to admit his wife was not happy about his dating Bethany. In fact, Lacy did not want Bethany around their young daughter. I asked Ray if there had been any specific incidents I needed to know about. Ray explained that one night, shortly before Bethany moved from Nome, Lacy showed up at his apartment. When Lacy saw Bethany there, Lacy became very upset. Bethany decided to leave the apartment in order to try and calm things down. As Bethany was leaving, Lacy picked up a glass and threw it at Bethany, striking her in the back. Bethany simply kept walking and left the house. A few weeks later Lacy called Bethany's parents in Talkeetna and called Bethany a "home-wrecker."

I asked Ray if Lacy was capable of hurting Bethany. Ray shook his head and said Lacy wasn't that "cunning." When I asked Ray who, besides his estranged wife, might want to hurt Bethany. He said no one came to mind.

Ray stated that he had returned from a trip to Hawaii the week before and that Bethany picked him up at the Anchorage International Airport just a few days before her disappearance. Bethany seemed happy to see him and was excited to show him her new place on M Street. Ray stayed with her there until his return flight to Nome two days before she vanished and he hadn't seen her since. Ray said that he'd bought a white puka-shell necklace as a gift for Bethany while he was in Hawaii and asked if we'd found it in her apartment. I told him we had not.

When I asked Ray where he was on Saturday and Sunday, he stated that he was flying his commercial routes. When I informed Ray we were going to check out his alibi with Bering Air, he showed no signs of surprise or concern.

I asked Ray to specifically go over the last time he spoke to Bethany. Ray stopped for a moment to compose his thoughts. He told me that he called Bethany's cell phone in between his flights early on Saturday morning, the day she went missing. He said it'd been a short call because he had to turn the flight around fairly quickly. Ray closed his eyes and strained to think back to that Saturday morning phone call.

After a moment he opened his eyes and said, "Bethany told me that she was awoken around 8 A.M. that morning by a phone call from Mike, her apartment manager and that he'd arranged for them to meet later to show apartments."

"Are you positive that is what she said?" I asked.

"I am absolutely positive," Ray said.

"Did she say when she and Lawson were supposed to meet to show these apartments?"

"No, she didn't say when. She was upset this guy Mike had woken her up and that he was pretty insistent about her showing apartments. She said he was being bossy."

I leaned forward to get as close to Ray as I could without touching him. I said to him, "I'm asking you to look me in the eye and tell me your conversation with her is exactly as you remember it... that you recall Lawson was the one who called her, not the other way around and that the idea was at some point they were to meet and show apartments."

I looked at Ray and waited for his reaction.

"I'm absolutely positive," he said without hesitation.

As the interview drew to a close, I asked Ray if he would be willing to take a polygraph examination. Ray shrugged his shoulders and said, "yes." When I asked him specifically how he would do on the lie detector test Ray looked me in the eyes and said without a hint of deception, "I would pass with flying colors."

Ray agreed to provide me with a DNA swab and fingerprints. I asked him to have a seat in the lobby and to wait until the rest of the Correiras had completed their interviews.

I walked back into the Homicide Unit where the rest of the detectives were waiting. I took a chair at the conference table and pulled out my notebook.

"How did the interview with the mother go, Phil?" I asked Detective Brown.

Brown shared with the group that Linda Correira appeared to be consistent with her earlier statements to patrol and to me. Consistent statements are the foundations of truth. People who have no reason to lie tend to be consistent with their stories and can repeat basic information back to you without much thought or radical changes to their memory of events.

I turned to Detective Mark Huelskoetter who had just finished interviewing Bethany's father, Billy Correira, "What did you think of him, Mark?"

"I like him," he said.

Huelskoetter said that Billy was dressed in jeans, a brown shirt and a brown Carhartt worker's jacket. Billy's long beard, round glasses and laid-back style gave Huelskoetter the sense that Billy was more comfortable outdoors than inside.

Huelskoetter said that he asked Billy Correira to tell him about himself and his family. Billy said he and his wife Linda moved to the rural area of Talkeetna in the heart of Alaska in the 1970s. The area surrounding Talkeetna is as rugged as it is beautiful. There are about seven hundred people who live in Talkeetna and the outlying areas. Billy said that he and Linda homesteaded on several acres of land just outside of town. They built a cabin with trees they harvested from the area. Soon he and Linda started a family. The Correiras had four children: Jamin, Bethany, Havilah and Brian. Bethany is the second child. All of the children were home-schooled by their mother, Linda. The family believes in faith and in prayer. Billy said they had sit-down dinners together every night. All of their children grew up being independent and self-sufficient.

"It wasn't an easy life," Billy said. "But they worked hard and they played hard."

All of the kids learned how to can vegetables and package moose meat. They hauled water to the house every day.

Bethany was probably the best example of being her own person. Bethany is kind but strong, her father said. Even before she was twenty years old, Bethany had gone to Nepal and done work as a Christian missionary. She had sailed in the South Pacific as a nanny for a doctor's family. She had worked in the base camps with climbers at the foot of Mount McKinley. She loved the outdoors and was "not afraid of anything," Billy said. She was tough but had a sensitive side and always tried to help those less fortunate than herself.

Bethany enjoyed running, hiking, rock climbing and was particularly fond of playing basketball. According to Huelskoetter, Billy appeared reserved during most of the conversation, but became more animated and engaged as he continued to speak about his daughter.

"Beth is a real athlete," he said with a smile. "She can bench press her own body weight. That's pretty good."

Billy described how growing up in Talkeetna, Bethany would play hockey on the boys' teams. She could even climb a rope hand over hand without using her legs. Billy told Huelskoetter that if Bethany had been abducted "she would have put up a real struggle. She is a fighter."

Bethany isn't just a jock from Talkeetna, he said. Billy described her academically as a straight-A student with aspirations of going to medical school someday. Bethany also has a memory for dates. She can remember everybody's birthdays. She goes out of her way to remember her friends' and her family's important occasions.

"Is she familiar with guns?" Detective Huelskoetter asked Billy.

"Growing up in Talkeetna, she has shot some," Billy answered matter-of-factly.

Detective Huelskoetter inquired if Bethany was predisposed to party.

"Beth is not one to drink very often. She's not into the party scene," her father said.

Billy described Bethany as a communicator. She wouldn't just "disappear," he said. She would let someone know where she was or she would call if she were going to be late.

"What else we got?" I asked the room.

Detective Pam Perrenoud spoke up, "We followed up on a lead of a girl similar to Bethany Correira's description leaving the apartment Saturday night." Perrenoud thumbed through her notebook, "A cab driver drove this girl to a bar near Northern Lights and Spenard Road."

Perrenoud explained that detectives went to the bar and met with the bouncers and bartenders. A check of credit card receipts confirmed the person they thought they saw was not Bethany. It turned out to be another girl who lived in Correira's apartment complex. Detective Perrenoud shut her notebook and sat back.

"A search of Bethany's car gave us nothing," Detective Brown added, "We only found Bethany's running shoes and her gym clothes."

"Okay, so she wasn't jogging and she wasn't out biking. She left her car, her keys, her wallet, her cell phone and her apartment unlocked," I said.

I then asked to the entire team at the table, "So where the hell is she?"

Nobody said anything. Not even Sarge. I knew the search teams had found nothing in the area including the Coastal Trail that runs in front of Bethany's complex.

Just then I noticed Captain Holloway standing off to the side of our conference. He was against the wall, with his arms folded, quietly taking it all in. I smiled to myself as I realized the presence of the captain must be the reason Sarge was being so quiet.

"What did the 911 call referencing the fire next door tell us?" I asked.

Another detective stated the caller, a Christine Bennett, was a newspaper delivery person for the Anchorage Daily News. She was working in the area when she spotted the fire early Sunday morning. Bennett reported that just as she drove by the empty duplex on M Street, the top floor window exploded and flames started pouring out. This was at approximately 6:45 A.M. She called 911 seconds later.

"Okay, let's break up and everyone head back to M Street," I said. "We need to canvass the area, talk to everyone who lives nearby."

As everyone filed out Captain Holloway turned to me and said, "Looking good, Klink."

He then added, "Klink, what do you think about the fire?"

"I think its bullshit. I think it was arson. I have absolutely no proof and I don't have any experience with fire investigations but I'd like a second opinion."

I realized I was being too blunt, so I added, "But I don't want to step on any toes."

The captain smiled. "Don't worry about it, Klink. This isn't going to be about protocol right now. This is your case, but I know who might be able to help with the fire. Do you mind if I call someone?"

"Not at all, boss." I smiled and added, "Thanks."

I left and managed to catch up with Huelskoetter in the parking lot.

"What about the landlord, Lawson?" he asked as we walked to my car.

"He's the number one suspect, but first things first. We need to interview all of Bethany's neighbors," I answered as I looked at the time. It was 4:30 P.M. I made a mental note to call home and let my family know I was going to be late again.

As we drove to Bootleggers Cove I noticed every telephone pole and street light in the downtown area had a poster attached to it. The posters read,

MISSING
Bethany Correira
If Seen Please Contact the Anchorage Police Department
(907) 786-8500

A colorful photo of a smiling Bethany Correira dressed in a blue colored shirt and jeans was printed on each of the posters.

As we pulled onto M Street I saw several large, white tents in the front yard of Bethany's apartment. People were milling about. Television crews were standing in front of the building trying to get people to speak on camera.

We found a spot about a block away from the building and parked the car. Huelskoetter and I got out of the vehicle and walked towards Bethany's apartment. Various people from all walks of life walked past us on their way out to search for Bethany Correira. Some of them held maps and radios. Other searchers in groups of two or more were getting into vehicles and driving out of the area. Still others were taking bikes out on the streets and following the trails that connect much of the city.

Huelskoetter and I headed up the stairs. We had to squeeze through more people who were going up and down the narrow stairway and into and out of apartment number three. What had been a nearly empty apartment when I had searched it yesterday was now abuzz with activity. Makeshift tables were set up all around the living room, piled with copies of Bethany's missing posters. People lined up to fill out forms and to get handfuls of posters. Several small black-and-white maps taken from old telephone books were taped on the walls. The maps were divided into hand-drawn search areas colored in with markers. I spotted Linda Correira behind one of the tables just outside of Bethany's kitchen. She looked at me and smiled.

"Hello, Detective," she said. "Is it okay?"

"Ok? Is what okay?"

"Is it okay that we use Beth's apartment for the search?"

Linda Correira looked at me with eyes straining for approval.

"Oh, of course," I said. "This is incredible. This is more than just putting up a few posters."

Linda Correira said, "God works in mysterious ways. We are so fortunate. When our friends in Talkeetna heard about Beth going missing, everyone came down. We didn't know what to do but we all knew we couldn't just wait around, so everyone went to work." She paused and took my hand, "There is someone I want you to meet."

I wasn't used to anyone holding my hand, let alone this small woman, but it seemed okay as she escorted me across the room. On the other side of the apartment was a couple standing at one of the makeshift desks. The man and a woman were handing out posters and writing down on pads of paper the names of volunteers as they came and went.

"Butch and Sandy, I want you to meet Detective Klinkhart," she said as she let go of my hand. A large, burly man with a light-colored beard and round face, stood up, smiled and extended his hand. His large hands dwarfed my own as he shook my arm up and down.

"Detective Klinkhart," Butch said, "It is a pleasure to meet you, sir."

Butch then turned to introduce me to the woman standing next to him who was still busy handing out posters to volunteers.

"Honey, this is Detective Klinkhart," he said

The woman smiled brightly. She was a tall beauty with long, curly, strawberry-red hair.

"It is so nice to meet you!" she said as she extended her hand. "I'm Butch's wife, Sandy."

I was thankful to her for giving me the opportunity to have Butch finally let go of my hand, which he was still vigorously shaking.

"How do you two know the Correiras?" I asked.

Butch answered, "Billy and Linda are our best friends. We've known Bethany since she was a baby. When Billy called and told us she was missing, we just had to come."

He continued, "I was in Talkeetna working on building a house when Billy called and said that he had to go to Anchorage because Bethany was missing. I drove down with him. My wife, Sandy, happened to be here in Anchorage and she came over to stay with Linda until we got here."

Butch explained how they had met up with the APD Auxiliary Search Team to learn everything they could about helping. With all the media exposure people had been coming over to the apartment and were asking how they could help find Bethany. There was no plan and nobody took a vote. The next thing they knew they were acting as unofficial search coordinators with Bethany Correira's apartment their command center.

"I'm going to have to get you guys some better maps," I said, "I have access to plenty of maps, really big ones. I will bring some over if you like."

"That would be so great," Sandy said. "We could use something better to organize the search volunteers. We also need one for poster distributions."

"Can do. Is there anything else I can help you guys with?"

"Yes, sir. I mean, Glen," Butch said. "The closest parking is at the park across the way but the sign says it's only two-hour parking. Is there something you can do to help with that?"

I shook my head. "No sorry, I can't help you there." I paused for a moment and smiled at the large man, "But, I happen to know it's not patrolled during the summer months due to budget cuts. So don't worry about it. Call me if someone gives you a problem."

I handed him my business card.

"Detective Klinkhart?" Butch asked. I turned around once more.

Butch and Sandy were standing next to each other but now I noticed they were holding hands. Butch lowered his voice and said, "We've heard about you. We are really glad that you are the one on this case."

Not knowing what to say, I simply replied, "Thank you. I'll bring you those maps tomorrow."

I turned and headed back across the living room and caught up with Huelskoetter who was now standing near Linda Correira.

I told her, "Mrs. Correira, we have some more work to do, but I will be by tomorrow. I will call you if we turn up anything."

She smiled and before I could turn, she reached out and with her small frame, gave me a big hug.

"Thank you," she said in my ear.

As she let go of me, I could see she was working hard to hold back tears.

ANCHORAGE POLICE DEPARTMENT
786-8500

MISSING PERSON

Bethany Correira
White Female
21 years old (DOB 8/29/81)
Brown Hair & Eyes
5'6" 120 lbs.

Bethany Correira recently moved to Anchorage from the Talkeetna area to attend college. She was living in a four-plex on "M" Street in downtown Anchorage at the time of her disappearance.

Bethany had daily contact with family members. She was reported missing when she failed to show up at the airport to pick up her brother on Saturday, May 3 and also missed a May 4th outing scheduled with her mother.

If you have seen Bethany Correira or have information as to her whereabouts, contact the Anchorage Police Department at 786-8500.

An early Bethany Correira missing poster. *Photo courtesy of the Anchorage Police Department.*

Chapter 14   The Dreams

It was late again when I got home. As I pulled up to the house I realized I had forgotten to call and let my wife know I wouldn't be home for dinner. The lights in the house were all off, including Evan's room. I walked upstairs and slowly opened the door to his bedroom. Decorated like a sports stadium, his room was lit only by a plastic soccer ball-shaped nightlight. I could see little Evan curled up under his covers, his round face softened by the low light. I took one step into the room and stopped. I stood there in the doorway and briefly watched him. His bed sheets rose up and down with his every breath. He looked so peaceful. I wondered what a five-year-old dreams about. Whatever it was, I'm sure it was nothing like my dreams. Thoughts of crime scenes, death and blood enter my dreams every night. Dead men do tell me their tales, but only when my eyes are closed.

I walked quietly over to his bed.

"Sleep tight," I whispered as I reached across the bed and kissed him gently on the cheek. I could feel the warmth of his breath on my face. I walked carefully out of his room and slowly closed his door behind me.

The master bedroom door was already shut. Inside it was dark. I crept across the wooden floor. Entering the clothes closet in the dark, I felt my way inside. I reached over to my gun safe and instinctively entered the combination by touch as I had a thousand times before. The safe opened with a soft "click." I put my gun inside and locked the safe back up. I hung my clothes up on the back of the closet door just in case there was another homicide that night. Many times I have gone to bed for a few minutes only to be woken up with a call from my sergeant informing me there has been another killing. I recalled one particularly bad week in the Homicide Unit in which we had to respond to five different murders over a period of five days. We had only gotten started on one crime scene when we would be ordered to move on to another. There was no sleep for anyone that week. I remember afterward going home and sleeping for two days straight.

I finished undressing and walked over to the bed. I could see my wife lying under the covers.

She was on her side, her eyes closed. She looked like she was asleep. I slid into bed. As I turned on my side to face her, she turned and rolled away from me. That was her way of showing her anger for my not calling. She was more distant than ever.

Why aren't I allowed to feel?

At least when I'm on a case I can feel something, anything.

At least when I'm working I feel like I matter.

I rolled back, closed my eyes and waited for the dreams to come.

Chapter 15   Follow The Clues

The next morning I was up and out of the house before my wife or son awoke. Arriving at the office, I went straight upstairs to the dispatch center. My daily ritual was to check and see if there were any overnight developments. Finding no new information about Bethany Correira's whereabouts, I strolled back downstairs to the Homicide Unit. The other detectives and Sarge were in the office drinking coffee and talking.

"Nothing overnight," I reported.

"This is a top priority with the Chief," the Sarge stated as he stared in my direction.

"Good," I replied curtly, before directing my attention to my fellow detectives.

"Did we get anything last night from the neighborhood canvass?" I asked them.

Each detective team had spent hours knocking on the doors of houses in the area. They noted who was home, who was not and what people said or did not say. Despite knocking on every door within a six block radius, they'd turned up no additional leads.

"We need to go back again tonight and contact those people who weren't home. Someone might have seen something," I said.

Many homicide cases are solved by what people in the area see or in some cases don't see. It's not uncommon in police work to talk to people who tell us they "didn't see anything." Further questioning can reveal a small piece of information that does not seem like much to the witness, but is a huge piece of the puzzle for investigators. I once had a case where I interviewed a couple who said they saw nothing that evening while they were out walking their dog at a local park. Later my suspect swore that he was at the park at the time and while there he was attacked by a bunch of gang bangers. He told me how he managed to bravely fight off their assault. He was trying to convince me that he was not at his ex-girlfriend's house at the time of her murder and he needed to explain his recent injuries, including the fingernail scratches to his face and neck. Unfortunately for my suspect his physical injuries were not only inconsistent with his story but the witnesses who "saw nothing" could show that the "gang fight" did not occur when and where the suspect said it did.

"What else do we have to do today?" Huelskoetter asked.

I could see the sergeant lift himself up in his chair and cross his arms. He was waiting for my answer.

I looked around the room and asked, "What's the word on her cell phone records?"

Detective Brown spoke up, "They should be in this morning. We had to get them through AT&T."

"Good. Let me know as soon as we get them," I said, too sternly. I had to catch myself as I could feel the effects of sleep deprivation grinding on my nerves. I stopped, took a breath and said with more control, "We need to tie down the boyfriend, Ray and his wife. That needs to happen today while he is still in Anchorage. If there is anything we need to hit him with I want it sooner rather than later."

Detective Perrenoud said that she would take care of it.

"I need someone to start working on any of her ex-boyfriends," I said.

I pulled from my notebook, a list of names that Bethany's mother had given me. I placed it on the table. "I need someone to do backgrounds on these guys and find out where they were over the entire weekend."

"What about video cameras in the area?" the sergeant asked. It was the first time in this case I actually liked something that he had to say.

Without missing a beat I asked, "Great, Sarge, could you please look into that for me?"

I turned away without seeing his reaction to my request. I was about to ask another question when my cell phone rang.

"Klinkhart," I answered.

"Klink, this is dispatch. We have officers over on Minnesota Drive. Someone found a pony tail on the side of the road."

"A pony tail? Like in a bunch of hair?"

"Yes, sir and it's still tied together with a rubber band," she confirmed.

"I'm en route."

Minnesota Drive is a major highway for connecting the downtown area, including Bootleggers Cove, to the rest of the city.

As I arrived at the scene I could see a couple of APD patrol cars parked along the side of the highway. Their overhead lights were flashing alternately red and blue. Two officers stood next to their cars waiting as I pulled over and parked.

"Whatcha got?" I asked as I approached.

"In a word... a ponytail," one of the officers responded.

He motioned for me to follow. We didn't have to go far. About eight feet ahead and along the shoulder of the road was a bundle of hair on the ground. The hair was approximately eight inches in length, dark brown, almost black, in color. The ponytail was tied together with a red rubber band. Above the rubber band the hair appeared to have been cut with a sharp object, likely a knife.

"Wow. It looks like someone was in a hurry, like they just yanked the hair back and cut it off," I said.

"And just threw it along side of the road?" the officer asked.

"Seems so," I said. The hair appeared too dark to be Bethany Correira's, but I had to be sure.

"Have you photographed it?" I asked.

"Yes, sir," the officer replied.

"You got gloves?"

"Yes, sir." He reached into his pocket and pulled out a set of black latex gloves.

"Great. Glove up and put the ponytail in a bag for me."

The officer quickly donned the gloves and placed the entire clump of hair in a brown paper bag. He sealed it and handed it over. I said thanks and flipped open my cell phone as I walked back to my car. The person on the line picked up.

"State Crime Lab this is Kristin."

"Kristin, this is Klinkhart."

"How's it going, Klink?"

"Good. How's my favorite scientist in the whole wide world?"

"You're so sweet, Klink. What you got?"

I stepped into my car and set the bag with the hair down in the front seat next to me.

"I need a favor and I need it now. I have some hair I need you to look at. Can you drop what you're doing?"

"Sure. Come on over."

"I'm en route." I didn't wait for a goodbye as I hung up my phone. I turned on my police lights and spun the car around in the middle of the highway. I pointed my vehicle northbound toward the State of Alaska Crime Lab.

Later that afternoon I returned to the homicide unit. Seated in the Homicide Lounge were the captain, the sergeant and the rest of the homicide unit. I didn't even bother to take off my coat.

"It's not her pony tail," I told the group. "It doesn't match the hairs I got from Bethany's hair brush in her apartment."

"Then whose is it?" Sarge asked.

"I don't know," I said as I suppressed my desire to add "and I don't care." I didn't think it was the right time to be flippant.

"What else do we have?" I asked.

"I guess I'll start then," said Detective Perrenoud, "I contacted Ray Betner's work, Bering Air in Nome."

She continued, "According to his flight records, he was flying a commercial route to Shishmaref, Saturday morning. He landed about 10 A.M. and then flew the second leg back to Nome. He arrived about 10:30 A.M. He also flew the same route again on Sunday."

"Did we get a copy of the flight log?" I asked.

"It's being faxed as we speak."

"Good. What about the wife?"

"According to her employer she was on Ray's flight to Shishmaref, Saturday morning. She arrived and checked into the hotel around 1 P.M. According to the people I spoke with she was in the village all weekend working and was seen at several venues."

Detective Perrenoud added, "There are very few flights in and out so she would have had a difficult time getting to Anchorage without anyone noticing."

"That doesn't mean she didn't have someone else do it," the sergeant said as he broke into the conversation.

"I'm not buying it," I responded. The thought of Ray's ex-estranged wife having someone else go after Bethany Correira was possible, but unlikely. This time I was going to do everything I could to prevent this investigation from going sideways on a single wild theory.

I turned towards the sergeant, "Even if the wife wanted Bethany Correira dead, she didn't know where Bethany was living. Correira had only been in her apartment for a couple of days before she disappeared. It would have taken a huge amount of time and effort to develop the kind of intel needed to locate Bethany, to quickly learn her habits, her comings and goings and then develop a plan and a method to extricate her without leaving a clue. I don't know of too many professional hit men willing to take on such a job with that kind of time frame."

"Did someone follow up your video camera lead, Sarge?" I asked.

I only asked because I was dying to know if he'd gotten out from behind his desk and done some actual police work.

"I called hotels in the surrounding areas, but none of them have outside cameras," he reported.

I smiled and nodded approvingly. It was only three o'clock in the afternoon but I was exhausted.

Captain Holloway noticed me slowing down and stepped in to assist.

"Based on a request from you guys, I contacted the Bureau of Alcohol, Tobacco and Firearms," he said. "The ATF said they are more than happy to lend a hand with the fire investigation. They are flying up their top guy to Anchorage. He should be here in a day or two."

"The Feds? This isn't their jurisdiction," Sarge said.

"Actually it may be," the captain explained. "The apartment fire was in a rental unit which is considered a commercial business. If Bethany Correira was hurt or killed there, or if the fire was arson, then the Feds could have jurisdiction."

I looked at the captain and nodded my thanks. Though his argument was a bit of a stretch, I was happy for any help I could get.

We broke and detectives scattered to work on their individual assignments. Some left to meet with witnesses, some logged onto their computers researching additional information and others worked the phones. As for me, I sat down at my desk and stared blearily at the stacks upon stacks of reports and notes.

What am I missing?

My notebook was already filled with hundreds of notes, many of them difficult to read. I hate it when I write too fast. My handwriting goes to shit when I'm in a hurry.

I found a scribbled note to myself to call Greg Branch, the owner of Branch Construction, the firm in charge of the M Street Apartments project. I got Branch on the phone. He said he was very concerned about "the missing girl." He sounded honest, but on the telephone it is difficult for even an experienced investigator to tell how forthcoming a person is, which is why I prefer face-to-face interviews.

Branch told me Bethany Correira had rented the apartment from his firm and that he'd authorized her to clean some of the properties, although he was unsure which ones. That was up to his Project Manager, Michael Lawson. Branch told me he personally had only talked to Bethany once or twice over the telephone and had never called her. He informed me some of the apartments were still for rent and they were running ads in the local newspaper. The renting of the properties was the responsibility of Mike Lawson.

"Whose responsibility were they before Lawson's?" I asked.

"His wife, Patty," Greg Branch answered.

"Where is Patty?"

"She up and quit about a week ago. Said she and Lawson were

getting a divorce. She gave me no notice. She just moved out of state. She kind of left me hanging."

"One more question before I let you go, Mr. Branch. Was Bethany hired to show the apartments to potential tenants?"

"No, sir, that was Mike's job," he answered.

I thanked him and hung up. I reached over and turned off my phone's audio recorder.

Detective Huelskoetter approached my desk with a stack of paper in hand.

"Here's Bethany's cell phone records, Klink," he said as he set them on top of my desk.

"Great. Have you looked at them yet?" I asked, already knowing Huelskoetter's penchant for numbers.

"Well, yes, I took a peek," he said with a grin.

"Well, don't just stand there, what the hell do they say, genius?"

He grabbed the documents back and went through the list of numbers, beginning with the night prior to her disappearance.

The records showed that Bethany Correira called her boyfriend, Ray, in Nome on the Friday night before she vanished at about 10 P.M. They spoke for 11 minutes. She then called her parents' house in Talkeetna at 11 P.M. The next call was to Ray again. That call lasted for 2 hours and 40 minutes. They hung up at around 1:45 A.M. on Saturday morning.

"That's consistent with Ray's interview," I said.

There were no more calls in or out of her phone until 8:05 A.M. Saturday morning, when Bethany received a call from an unknown number. It lasted only one minute. The next call was at 8:58 A.M. and was also from an unknown number. It took only two minutes to complete.

"How come we don't have the caller ID on those last two numbers?" I asked Huelskoetter.

"It could be any number of reasons. The caller ID may be blocked on the originating number or the billing company may not care as the calls might not have been billable."

Huelskoetter flipped through the rest of the pages looking for additional calls.

"That's all there is," Huelskoetter said, "There were no more calls after that. The records start showing activity only after her mother starts trying to reach her the next day."

"So whatever happened to her occurred after that last call at 9 A.M. on Saturday, May 3rd," I said.

"Sure, but her mom showed up at 10 A.M. the next morning. That's a twenty five-hour window Glen."

"I know… our timeline sucks," I moaned, as I threw the phone records on top of a pile of paperwork. I wondered how the hell we were going to tighten up the timeline. If Bethany was really showing apartments, then every guy in Anchorage looking for a place to rent was a suspect. My worst case scenario was an abductor with no prior connection to my victim. It all seemed so overwhelming as I continued to stare at the enormous piles on my desk.

One thing at a time, one thing at a time.

I caught my breath and looked at Huelskoetter.

"Okay, if this is the way it's going to go, then so be it," I declared.

Huelskoetter looked puzzled.

"What I mean is, if this is going to be a case where we have to eliminate everything and everyone one at a time, then that is what we have to do," I explained.

"Oh, old school huh?" my friend said. I looked at him inquisitively.

He continued, "I think it was Sir Arthur Conan Doyle who wrote in his Sherlock Holmes books, 'Once you eliminate the impossible, whatever remains, no matter how improbable, must be the truth."

I shook my head. "Do you stay up late at night coming up with this crap?"

"No, I just like to read," he said with a smile.

"Let's get someone working on obtaining more cell phone records," I said. "I want to know who those last two callers on Bethany's cell phone were and what she said to them."

I looked at my watch.

"Damn," I said as I stood up.

"Where you going now?" Huelskoetter asked.

"I almost forgot to drop off the maps."

I grabbed the pile of rolled up posters propped up next to my desk.

As I was driving to M Street, I was again reminded of Bethany Correira by the hundreds of missing posters hanging up along the way. It was only the third day of my investigation, but I was already starting to see posters of Bethany in the midtown portions of Anchorage. By the next day the entire town would be covered with her face.

Bethany's family and friends certainly are efficient.

It was around dinnertime when I arrived on M Street. There were more tents out front of her apartment. People were again coming and going from the area, each appearing to be on a mission. Several of the folks leaving were wearing backpacks, safety vests and canteens.

As I entered Bethany's apartment, I heard a loud but familiar voice call out, "Detective Klinkhart!"

Butch greeted me with a broad smile and his usual firm handshake. "Oh, thank you for the maps!" he said, "These are going to be awesome!"

"Butch, what's with all of the people with the gear?"

"Oh, those are friends from Talkeetna," he explained. "Some are friends, family and others who just wanted to help and some of them are professional mountain climbers. Most of these folks are usually up at the mountain base camp right now."

Talkeetna is the staging area for adventurers who want to climb Mount McKinley. During the summer months hundreds of people from around the world come to Alaska hoping to reach its summit. Many of the people in Talkeetna offer support and services for those adventurers. Some of the daring climbers succeed, some fail and a few die trying. Some of those killed on the mountain are never found.

"So you guys are searching the city for Bethany like you'd search the mountain for climbers?" I asked.

"Yep... that's the plan... is that all right? We just figured it was a good way to do it." Butch asked nervously.

"Absolutely, it's all right," I said trying to reassure him. "Keep up the good work."

I wasn't about to tell Butch or anyone else, that at this point finding someone lost on the face of the tallest peak in North America might be easier than finding Bethany Correira.

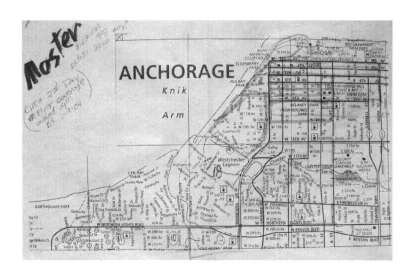

An early volunteer search map and missing poster distribution sheet.
Photo courtesy of the Anchorage Police Department.

Chapter 16   A Drive

The morning of the fourth day brought no fresh clues. There were, of course, the "crackpot" leads. We had wasted hundreds of man-hours in the Johnson case tracking down every tip with little or no attention to their validity. I never want to completely dismiss a lead, however my trick is to separate them into two piles: one for high priority leads and the others go into a secondary, "we'll get to it when we have nothing left to do," pile that included virtually all the nut job leads.

Today my primary lead list was looking pretty bare so I began to look through the secondary pile.

There was a lead from Sunday night about someone seeing a girl matching Bethany's description hundreds of miles north of Anchorage in a diner. It turned out the person making the report was clearly not able to describe Bethany. He had her hair color and length completely wrong. I pulled the lead sheet out and tossed it into a trash pile behind my desk.

There was another lead in the pile from a citizen about a silver colored Blazer SUV parked near the M Street Apartments a couple days after Bethany vanished. The driver was an adult Alaska Native male in his thirties or forties. Nothing else in the report was helpful, but I decided to assign it to another detective anyway.

The next lead was a call from a citizen about seeing some sort of green colored can on the roof of a building near M Street. That was it. Just a suspicious green can. I set that one aside for later follow-up as well.

The last lead sheet in the secondary pile was from a concerned citizen who wanted us to know Bethany was seeing a married man up in Nome. I smiled to myself as I tossed it aside.

I turned to Detective Huelskoetter.

"Want to take a drive out to Bayshore?" I asked.

"Sure? Who's in Bayshore?"

"Mr. Lawson," I said. "We're going to go visit him at work."

I love to drop in on suspects at work. It's not as good as having them at the police station in an interview room, but there is a different kind of pressure a suspect feels when the cops show up at his place of employment. Typically a suspect is more likely to talk with the cops at work than at home, because they don't want to appear uncooperative in front of their co-workers. They are also less likely to run or become violent.

Detective Huelskoetter and I drove along 100th Avenue and into the area of Bayshore, a popular residential area of diversely styled single-family homes along Campbell Lake. We turned onto Voyager Circle. Along the street I could see the newer homes here were much larger than most others I had seen in the area. As Huelskoetter drove into the cul-de-sac, I could see an empty lot of land at the end of the street. A new foundation was centered in the middle of the property. Stacks of lumber had recently been delivered and were sitting in the middle of what would someday be the front lawn of a new house. Several pickup trucks and cars were parked along the dirt entrance to the driveway. Huelskoetter parked the police car in the middle of the cul-de-sac. He switched on his new digital audio recorder and placed it in the front pocket of his coat. I pulled a notebook from my pocket and jotted down the time. It was 11:45 A.M.

"How ya doing, Mike?" I called out as we walked up the dirt driveway.

Lawson had seen our approach and walked over to meet us. He was wearing a blue-colored jacket with a logo that read "Lawson Roofing" on the chest. His hair was combed back and instead of looking like an Italian mafia boss, he now reminded me more of a wannabe Elvis, more specifically Elvis in his declining, Vegas lounge act years, considering Lawson's pudgy physique. Lawson smiled a broad smile and reached his hand out to me. I shook his hand and introduced Detective Huelskoetter.

"Mike, this is Detective Mark Huelskoetter," I said.

"Hi, Mark, pleased to meet you," Lawson said with a big grin.

Attempting to make small talk, Huelskoetter asked Lawson about the construction site. Lawson explained the foundation was in and that they were about ready to start putting up the walls. The home was going to have a three car garage and parking pad for a motor home.

While Huelskoetter was talking with Lawson, I surveyed the area. I was looking for anyplace someone could hide a person or a body. The homes on both sides of the construction site were right next-door and were clearly occupied by families. It wouldn't be impossible at night to get into a site like this and bury someone, but the probability of being seen was very high. I took some notes and turned to Lawson and Huelskoetter who were still talking construction.

"Let me see, Mike, when we talked on..." I paused.

"Sunday," Lawson answered for me.

"Sunday, yeah right," I said, flipping through my notes purposefully to give Lawson the impression we were unprepared to talk with him.

"Now, let me see... according to my notes," I said as I continued to fumble around, "you got a call from Bethany."

"No, I called her," he corrected me. That was good, because it showed he was paying attention.

Lawson continued to talk, "I called her around eight o'clock that morning. I was returning a call from her from Friday. She told me that she was having problems with keys to the triplex. I just called her to make sure she had gotten it taken care of."

I reached into my pocket and pulled out the set of keys I had found on Bethany's counter in her apartment. I held them up in front of Lawson.

"Do these look familiar?"

"Yeah, those are the master keys to the triplex," he said.

"Is there anyone living in the triplex?" I asked.

"Yes, Ted and Victoria Willette live there. They're on the first floor."

Lawson continued by saying the keys in my hand fit the triplex, not the duplex, where the fire was or the fourplex where Bethany lived. Lawson was being very thorough and was giving me a lot of detail. Perhaps too much detail, I thought.

"She was supposed to clean the hallways and laundry room and get it ready for the Willettes to move in on Saturday," Lawson said.

"Did she ever do that?" I asked.

"I don't know, but to the best of my knowledge, I'm sure she did, Detective," Lawson answered.

"Okay, but she said she was having problems with the keys, is that right?"

Lawson repeated, "That's what she said. She said she was having problems with the keys, but when I asked her Saturday she said she got it taken care of."

I asked Lawson if Bethany had called him on his cell phone and he indicated that yes, she had called his cell phone sometime Friday afternoon.

"Did you drop off some cleaning supplies for her?"

"Uh, um, Tuesday, Wednesday, somewhere in there," he said.

"So, Bethany's deal with you was to just clean the apartments then?"

Lawson thought for a moment and said, "Clean and keep the

yard up. You know, change light bulbs, whatever needed to be done. It was my boss Greg that wanted to give her a job. Told me to get her what she needed."

"It looked like she was going to be paid about 10 bucks an hour..." I said, "Were there any plans to give her a break on the rent or anything?"

"No. Not to the best of my knowledge, no. Greg is pretty tight when it comes to that," Lawson chuckled.

I smiled back.

I started flipping through my notes again, not for any real reason except to get Lawson to again tell me about Saturday.

"Okay, let me ask you this.... There was no plan to meet with her over the weekend then?"

"Nothing at all," Lawson said without wavering.

"And was there a plan for Bethany to ever show apartments?" I asked.

"No, that's my job" Lawson answered.

"And so that Saturday morning call about the problem with the keys being solved, that was the last time you talked to her?"

"That was the last time," he answered.

"When was the last time you actually saw Bethany?"

"That would have been Thursday when I dropped off the cleaning supplies," Lawson said.

I explained to Lawson we were talking to everyone who knew Bethany and I was just working on eliminating as suspects, her friends, family members and anyone who had contact with her over the weekend. It was standard procedure, I said. Lawson smiled and nodded that he understood. He added he was nowhere near M Street on Saturday.

Lawson went on to explain that he too is a father. His own daughter is Bethany's age.

"I'm heartbroken. It's sad. Really sad. I don't know what could have happened," he lamented.

Feeling I had enough for now, I was preparing to give Huelskoetter the signal for us to leave, when I thought I might see just how cooperative Mr. Lawson was going to be. I put my notebook away in my coat pocket and I asked Lawson, "So Bethany Correira has never been in your vehicle has she?"

Lawson clearly did not expect that question.

"No," he answered with a slight nervousness in his voice.

I began to give Lawson my speech to see if he would bite.

"Okay, Mr. Lawson what we're asking people to do, the family, the friends and everyone else who had contact with her is to allow us to search their vehicles…" I smiled and I paused for effect. "We just want to make sure she's not hiding in the backseat of your car."

As I talked, I walked over to the dirty white Mercedes SUV parked on the edge of the construction site. It had not been parked outside the Lawson residence when Officer Chris Ritala and I were there the other night. The plate on this car was one I had already run before we arrived. It showed the owner of the white Mercedes SUV was Michael A. Lawson.

"I can already see from here that she's not tied up in the back of your car," I said to Lawson. Both he and Detective Huelskoetter laughed.

"Do whatever you want to do," Lawson said. "I'll cooperate 100 percent."

I reached into my coat pocket and with one motion pulled out the latex gloves I had placed there for just this moment. I snapped them on and opened up the driver's door of the SUV.

Huelskoetter stood next to Lawson and watched for any reactions from him as I searched.

The vehicle struck me as quite a contrast. It was a newer, luxurious, white, Mercedes 320 SUV. And yet here it was at a construction site, dirty, messy and filled with trash and random items including cigarette wrappers, fast food bags and tools. I looked and then felt with my hands along the front areas of the interior. I didn't really know what I was looking for. I suppose it could have been anything or nothing at all. I was hoping if Bethany had been in this car something would catch my eye. To really search the car right I was going to need a crime scene team to take it apart. That wasn't going to happen here and it likely wasn't going to happen without a search warrant.

Finding nothing in the front, I moved to the rear passenger seats. The rear of the vehicle looked cleaner, but not by much. I bent down and looked from side to side. Seeing nothing, I moved to the back portion of the SUV. As I opened up the rear door I saw a couple of tools and a toolbox. More food wrappers and some receipts were the only other items present.

I closed the hatch of the vehicle.

"Thank you, sir," I said as I peeled off my sticky latex gloves.

Lawson nodded just as a large, burly man approached. From his baseball cap, his unshaven face and his well-worn tool belt, it didn't take a detective to figure out he was one of Lawson's construction workers.

Lawson introduced him.

"This is Franko."

"Hi, I'm Glen Klinkhart, APD and this is Detective Huelskoetter," I said.

"They're asking about that missing girl," Lawson explained to Franko.

"Oh, ya, I did some work in fixing up the places on M Street this winter," Franko said. "We had some wind damage and some broken pipes."

"Did you know Bethany Correira?" Huelskoetter asked.

"No, I never met her," Franko answered.

"Where were you this weekend?" he asked.

"I was in Chickaloon helping some friends build a cabin," Franko said.

Chickaloon, Alaska is about an hour and half northeast of Anchorage. I thought to myself it wouldn't be too difficult to confirm Franko's alibi. I wrote down Franko's information and telephone numbers. I handed Franko one of my business cards.

I then asked Lawson if he was free this afternoon. He said he was.

"The reason I ask, Mr. Lawson, is my boss is having us do more than just visit people at work. Anyone that had contact with Bethany Correira last week is being asked to come down to the police station to do a full taped interview." I tried to reassure Lawson by adding, "Basically, just to go over what you've already said, except do it on tape. Just to get it all down on the record. I'm sure you understand."

Lawson paused. All of a sudden he said he wasn't sure if he was free after all. He quickly explained that some contractors were coming to the job site and he'd have to check with his boss to see if the appointment could be changed or if someone else could cover for him.

"What time can we meet then?" I asked.

"I don't have your card with me, it's at home," Lawson said.

I smiled and grabbed for my wallet, "Oh, don't worry about it Mike, I have lots of cards. Just give me a call this afternoon." I pulled a card from my wallet and handed him a new one.

"Thanks, guys," Lawson said.

"Thank you, Mike," I said. Huelskoetter and I turned and walked back towards our car. We drove out of the cul-de-sac and began making our way out of the middle class neighborhood.

"What do you think?" I asked.

"Creepy. You think he did something to her?"

"I don't know yet," I replied.

I kept my real thoughts to myself.

Chapter 17   He Will Only Talk To You

By the time I got back to my desk I had a voice mail from Mike Lawson. His message said he was calling to inform us he had spoken to an attorney and on the advice of his counsel he would not be coming in for a taped interview. I chuckled and pressed the number seven on the keypad to save the voicemail.

"Hey guys! Guess who got an attorney?" I yelled across the room to anyone within ear shout.

"Lawson?" Detective Huelskoetter responded.

"Yep. He just left me a voicemail," I said. "He doesn't want to come in for an interview."

I stood up and grabbed my notebook.

"I think we should go see him," I said.

"But didn't he say that he had an attorney?"

"That's right," I said. "But he didn't say not to come over to his house. We would be doing a disservice to the man if we didn't go over there right away and give him an opportunity to explain himself now, wouldn't we?"

Huelskoetter smiled. When people "lawyer up" it doesn't necessarily mean they're guilty, but what it does tell me is they are scared of something. Some people call an attorney because they actually did the crime. Others do so out of fear we will find out about other illegal things they are doing. Others still are simply fearful of the police. My strategy when a suspect lawyers up is to ask them to their face why they didn't want to talk to me. People have a right to an attorney and they have the right to remain silent, but they also have the right to tell me the truth.

We knocked on the door of Lawson's residence around 3:45 P.M. It took a while, but he finally answered the door.

"Hello, Mike," I said. "I got your message. Can we come in?"

To my surprise, he invited us inside.

We walked through the kitchen area and into the dining room. This room definitely had a woman's touch. The walls were painted a flowery pink and white. Small ceramic figurines of animals sat on the shelves. This was in stark contrast to the swords and NASCAR memorabilia in the entry and the living room. We all sat down at the table with Huelskoetter on one side of Lawson and me on the other.

"Can we ask you a few questions, Mike?" I said.

Lawson, now sweating profusely, replied, "I really want to talk to you guys." He was about to say something else, but he quickly changed his mind. Lawson became even more uncomfortable when Huelskoetter pulled out his audio recorder. At that point he asked if he could call his attorney.

"Sure, please do," I replied.

Lawson got on the phone and spoke with his attorney, Rex Butler. After a few minutes, he handed the phone to me.

After a short conversation with Mr. Butler, I hung up the phone.

"Your attorney tells me you don't want to talk with us, Mike," I said. "I heard your attorney, but I need to hear from you. What do you want to do? What is it that you want, Mike?"

Lawson thought for a moment and then said, "I want to explain why I'm hesitant to talk to you guys."

Lawson stated he was concerned about all of the questioning and felt like he was being treated like a suspect. I explained that we just wanted to get a taped statement about his activities on Saturday and Sunday. Lawson clasped his hands together and put his head down. He said nothing.

I asked Lawson if he would be willing to provide us with a DNA sample. He said he would absolutely be willing to provide his DNA as long as it was okay with his attorney. Lawson asked to call Rex back again. We told him that was a good idea. It became clear to me that he was not going to talk to us, so as Lawson attempted to call his attorney back, Huelskoetter and I stood up and walked to the front door. We let ourselves out and headed back to the police station.

"That was very interesting, Mark. What do you think?"

"It doesn't matter what I think," Huelskoetter said as he looked at me. "All that matters is what the case detective thinks."

I checked my watch. By now it was well past four o'clock.

"Mark, can we drive up to M Street for a minute?"

"Sure, Klink."

We arrived on M Street little after 5 P.M. The sun cast a warm glow on the M Street apartments. Although I wanted to go into Bethany's apartment and see how the search teams were doing, I first directed Huelskoetter to the corner of 6th Avenue and M Street. I knocked on the entrance to the triplex. Hearing no answer, I pulled out the keys I had recovered from Bethany's apartment. I tried each of the keys until I found the one that fit the front door. We entered and worked our way upstairs. I checked and tested each of the keys along the way. When we got to the third floor I could hear banging coming from the top apartment. I knocked on the apartment door and called out, "Mr. Branch? Are you in here?"

As we entered the third floor apartment, I saw a man in the living room, standing in front of a large set of sliding glass doors. He was an older gentleman with a short, light-colored beard and thinning hair. He was trying to remove a series of curtains and was having trouble getting them off the rails.

"Mr. Branch, we talked on the phone. I'm Detective Klinkhart."

Greg Branch reached out and shook my hand. "Greg Branch. Nice to finally meet you, Detective."

I introduced Detective Huelskoetter. Branch reached up and pulled down on the curtains. With a bang, the entire set of curtains, the holders and the rod came crashing down. Twenty years of dust kicked up over the entire living room floor.

"Mr. Branch?" I asked, trying desperately not to cough. "Have you talked with Mike Lawson recently?"

Branch raised his hands up and tried to pick at the remaining parts of the curtain.

"Yeah," he said. "He called earlier and told me he needed to take the rest of the day off."

Branch stopped working and turned towards me. He said that Lawson had sounded upset when he called, ranting about how the police were harassing him and how much he was afraid because he had a past and it was all over some girl. When Branch asked Lawson for specifics, he said, Lawson said that he'd been in prison years before and that it had to do with drugs, but wouldn't elaborate.

Just then my cell phone rang. I flipped it open. It was the Crime Stopper Tipline operator. She said we needed to return right away. There was a witness at the station who had information about the Correira case but he would only speak to me. I hung up the phone.

"Thank you, Mr. Branch," I said.

I looked at Detective Huelskoetter and nodded that we had to go.

Sarge was waiting for me when we arrived wearing his usual frown.

"There is someone here to see you," he said.

"Who is it?"

"I don't know," Sarge said. "He would only talk to you."

Huelskoetter and I went around to the back of the interview rooms to take a look. I stood there as Huelskoetter turned on the video feed to Interview Room number 2. Inside the small room was a large man, sitting forward and wringing a baseball cap in his hands.

"Franko," I said.

Detective Huelskoetter and I walked into the interview room. Franko looked up as I said hello. He smiled and looked relieved to see me.

"Hello," he said.

"I understand you want to talk with me," I said.

"Yes, sir," Franko replied.

He looked down again. It was interesting to see this large man, still wearing the same dirty work shirt, torn jeans and large boots from before, looking almost shy and timid as he tried to keep from making eye contact with me.

I pulled my tape recorder out of my pocket and turned it on. I didn't need it, since video cameras were already recording our audio on the other side of the two-way mirror, but I wanted to gauge Franko's reaction.

As I set the small device on the table, I looked at Franko. Unlike Lawson, who'd practically jumped out of his skin at the sight of a mini-recorder, Frank didn't so much as flinch as I turned on the recorder and said, "What I've done Franko, is I've turned on a tape recorder."

Franko continued to look straight ahead, which I took as a good sign.

Talking into the audio recorder I said, "This is Detective Klinkhart, Anchorage Police Department. It is May 7th. I'm here with Detective Mark Huelskoetter, also with the Anchorage Police Department and we are here with Franko. And Franko, can I get your last name for the record?"

"Besinaiz. B as in boy, E-S-I-N-A-I-Z," he spelled out.

After getting Franko's basic information I leaned forward and got down to business.

"Okay, Franko. I want you to start from the beginning and tell me why you came here today to speak with us. If I have any questions, I will cut in, okay?"

Franko nodded again and began to speak in a soft voice. He said that about a week and a half ago Mike Lawson had called him. Lawson said that his wife, Patty, had left him and that they were getting a divorce. Lawson told Franko that he and Patty had had a "big" fight. When Franko asked him what the problem was, Lawson told him that it was over Patty's son living with them and other stuff that he didn't want to go into.

Franko was beginning to loosen up a bit more as he talked but continued to wring his hat with his hands. Franko told us Lawson has an auto detail shop that he owned called BRAM Auto Detailing. He told Franko that after his wife left him, he went out to the bars and got drunk. Lawson told Franko that he met up with a girl at one of the bars. Franko paused for a moment and then nervously said, "He told me and this is a quote... that he 'grudge-fucked' her and he took it out on her. He was doing it to get back at his wife."

Franko struggled to get the words out.

He continued, "Mike said that he did her while he was beating her. Taking his frustrations out on her."

I looked up from my notepad.

Franko continued, "The next day, Mike asked me to call Greg Branch and cover for him. I told Mr. Branch that Mike was at the job site all day, when he really wasn't."

Franko dropped his head and looked down at his feet.

"So this was Monday?" I asked. "About five days before Bethany's disappearance?"

"Yes, I believe so," Franko answered.

Franko went on to tell us how Lawson had been bragging that his car-detailing shop was a front for drugs. Lawson ran the business with a "black guy named Big Al," Franko said, adding that Lawson often talked about having two choices when it came to partying, that he could either drink or "grab a straw," which Franko took to mean cocaine.

Franko told us Lawson and his brother, Bob, used to have a roofing business and that Lawson liked to brag about how he used to be a millionaire with houses in Fairbanks and Anchorage. According to Franko, Lawson said the company got too big and spun out of control, eventually forcing him to file for bankruptcy.

"What does all of this have to do with Bethany?" I asked.

Franko stopped and thought for a moment. He told us that after the fire at the duplex in Bootleggers Cove, Lawson suddenly announced to Franko that he wasn't going anywhere near the M Street buildings anymore, because with "everything going on," including "that missing girl," it was all just too much for him to handle. Lawson said he didn't want anything more to do with the properties.

Franko confirmed what Greg Branch had told us about Lawson's wife, Patty. She was employed by Branch to oversee the renting and upkeep of the M Street apartments for the summer, as well as how those responsibilities shifted to Lawson after Patty abruptly left him. Franko said Lawson told him that he was getting "tired of being Greg's bitch on the weekends," for having to show apartments. Franko also said that after Patty and Lawson's big breakup, she not only left the state and flew to Minnesota, but when she left she took their two dogs and dropped them off at the pound on her way out of town. Franko said that as far as he knew, Patty was Lawson's fourth or fifth wife.

Lastly, Franko said he'd covered for Lawson a couple more times last week and again that very day.

"Today?" I asked.

"Yes," Franko said. "He asked me to cover for him, right after you two guys left. He told me that he had to go see an attorney. Lawson said he already had a strike against him because he'd been arrested for cocaine and had been in prison for it. Said he did three years."

I turned and looked at Huelskoetter. He was looking right at me. This was getting good. We turned back and asked Franko if Lawson had said anything else about Bethany Correira.

Franko said that on the Monday after Bethany was last heard from, Lawson talked about how the cops had come to his house and grilled him about "the missing girl" because Lawson had rented Bethany her apartment.

Franko stopped and looked down at his feet again.

I leaned over and looked up into Franko's face. I looked him in the eye and asked, "What else did Lawson say, Franko? I need to know."

Fighting back tears, the large man in front of me said, "Mike told me, 'I didn't know the fucking bitch.'"

"Are you okay?" I asked Franko.

"You know, detective, I don't care what you say, even when I hardly know somebody, I'm not gonna call them no bitch, especially some girl who's missing. It ain't right."

"Did Lawson say anything else about Bethany Correira or her disappearance?" I asked.

"No, sir," Franko answered. "All he said was that she had some problems with her keys. He told me he called her Saturday morning. That was it."

I paused and felt a slight twinge of disappointment. Detective Huelskoetter and I had worked together for years interviewing hundreds of witnesses and suspects alike. A good interviewing team learns to give and to take. While one asks the questions, the other watches the reactions of the person being interviewed. It allows for better analysis of the suspect and it makes for more accurate interviews. It also happens that some people may respond better to one interviewer than the other. In those cases, the other detective can quickly and seamlessly take over the lead role of interviewer without a glaring delay or change in direction.

Detective Huelskoetter picked up on the tiny lull in the conversation and without a missing a beat asked, "What did Lawson do after we left your job site this morning?"

"That was the other reason I called you guys," Franko recalled.

Franko went on to describe how before we arrived at the job site, Lawson seemed focused on what needed to be done. After Detective Huelskoetter and I left however, Lawson couldn't focus on anything.

"He couldn't even eat when the rest of the crew brought him lunch. He just threw his burger, fries and soda in the trash."

I smiled and added, "And Lawson looks like he's never missed a meal before in his life."

Franko smiled and laughed for the first time.

"Besides that, what else did Lawson do after we left?" I asked.

"Oh, yeah. After you guys left, Lawson searched his own car, the Mercedes."

I was puzzled. "What do you mean he searched his own car?"

"After you guys left, he opened up the back of his car, just like you did. Then he opened up each of the other doors. He was looking in his car just like you did."

"Was he looking for a tool?" Huelskoetter asked.

"Hell, no. Mike doesn't even swing a hammer," Franko said.

"What happened next?" I asked.

Franko described how Lawson then got on his cell phone and how a little while later, Lawson's brother, Bob showed up in a white pickup truck. Lawson got into Bob's truck and the two of them seemed to be in a heated conversation, but Franko couldn't hear what they were saying. After a few minutes, Lawson got out and Bob left. At that point Lawson told Franko that he needed to go speak with an attorney, which Franko thought was strange.

Lawson asked Franko to cover for him at the construction site. After Franko agreed, Lawson left in his Mercedes.

"Franko, I need to know about your criminal history." I said.

Without hesitating, Franko said, "Sure I have, ah, I have a record. I received stolen property. Also I was a felon in possession of a firearm and I got into a bar fight. It was all in California. I'm up here in Alaska on probation."

"Thanks for telling me that," I said. "I'm sure you can figure out that I was going to check, so it's good for you to let me know up front."

"That's what I figured, sir," Franko replied.

We'd reached the point in the witness interview where usually Detective Huelskoetter and I would leave the room to talk about what to do next. I looked at Huelskoetter and he nodded. There was no need for us to confer.

"Franko," I asked, "Would you be willing to tell everything you just told us to a judge?"

Chapter 18   The Bureau Of Alcohol, Tobacco and Firearms

By the fifth day of the investigation into the disappearance of Bethany Correira, our morning meetings in the Homicide Lounge had become routine. I began this day by going around the table, asking for input. To my surprise the Sarge didn't have much to say. Captain Holloway informed me the Bureau of Alcohol, Tobacco and Firearms expert had arrived and was at the scene of the M Street fire along with Anchorage Fire Department investigators. We had already received permission from Greg Branch and his company to search the duplex again, so there was no need for a warrant.

After the meeting ended I decided to head back to the fire scene. I arrived on M Street around 10 A.M. The sun was out, but rain clouds were gathering along the mountains to the east.

Even though it had been five days since the fire, I could still smell the odor of scorched plywood and sheetrock emanating from the scene. In front of the burned-out duplex were several large SUVs with blacked-out windows. Feds love tinted windows. Next to the SUVs was an enormous blue and white box van, new and polished to a shine. Large letters were printed on its side that read "ATF." Men in fire turnout coats and pants were going in and out of the back of the van. I could see other investigators in helmets and fire gear up on the roof of the building. They were hauling out pieces of burned lumber and bags of debris and then placing it all on large tables with screened tops. They appeared to be sifting the rubble through the screens attempting to separate the burned items.

I ducked under the crime scene tape and approached the building. A fireman I recognized came out of the front door.

"Detective Klinkhart," he said as he removed his work glove to extend his hand.

"Hello, Investigator King" I replied. "How's it going?"

Anchorage Fire Investigator Bob King looked troubled. He paused and looked at the ground.

"Well, Klink, I sure called this one wrong," he said.

"What do you mean Bob?"

"The ATF and I both now think it was arson."

At the word "arson" I froze. I was right. Someone had deliberately set the fire.

But when, how and why?

And where is Bethany?

"Let me introduce you to someone," King said. "In fire circles, this guy is a legend."

King walked me over to the large ATF van. Standing in the doorway of the vehicle was a man looking over some photographs. He was in similar fire gear as the others, but his coat said ATF. His blond hair and dark tan told me this man didn't live in Alaska. He looked up from his photos.

"Special Agent Lance Hart, I'd like you to meet Detective Klinkhart," King said.

"Nice to meet you, detective," Agent Hart said.

"Please, call me Glen. Where are you in from?"

"Spokane, Washington," he replied. Special Agent Hart went on to explain that he worked out of Spokane but was the senior special agent assigned to the ATF National Response Team, specializing in arson investigations. Without boasting, he let it be known he was a seasoned agent with more than 500 arson investigations to his career. He motioned for me to enter the van.

"Come on in," he said.

I excused myself from Investigator King and stepped up into the van. Inside were brand new computers, electronic monitors, testing stations and row after row of fire and lab equipment. Each piece of gear looked new and each was professionally labeled and in its own place. It was clearly a top-of-the-line crime scene van.

Agent Hart laid out a series of photographs on the table in front of me.

"It's really been a process of elimination," he said as he showed me photo after photo of what appeared to be electrical boxes and wiring. Agent Hart explained to me how investigators under his direction had tested and pulled every wire in the house and then tested them all again for faults that could have caused the fire. Every wire, every junction box and every outlet had been checked and re-checked. Everything worked fine and therefore he'd ruled out any problem with the house's electrical system as the source of the fire.

"And thus I cannot find an accidental source," he said.

Agent Hart must have seen confusion flash on my face at the term "accidental source," because he took a breath then clarified, "If the fire was not caused by something, then it was caused by someone. That someone makes it arson."

"Do you know how it started? Or where?" I asked.

"We're still working on those questions. It's going to take a bit more time," Agent Hart answered.

I thanked him and climbed out of the van. I walked across the driveway and stopped to survey the action at the crime scene. A short man in a full fire helmet, mask and fire retardant gear approached me. He started to say something before realizing he still had on his breather mask. He unclipped the mask and removed his helmet. I was shocked to see that instead of a fireman, it was a woman underneath all of that gear. Although she had soot and ash all over her, I could see this woman was as beautiful as she was tough, with soft features and long brown hair. I did not recognize her and I was sure I'd remember if we'd met before.

"Special Agent Rebecca Bobich, ATF," she said as she reached out a dirty hand for a firm handshake.

"Detective Glen Klinkhart," I replied, "And you can call me Glen."

"I'm the assigned Anchorage ATF Agent in charge. I was so lucky to get Lance Hart up here to help," she said.

"Yes, thank you. I'm quite impressed with him." I stopped and added, "And with the rest of your crew as well."

"Would you like to go inside the scene?" she asked.

I looked at the building. The blackened windows and the charred exterior of the building seemed darker than I remembered. The smell of the fire was more pungent up close.

"Show me the outside first," I diverted.

Agent Bobich and I walked around the exterior of the building. She showed me the various outdoor electrical cables and wires that were tested and eliminated as the source of the fire. We were standing near the outside gas meter when I noticed something curious. Along the outside wall about six feet above the ground were four staples. Underneath two of the staples were tiny pieces of plastic. I pulled out my pocket knife and pried one of them loose.

"What is it?" Agent Bobich asked.

"It's bit of hard plastic." I continued to look at the small plastic piece. "It looks like a corner to a sign that was posted up here."

"What kind of sign?"

"Perhaps one that said, 'For Rent,'" I replied.

We walked back around the front of the apartment and found another set of staples on the building near the front door. These too also had torn white corner pieces of plastic wedged underneath them.

"That's interesting," I said. "Looks like someone ripped the signs down in a hurry.

By now we were standing next to the garage doors. Every time I had been to the duplex these doors had been closed, but now they were wide open. Several crime scene team members were photographing and measuring the interior of the two-car garage.

"Do you see that?" I asked Agent Bobich as I pointed.

"What?" she asked.

"The floor. Look at the floor," I said. "See there on the left?" That side of the garage looks like it has been swept, while the other side is dirty and undisturbed."

Agent Bobich turned and pointed to her left.

"And there is a broom," she said.

Sure enough there was a broom in the corner near a side exit to the garage. Next to the broom there was a square shaped, red-and silver-colored can. I had missed both items in my initial scan of the garage. Agent Bobich and I both looked at each other. We both recognized the metal can as a container of Coleman Fuel. Also called "white gas", it is a fuel that burns well even in cold temperatures. It is commonly used in camping stoves. I turned back to the agent.

"You want to see the inside, Detective Klinkhart?" she asked.

"I'll take a rain check."

Agent Bobich smiled and put her helmet back on while I motioned to the crime scene team members. I asked them to photograph the items and to seize the broom and the can of fuel for testing.

I waved goodbye to Agent Bobich and walked over to my car.

Broom and can of Coleman Fuel found in the empty garage of the burned out duplex on M Street. *Photo courtesy of the Anchorage Police Department.*

As I drove back to the office I ran through a mental checklist of what evidence I had and what I still needed to do. I wanted the phone records of everyone involved in this case. I wanted to search Mike Lawson's car again and I wanted to search his house. But to do that I needed search warrants.

What Franko had told us the night before was a good start, especially since he'd agreed to talk to a judge if asked, but his accounts of Lawson's suspicious behavior and statements weren't quite enough to get the warrants I wanted.

Obtaining search warrants when you're a homicide investigator is usually pretty straightforward. You get a call to a scene. Someone is dead. You have a body. He's been shot, stabbed, strangled or whatever else and it's clearly a homicide. That's what you call probable cause and probable cause gets you the warrant.

I learned about probable cause in my police academy days. Our legal instructor, a local attorney, drilled it into us.

"You need probable cause to convince a judge to let you search somewhere that you aren't normally allowed to be, so you damn well better know what probable cause is and what it is not," she told my academy class.

"Someday your ass will be on the stand and a defense attorney is going to ask you why you were in his client's home. If you say that you had probable cause to be there, you'd better know what the hell you're talking about."

She went on to teach us that forcibly entering someone's home or business means temporarily suspending the United States Constitution "Think about that for a moment,' she said. "You are asking for the power to, for a short period of time, put the fourth amendment of the constitution on hold while you obtain the information that you need to solve a crime. That is an incredible power and you as a police officer have a responsibility to use it carefully and sparingly."

Some of my fellow classmates later mocked the instructor for making all of the recruits repeat out loud the definition of probable cause as if we were a bunch of seven-year-olds learning our multiplication tables.

"Probable Cause is reliable information, in sufficient quantity and detail as to lead a reasonable person to believe that a crime has been committed and the person has committed the crime or that there is evidence of the crime present at the place to be searched."

She made us repeat the definition over and over again. I thought it was a powerful statement and something I should never forget. To this day, I can still recite the definition of "probable cause" word for word.

The biggest problem I faced now was I didn't have concrete evidence a crime against Bethany Correira had occurred. I didn't have a body. I had Franko's statements, I had Lawson acting suspicious, I had arson next door to her apartment and I had a powerful gut feeling. Was it enough?

Back at my desk, I rubbed my eyes with my hands, hoping it would help my morning headache. I knew I needed help.

I picked up my cell phone and dialed.

"Good Morning, District Attorney's office," the receptionist answered.

"Sharon Marshall's office, please."

I'd first met Assistant District Attorney Sharon Marshall the same way I meet a lot of District Attorneys, at a crime scene. It was the Cynthia Henry case, the homeless woman found stabbed to death beneath the interchange bridge in downtown Anchorage. I was in the mobile crime scene van with the rest of the investigative team when the acting district attorney arrived with Sharon, a new attorney in the DA's office.

My first impression of Sharon was that of a short but powerful woman with brown hair, glasses and round cheeks who seemed to have only two speeds: fast and faster.

I learned that Sharon came on strong at times and would not hesitate to tell you exactly what she thought of a situation, a case or your competence as she did not suffer fools well. She could scare a lot of people, cops included. Every once in a while she even scared me, but I respected her and I was pretty sure she respected me as well.

Sharon Marshall had grown up on the east coast, in New Jersey. She practiced law in several other states before coming to Alaska with her husband. Sharon's husband was an oil company executive, which meant Sharon was in a rare position for an assistant district attorney, she did not have to work for the District Attorney's office. She chose to work there. Most prosecutors in the DA's office make far less than what they could make in private practice. Sharon would never tell me any of this, but the more I worked with her the more I realized that, like me, she did the work she did because she wanted to handle the tough cases and, like me, I suspected she had something to prove. If anyone could help me figure out how to put enough pieces together to get a legal search warrant it was Sharon Marshall.

She picked up on the second ring.

"Sharon, it's Klink, I need your help. It's about this Bethany Correira case."

"Tell me what you have."

I summarized the case findings to that point, including the interview with Franko. I told Sharon that after we talked to Franko, we did a nationwide check on Lawson. According to criminal records for the State of Indiana, fifteen years ago Mike Lawson was convicted of aggravated sexual assault. He was sentenced to seven years in prison. We were still waiting for copies of the police reports.

Sharon listened on the other end of the line intently. She didn't say much, nor did she interrupt, which for her was unusual. When I finished she asked, "What is the status on the search for her?"

I told Sharon it was day five and the search teams on M Street had reported their progress to me every night and every morning. Butch and Sandy and their teams of searchers were under specific orders to call me or 911, if they found anything at all. Hundreds of volunteers from Talkeetna and Anchorage were spread throughout the entire city including the coastlines, the biking and hiking trails and the creeks. They had recently expanded north of the city to the town of Eagle River and as far south as Girdwood, a ski town about 45 minutes from Anchorage. They had found nothing. It was as if Bethany had simply walked out of her apartment and disappeared.

"Do you think you know this girl yet, Glen?" Sharon asked.

"I think I'm starting to get a good idea who she is, why?"

"Well, that's how we present it to the court," she explained. "This isn't only about what you found. It's about what you didn't find. You and I need to present this case as a girl who is more than

149

missing. She is a girl who should not be missing. Everything else has been eliminated."

Sharon was on a roll. "She's not a runaway; she is not a druggie or a drunk. Bethany Correira would want to be found. There has been no accident and the only logical, reasonable and probable reason for her to disappear is that something criminal has happened to her."

"Can we put something together quickly?" I asked.

Sharon could hear the urgency in my voice. "Get everything you have together and come over. Let's start typing up some search warrants."

As soon as I hung up my phone rang.

"Detective Klinkhart, APD."

"Klink, it's me, Franko."

"What's up Franko?"

"It's about Mike," Franko said. "His car... It's clean."

"What do you mean it's clean?"

Franko spoke at a rapid pace. He said he was at the job site working when Lawson showed up. The job site was a complete mud pit as it had been raining all day long. Lawson arrived driving his white Mercedes SUV. According to Franko, the car was immaculate. It had been cleaned and detailed from top to bottom. When Franko got into the car with Lawson to avoid the rain and talk about the work for the day, Franko noticed that the interior had been cleaned and detailed as well. Franko said that the smell of the cleaning chemicals was so strong that it actually gave him a headache. He could even see pools of water and cleaner still in the cup holders.

I felt sick to my stomach.

What had I done?

Why didn't I take the Mercedes?

No, I couldn't have taken the car, I had no proof then.

I asked Franko to meet me downtown. He agreed and I hung up the phone.

I was hurriedly packing up when Detective Huelskoetter walked in.

"I can't talk now Mark, I have to get my shit together and get down to the DA's office," I said quickly.

"If it's okay with you I'd like to come along," he replied. "In our neighborhood canvass last night we talked with a neighbor who gave us some good information that you need to know."

As I drove, Detective Huelskoetter briefed me about his interview with Victoria and Ted Willette. The Willettes had recently rented an apartment in the white triplex next door to Bethany's apartment building.

Victoria and her husband, Ted, had been looking for temporary housing while their own home was being renovated. They had seen an ad in the local newspaper and that was how they met Patty Lawson. Victoria told Detective Huelskoetter that she and Ted had been dealing with Patty Lawson for a week or so about renting the apartment in the triplex when Patty quit answering her cell phone.

Victoria told Huelskoetter that after a few days of futilely trying to reach Patty, she'd called the number again, expecting no response as usual, except this time Mike Lawson answered the phone. Victoria said that Lawson had almost immediately started ranting about his issues with his wife, how she had left him and that they were going through a divorce. Victoria said she told Lawson they were still interested in renting the apartment in the triplex and they'd agreed to meet on Thursday evening, just days before Bethany went missing.

Lawson drove a white Mercedes SUV to show Victoria and her husband the apartment, she recalled. Victoria knew the vehicle make and model well because she'd recently considering buying the exact same Mercedes and had even taken one for a test drive. She remembered thinking it was strange that Lawson was driving the white SUV because Victoria thought it was a "girl's car."

"Bethany was inside the triplex at the time," Huelskoetter told me. "She was cleaning and sweeping the floors. Mrs. Willette said that she clearly remembers Bethany. Mrs. Willette has a daughter who is also Bethany's age. I asked Mrs. Willette what else she remembered and she said that Bethany was very polite, but quiet. She also said she remembered the way Lawson looked at Bethany."

"Looked at her?" I asked as I kept on driving.

"Yes," Huelskoetter said. "Victoria Willette said Lawson told them he was giving Bethany Correira a reduced rent for cleaning, but Victoria said it was the way Lawson looked at Bethany that made her very nervous."

"Go on," I said.

"Victoria told me the way he looked at Correira was weird. To her he seemed like a letch." Huelskoetter said. "Mrs. Willette just thought Lawson was slimy and that after meeting him only once, she wasn't surprised his wife left him."

"Sounds like Mrs. Willette is a good judge of character," I said.

"And that's not all," Huelskoetter continued.

Victoria went on to report that Lawson failed to give them their rental agreement. He told them he would bring the document over, along with some light bulbs for the apartment on Saturday, the day Bethany vanished.

"Let me guess... he never showed up?" I said.

"Well, yes and no," Huelskoetter said. According to Victoria, on Saturday she and Ted were going back and forth moving furniture from their old house to a storage unit and then back over to the triplex in Bootleggers Cove. Victoria recalled that about 11 A.M. that Saturday she left the triplex to get another load of furniture and it was then she noticed that Lawson's white Mercedes SUV was parked in the driveway of the empty duplex.

When Victoria returned about an hour later, the white SUV was gone. She remembered it because she thought it was weird that Lawson or at least Lawson's car, was there on Saturday, but that Lawson still hadn't delivered the paperwork or the light bulbs as promised.

"Is she absolutely sure it was Lawson's Mercedes parked in the driveway on Saturday?" I asked.

"Glen, this woman is positive. She is a good witness."

I parked the car outside the DA's office and we grabbed my three boxes of files. After meeting up with Franko and Sharon Marshall at the DA's office and after spending a couple of hours going over all of our testimony, we were ready to present our case to the judge.

The judge was good, very good. He listened intently to everything I had to say about the case and about Bethany. He heard what Sharon Marshall said and he paid close attention to Franko. Franko did very well. He appeared sincere and honest; just as he had with Detective Huelskoetter and me the day before. The judge rightly asked Franko about his criminal past and Franko put it all on the record. In applying for a search warrant it is vitally important to put all your cards on the table. We told the judge everything we knew, including all of the things we had done, all of the leads that hadn't panned out and all of the suspicious actions of Mike Lawson.

The judge paid especially close attention to what I told him about Bethany and who she was. I deliberately used the past tense – was – because given everything I knew about homicide and missing person cases, I was certain that after five days of being

153

missing, our chances of finding Bethany alive were close to zero.

For obvious reasons, I hadn't shared this dark calculation with Bethany's mother. How could I? Linda had said to my face that she knew in her heart that Bethany was still alive and that she prayed every day for Bethany to come home safe. What could I say to that? I remembered telling Linda that it was my job as the detective to assume the worst and that when Bethany showed back up safe and sound, all I would have lost was some time, so not to worry.

That's what I always tell parents. But never had those words felt like such a lie. I had no direct evidence Bethany was dead. I had my suspicions, but I had no proof. I knew where she wasn't, but I had no idea where she was. Every fiber in my being told me this girl was dead and yet I had no body. I felt in some ways that Linda Correira's hope and faith were more tangible than what I had in all of the stacks of paper on my desk back at my office.

The judge signed all of my search warrant requests. I walked out of the courthouse with ten warrants. All I could do at that point was hope our work was good enough to stand up in court and that we would get something, anything, that would lead us to Bethany.

Arriving home late again, I took off my coat and headed up the darkened staircase. As I got to the top I noticed a light coming from Evan's bedroom. The door was partially open. I slowly opened the door and crept inside to turn off his light.

"Hi, Dad," a little voice said from the bed.

"Hey, Buddy," I said, as I walked slowly across the room. "It's kinda late. You should be sleeping."

I sat down beside him and pulled the covers up to his tiny chin.

"I can't sleep," he said.

"Well, then just rest your eyes for a while."

"Mom says you're looking for someone," he whispered.

"Yes, I am. Her name is Bethany. She's missing, but I'll find her."

"I was wondering where you were today. We went looking at schools," he said as he looked up at me with his big blue eyes.

My heart sank.

I was supposed to have helped look at schools for Evan that day. He was going to enter kindergarten in the fall. His mother had several schools she wanted me to see. I had completely forgotten. A wave of frustration washed over me.

"I'm sorry, Buddy," I said. "Did you see some neat schools?"

Evan smiled and said, "Yeah, there was one with a big playground. I can't wait for you to see it, Dad."

"I'd love to see it, Buddy," I said. "Now, go to sleep."

I touched the side of his face and stroked his soft blond hair. Evan closed his eyes. I continued to stroke his hair until I was sure he was asleep and then I crept out of his room and slowly closed the door.

Chapter 19   The Wire

Inside the surveillance van I held up the wireless transmitter.

"Okay, Franko, this is the wire." I said.

"That thing is huge!" he said as his eyes widened.

"That's just the transmitter," I replied. "The microphone itself is this thing here."

I held up the small microphone and its wire attachment. I asked Franko to pull up his shirt as I wrapped the transmitter around his waist. I then affixed the device tightly to his belly with some medical tape. I fed the wire and the microphone under his shirt and up over his collar. I added a secondary digital audio recorder under his shirt, as well.

"Don't worry, Franko, this only hurts when we rip it off," I said.

"That's funny, Klink."

"Okay, you are all set."

With the help of Detective Huelskoetter we tested the wire and the receiver. The receiver was housed in a suitcase-sized box that I placed in the back seat of the van. The case had a built-in tape recorder and an external cable that led to a roof-mounted antenna. The vehicle, a borrowed minivan from our drunk driving impound lot, had tinted windows.

The plan was simple.

Franko was to go over to Mike Lawson's house in south Anchorage and try to get Lawson talking about the police investigation into Bethany's disappearance, why he'd cleaned and detailed the Mercedes SUV or anything else regarding the case. I advised Franko not to push the conversation too far or too fast.

If it became clear at some point that Lawson had said all he was going to about Bethany or if at any point I thought Franko was in danger, I'd give the signal for the other officers waiting outside to move in.

Once inside they were to seize control of the residence and place everyone, including Franko, into handcuffs. Franko was supposed to play ignorant as he was taken away in police custody. Lawson's white Mercedes was to be impounded for a thorough search and examination back at the lab. Despite Lawson's detailing of the car I wanted to see if there was anything still left that might connect it to Bethany.

Franko had previously told me he and Lawson had been talking about going into business together and that Franko had an open invite to visit him at home, so his stopping by wouldn't be seen as being all that suspicious.

"Franko, you set?" I asked.

"Yes, sir," he answered.

Franko got out of the van and started walking up the road. As he moved I could hear his footsteps echo in my headphones. Even his breathing was loud and clear. Franko walked up to the house and rang the doorbell.

"Hey," Franko said.

"Come on in," a voice replied. I could tell it was Lawson. I held the earphones tight against my head. The signal became more difficult to pick up once Franko entered the house.

"Cute dog." Franko said. "I thought your ex gave that dog away?"

"I got one of them back from the pound. The other one got fucking adopted," Lawson said.

I could hear two sets of footsteps as they walked across the entry floor.

"Oh, do I need to take my boots off?" Franko asked.

"Don't worry about it," Lawson said.

"Nice place, Mike," Franko commented.

"I talked to my ex yesterday," Lawson said. "Ya the fuckin cops have called her four or five times already."

Lawson was right about that. We had contacted his wife, Patty Lawson, after locating her in Minnesota where she'd gone to live with relatives. When we spoke to her, it was clear she was minimizing the trouble between her and Lawson. She was hesitant to describe their blow-up as anything more than an "argument." When she was confronted with the facts that she'd left Anchorage quickly with little but the clothes she had on, she insisted that "it wasn't any big deal."

My experience is that it isn't uncommon for women who are in abusive relationships to minimize the situation, including the violence, even after they have left. I decided not to tell her anything except we were interviewing everyone that had contact with Bethany. Perhaps when she was ready, Patty Lawson will open up and tell us more.

Lawson kept talking, "Patty told the cops that it's a witch hunt going on… and that's coming from the lady I'm divorcing! But I'm not worried. Patty will always stand up for what's right."

"What did she tell the cops?" Franko asked.

"She told them they were fucking idiots." Lawson said, "The cops asked her about a fight between me and her son and that I supposedly had a gun… There's a motherfucking rat out there somewhere."

I froze. Franko had to be careful.

"Fuck that shit," Franko said.

"Good boy," I said out loud.

"I don't know, I don't care," Lawson said. "I have got nothing in this fucking world to hide. I know it looks guilty because I went and got a lawyer. I got the same one as that mother, the Johnson brothers."

"The Johnson brothers?" Franko asked.

Lawson continued, "Ya, them two little boys who drowned. Them fucking cops made her feel like a criminal, too."

My stomach dropped. Malcolm and Isaiah Johnson rushed back into my mind. The pain, the hurt, the frustration. I fought to stay focused.

"So you got the same lawyer?" Franko asked.

"Yep, same one as my son, too. My kid got into trouble downtown. He and his buddy shot a guy a while back… They were supposed to just hit the guy with a bat but some dude gave them a gun and he got arrested about a year ago. I haven't seen my son in six months."

Lawson continued to rant about his son's legal problems and how the cops had no idea what was going on, "The cops couldn't find their way to the bathroom!"

I laughed and gave Detective Huelskoetter the thumbs up. Lawson may not be admitting much, but I sure was learning more and more about his family issues and attitude toward law enforcement. He'd certainly dropped all pretenses of politeness.

Keep talking, Mike.

Franko and Lawson started talking sports and about the Los Angeles Lakers game from the night before. They talked about the construction project in Bayshore for a while, but soon Franko was able to drift the conversation back to Bethany.

"The cops are only asking 'cause you had contact with her, right?" Franko asked.

Lawson gave Franko the same old story about Bethany having problems with the keys to the triplex on Friday, about his calling her on Saturday morning to check back and her telling him the key problem was handled.

"It wasn't even two minutes long," Lawson said. "The conversation was, 'Your keys, did you get them straightened out? Yes. Okay, well then have a nice day.' Bye. That was it!"

Lawson told Franko he didn't even know Bethany was missing until the next day when Bethany's mother called him. He described Officer Ritala and me coming to visit.

"The motherfuckers came here that day. The lying son-of-a-bitch cock suckers said that she called me," Lawson said as his voice got progressively more animated, "And I told them they were lying motherfuckers. One fucking cop was sitting right here. He had a recorder going under his jacket. I told them don't twist this shit in my fuckin' ass."

Franko laughed.

"Then they came over to harass me some more. That's when I told them to get the fuck out," Lawson said. "I told them to get the hell outta my house when they asked me if I fucked her... that's when I told them to get the fuck out."

"They asked you that straight out?" Franko asked.

"Yeah, just like that... General Klinkert or whatever his fuckin' name is... he asked, am I'm going to find your DNA on her? That's when I told them to get out."

I turned to Detective Huelskoetter, "Hey, Mark, I just got promoted to General!"

Huelskoetter smiled.

Lawson and Franko began to discuss the building trade and exchanged ideas about perhaps starting their own construction business. After a few more minutes it seemed pretty clear to me that Franko couldn't push the conversation any further.

"Time to move in," I said.

Huelskoetter keyed his radio and gave the go signal.

A minute later I heard Lawson on the wire as the doorbell rang.

"You know, Franko…" Lawson said and then stopped in mid-sentence. He must have looked out his front window as I next heard him say, "Son-of-a-bitch!"

Lawson opened the front door and was greeted by the Sarge.

"APD. I'm in charge here," Sarge growled. "We've got search warrants for your DNA and your car."

I smiled to myself as I could hear the tension in the voices between Mike Lawson and the Sarge. Despite my problems with Sarge, I had no doubt he was the first one I wanted at Lawson's door. I didn't love Sarge, but I was pretty damn sure Lawson was going to hate him. I wanted Lawson kept on edge and pissed off and Sarge was the perfect man for the job.

Sarge started with Franko.

"What's your name, Bud?" Sarge snapped.

"Franko," he answered.

"You got I.D.?" Sarge asked.

"Yeah," Franko said timidly as he handed Sarge his driver's license.

Sarge then had the other officers pretend to run the identification card for Franko. I could hear other police officers escorting Lawson's brother Bob downstairs. Both of the Lawson brothers and Franko were moved into the living room. Sarge turned his attention to the brothers.

"We have a search warrant for you," the sergeant repeated.

162

"I want to call my lawyer," Lawson said. He began moving toward the kitchen.

"Whoa, wait a minute there, partner," Sarge snapped. "Just sit your ass down."

I could hear movement as the sergeant continued to lecture the Lawson brothers.

"Now, listen to me," he scolded. "Look at me when I'm talking to you. I'm trying to be as nice as I can about this. If you two want me to be a jerk about this, I'll be a jerk. I'll put everyone in this house into handcuffs and I'll throw you out in the rain. Do you understand me?"

I wished I could be there just to watch Sarge dealing out his daily dose of attitude to someone other than myself.

Sarge had a phone brought to Lawson, so he could make a call to his attorney. Just then Franko was strongly and convincingly ordered out of the residence.

I could hear the footsteps on the wire as Franko was escorted by officers out the door and down the driveway.

I grabbed my cell phone and dialed Franko's number. Franko picked up. Before I could speak, he said, "Hey listen, Klink, I'm telling you what, I know that when they find out what I'm doing I'm going to be a target, I know that. My family has already told me they're scared. I don't want to have to deal with this. Mike knows where I live. Did you hear what he said?"

"I know, I heard it all," I said. "Get back to the van and we'll talk about it".

Franko hung up the phone.

Chapter 20   A Promise

One warrant down and nine to go.

I pulled into the parking lot of the crime lab, officially known as the State of Alaska Scientific Crime Detection Laboratory. I had the car towed to the crime lab while Lawson was escorted to the station.

Taking Lawson to the station served a couple of purposes. First and foremost, I wanted a copy of his DNA and fingerprints. Someday, if I find Bethany, I desperately hoped I would have a chance to locate something, anything, like hairs or fibers that would tie her to an abductor. Secondly, it put Mike Lawson on notice that he was a suspect and he was going to remain as such. I wanted to let Lawson know I wasn't going away anytime soon. His activities and statements were suspicious for damn sure and, one way or another, I was determined to find out why.

My old friend Kristin Denning greeted me as I walked into the crime lab. She wore a lab coat, slacks and a bright colored blouse. Kristen smiled her usual broad smile and her blue eyes lit up as she opened the security door.

"Klink," she said with a song in her voice. "How ya doing?"

"Great," I said. "How is my favorite mad scientist?"

"I'm good for now. Ask me again after I spend my entire weekend going over this Mercedes you just brought me."

I smiled and followed her to the crime lab warehouse.

As we walked into the bay I could see members of the Anchorage Police Department Crime Scene Team and State Crime Lab technicians working on the white Mercedes. I looked at the car. Franko wasn't kidding. Instead of the dirty, messy, construction vehicle I had seen a few days before this car looked like it had just come off the showroom floor. The white metal exterior was bright and every piece of chrome from bumper to bumper shined. The rear hatch was open and I could see into the back. Instead of tools, old fast-food wrappers and other various pieces of garbage, there was nothing but track marks from a vacuum cleaner.

Kristen saw the disappointment on my face.

"Don't worry, Klink, we'll find something, even if we have to take it completely apart."

I left so the searchers could go about their work undisturbed.

Mike Lawson's white Mercedes SUV at the State of Alaska Crime Detection Laboratory. *Photo courtesy of the Anchorage Police Department.*

The newly cleaned interior of Mike Lawson's SUV.
Photo courtesy of the Anchorage Police Department.

I'd planned to go back to the station to check in, but instead I found myself headed downtown. It was Saturday, one full week since Bethany had vanished. I had talked on the telephone to Linda Correira a couple of times in the past couple of days, but had been so preoccupied with Lawson and the search warrants that I hadn't been to M street in person.

I arrived on M Street to once again find a hive of activity, with searchers coming and going. The ATF mobile lab and the SUVs with tinted windows were still at the burned out duplex building next door.

One of the local news stations had a large television van sitting across the street. I pulled my car up behind it and parked. I wanted the news people to notice the detective car behind them. Bethany's disappearance was now a statewide media event. I had even heard it made some of the national news outlets. The police often bear the brunt of the news media, especially when things go slowly and the news people have little to publish. It makes better headlines to say the police aren't doing enough or they have no clues, than to say the investigators are working hard and are lucky if they have time to eat. My personal lack of a home life or food intake didn't make for riveting television.

I spied Linda and Billy Correira near the top of the driveway of Bethany's apartment. They appeared to be looking over at the burned out duplex and the large ATF truck parked in the driveway. They turned and smiled as I approached.

"Hi, Billy, Hi, Linda," I said as I walked up.

"Hello, Detective. I mean, Glen," Linda said, laughing at her mistake.

Billy nodded.

"How are you guys holding up?" I asked.

"We are doing okay. We have our friends here and lots of people from Talkeetna came down to help," Linda said and then added, "we have prayers and we have hope."

"That's what I told you right? Your job is to be strong and to hope."

Linda paused and said, "Glen, I just wanted to tell you thank you. Thank you for believing in us and in Bethany. And thank you for having them check the fire again."

"No worries, it was my pleasure, Linda."

I explained to Linda and Billy I wanted to make certain the fire was accidental as the fire department had determined earlier. I explained the ATF had flown up a fire expert. Without letting on that Agent Hart found it was arson, I tried my best to give Linda and Billy a pep talk, assuring them that lots of people from APD, the ATF and the State Crime Lab were working overtime to find their daughter.

I took a deep breath and gave myself a moment to think about how to word my next question.

"Linda, do you remember our talk where I told you that my job is to assume the worst?"

"Yes, Glen."

"Along those lines and please don't read anything into this, it's just part of my job, but I need the name of Bethany's dentist. I need to get a copy of her dental records." I paused. "Hopefully I will never need them, but I should have them on file, just in case."

I looked at this mother's face, waiting for some terrible reaction. There was none. Linda paused, looked up at me and said, "I'll make a call for you. I can have someone in Talkeetna go over to Dr. Little's office. They can bring them down on Monday. Is that too late?"

"No hurry," I said, trying to assure her it wasn't a priority.

"And Linda," I said. "I am going to find Bethany. I promise."

I'm not sure why I said those words. I couldn't believe those words had just come out of my mouth.

How could I make such a promise?

That was not a smart thing to say.

Maybe I said it because I felt bad asking the mother of a missing girl to hand over her daughter's dental records. Or perhaps standing there in the middle of a dirt driveway, looking at the parents look at me, I needed to hear it myself.

"Thank you, Glen," Linda said.

She reached over and gave me a hug. I hugged her back. A warm sense of peace rose up through me.

I'm going to find her.

The three of us went upstairs to Bethany's apartment. Butch and Sandy were there, still working hard coordinating volunteers.

169

The makeshift maps had been replaced by the larger, professionally printed ones I had brought over. The entire city and the outlying areas were represented on each of the walls in Bethany's living room. Several more tables had been set up since I'd last been there. A young boy, perhaps no more than 12 years old, was seated behind one of the tables, carefully folding copies of Bethany's missing poster and placing them in envelopes for distribution. His unkempt hair drooped over his eyes, but he was obviously focused on the task at hand.

Motioning towards the boy at the table I asked, "Whose kid is that?"

"That's Joshua," Butch said. "He's our youngest volunteer."

"Where are his parents?" I asked.

"They aren't here. Joshua's mom brought him here on Thursday. She gave him permission," Butch explained. "Apparently Joshua heard about Bethany on the TV news and told his parents he really wanted to help find her. He doesn't even know Beth, but he has been here every day since. He takes the bus across town all on his own. He's too young for us to let him go out and search so we give him odd jobs to do around here until his mom comes to pick him up after work."

I watched as the boy continued to ever-so-carefully place each sheet of paper, as if it were the most important document he had ever held, into yet another envelope. His dirty jeans, shirt and black tennis shoes were as unkempt as his hair and yet there he was in a metal folding chair sitting behind a table for hours on end. He was doing whatever he could to help someone that he didn't even know. Here was a boy with little or nothing to give but his time. I became lost in watching his dedication. I stood there as he again and again took one poster after another, folded it, placed it into an envelope and then stacked them neatly into rows. Each motion was moving him forward, closer to his goal of finishing the pile of missing posters in front of him.

Butch and Sandy led me away and over to tables near the far end of the living room. They went on to explain how the search had expanded to all over the city. People were being sent out in parties of at least two, sometimes more. Teams were to check in, take some posters, tape, staplers and a map and go and search a designated part of town on foot or on bike. When they were finished with that area, they checked back in at M Street and depending on the time of day, go out again. Sandy said many groups would do two or three searches a day. She explained hundreds of people from all over Alaska had come to lend a hand.

"That explains why I can't drive anywhere in this town and not see a poster of Bethany," I said.

"Exactly," Butch said with a hint of glee in his voice.

I looked out of the apartment window and saw the TV crew filming the side of the apartment.

"What are you guys doing about the media?" I asked.

Sandy said that while she and Butch were coordinating the search, they'd asked a friend they knew from Talkeetna to handle the media.

"We are trying to keep as much of the outside stuff from affecting Billy and Linda," she explained.

I motioned for all of them to follow me into what was Bethany's bedroom. I asked Butch to close the door behind us. Linda, Billy, Sandy and Butch gathered around to listen.

"There is something I need you guys to do for me."

"You need to keep Bethany's disappearance in the media. Keep putting up posters. Don't stop." I said.

All of them looked at me intently. I went on to explain how they needed to keep the TV and the newspapers talking about Bethany. We need everyone in town looking for her. Even if it's someone on the way to work, they need to be on the lookout for her.

As impressed as I was with these four best friends from Talkeetna, I wanted them to understand what they were going to be in for. I spent the next few minutes explaining to them that this was not going to be an easy or fast process. I told them the media is great for getting the message about Bethany out. There is no way better than using the media, but the media is not always looking out for their best interests. I explained that dealing with the news was a bit like playing with a snake. If you aren't careful and if you don't pay attention, you can get bit. The media will eventually get tired of the same old message of "please help us find a missing girl." They will begin to want to know more about the investigation. I explained the media outlets will soon begin to contact each of them individually, if they haven't already. They will call their families, their friends and their friends-of-friends looking for some small bit of information. The media will try to get one piece of information from one of you and try, unbeknownst to you, to leverage that against the others.

"Don't fall for it. You have to be strong and keep Bethany in the spotlight."

I could tell by all of the eyes on me they were listening.

I continued to explain, "Some reporters might even lie to one of you and say something like 'Linda Correira told me this, can you confirm that?' They will do this in order to get you to say something they can use. They may even say they talked to me. They will try to ask you about leads, rumors or things that are flat out not real, just to get reactions from you and your volunteers. In order to make sure you keep Bethany's story alive, each of you needs to look at the larger picture and realize this is not about any of us... it's about finding Bethany. Let me deal with the investigation. You guys continue to make Bethany the focus."

"Can I trust you guys on this?"

All of them agreed wholeheartedly.

"I tell you guys what," I said. "I will make you a deal. If you hear something or someone says something or makes an accusation or maybe it's just a rumor... call me. I may not tell you everything as it might jeopardize the case, but I will never let a rumor upset you or your family. If there is something or someone bothering you, call me and I will handle it. Okay?"

I looked up at the four people standing in front of me, waiting for a reaction. A few moments later a single voice spoke up.

"Thank you, Glen, you have our word," Billy Correira said.

It was the first time Billy spoke the entire time I had been there.

Before I could say anything else, Linda Correira stepped forward and extended her arm. She handed me a thick, green, spiral-bound notebook with a worn cover. I flipped through the wrinkled pages, each filled with handwritten notes. I recognized the handwriting on the pages to be that of a girl.

"It's Bethany's journal," Linda said. "We found it among her things. We thought it might help you."

"Thank you," I said.

I tucked the notebook under my arm and headed back outside.

From left to right, the Triplex, the Fourplex (where Bethany lived), and the Duplex where the fire was discovered. *Photo courtesy of the Anchorage Police Department*

Chapter 21   Cell Towers And Hairs Of A Dog

By the time I got back to headquarters it was already late afternoon.

Huelskoetter reported he was able to reach the phone company. The Pen-Register and the Trap-and-Trace warrants were in place. A Pen-Register and a Trap and Trace give real-time records of all incoming and outgoing calls through a specific phone number. Although I still wanted to see Lawson's phone records for the weekend that Bethany disappeared, I also wanted to know whom he was calling now that he was under suspicion and who was calling him.

In the old days of telephones and police work, a detective would have a physical Trap-and-Trace instrument installed on the actual phone line. It would gather all of the incoming telephone numbers as well as the time and date. It would print the phone numbers out on long rolls of white paper strips. A Pen-Register performed the same operation but for outgoing calls.

These days however, mechanical phone switches have been replaced with electronic ones. Trap-and-Traces and Pen-Registers are now done via computer and are instantaneous. The phone call records can even be emailed to investigators for quick analysis.

Unfortunately for me, Lawson's phone records would not tell me what was being said in his conversations, only the numbers being dialed in and out. I still didn't have enough evidence for a warrant to monitor to his private phone calls.

We would likely not be getting any phone data back until Monday as most of the offices were closed on the weekend. Huelskoetter said he did get some records back from the cell phone that Branch Construction used when they placed ads in the paper for the rentals down on M Street.

"The records are on your desk."

"Great," I said, "now that the trace is up, when can we hit his house?"

We did not actually search Lawson's house yesterday when we grabbed his Mercedes and brought him to the station for hair and DNA samples. I wanted the trace on his phones up first. I also wanted to spread out the searches so we would get multiple tries at seeing whom Lawson called whenever we pushed his buttons. Upsetting him was not my specific intent, but I knew that if I managed to piss him off I'd consider it an added benefit.

Maybe Creepy Mike should have cooperated with me when he had the chance.

The team decided we had to hit Lawson's residence and Bram Auto Detail shop, where he cleaned the car, simultaneously. We would need about a dozen people in each location in order to properly search and document what we found. As this was my first opportunity to potentially gather some real evidence, I wanted everything in order. I would prepare an operations plan for both searches. A search warrant operations plan contains all of the law enforcement personnel who would be involved, what each person's role was, how entry was to be made and any contingency plans, including what will happen should things go bad. We even plan, should an officer get injured, what hospital to take him to.

"What are we missing?" I asked the team and then added, "other than Bethany, of course."

Hearing nothing constructive, we decided to call it a day. It was, after all, a Saturday.

Looking out the tiny windows above the Homicide Lounge I could see it was a beautiful early summer day in Alaska. We were on the seventh day of the investigation and it looked like it was going to be a busy week starting up again on Monday. We broke up and most everyone packed up their things and headed home to enjoy the rest of the weekend with their families.

As for me, there was something else I needed to get done. Hoping it wouldn't take but a few minutes, I headed down the hall with a large white cardboard box I had grabbed from the crime scene team. I turned to my right and walked through the door of the Anchorage Police Department fingerprint lab. The main lab door was closed.

"Hey, Houseman, open up," I yelled as I knocked.

The lab door opened and Fingerprint Examiner David Houseman's bearded face and big smile poked out from behind the lab door.

"Hey, Klink! Come on in," he said as he held the door for me.

I stepped inside the Anchorage Police Department's forensics laboratory. This was where Houseman and the rest of our forensics crew would work on developing latent prints. They use any number of techniques including powder, super glue and ninhydrin to reveal hidden fingerprints.

"Whatcha got?" Houseman asked as I carefully handed him the large white box.

"Keep it level, don't spill it," I said.

Houseman set the box down, put on a set of latex gloves, broke open the evidence tape seal and reached into the box.

"A Coleman fuel can? Does this have to do with the missing girl?" he asked.

"Yep. It was in the garage of the house next door that burned down."

Housman held the container up. He slowly turned the red and silver can around in the light.

"We need to get the fuel or whatever is in it out before I hit it with my stuff," Houseman said.

"Good idea. I don't want you blowing yourself up on my account,"

I said, "And please find me some prints."

"Sure, as soon as I get this animal hair off of it," Houseman said as he turned to me.

"Animal hair?" I asked. "What animal hair?"

Houseman set the can down. He reached over to a tray on the table and seized a silver pair of tweezers. Houseman moved over to the fuel can and carefully removed a single hair from the side of it. He placed it on a slide and motioned for me to follow. We walked over to the microscope on the other side of the table and he clamped the slide in place. He looked through the eyepiece and adjusted the focus knobs.

He paused, moved back and said, "Take a look for yourself, Klink."

I looked through the eyepiece. I could see a single semi-translucent hair. It looked like any other hair I had seen close up except for one thing, the color. The hair was colored white on one end, black in the middle and white again on the other end.

"What do you make of it?" I asked.

"Does your suspect have any pets?"

"Yep. He had two dogs. Both happen to be black and white," I said as I smiled and thanked him for his help.

Houseman was still pulling hair and fibers from the can when I left the lab. As I walked back towards the Homicide Unit, I pulled out my cell phone and dialed. The line started ringing. Finally, the phone on the other end picked up.

"Sharon Marshall," the voice said.

"Hey, Sharon. It's, Klink," I said. "Are you in a good mood?"

"Yes... why?" Sharon said with a long suspicious Jersey tone in her voice.

"Are you sitting down?" I asked.

"Klinkhart . . . what do you want?"

"I want a search warrant for a dog," I said.

"You what?" She asked, "You're joking right?"

"No, I'm serious," I answered.

I explained to Sharon how we found the can of Coleman fuel in the garage at M Street and how Houseman found this unusual white and black colored hair on it. When I had finished, I paused and waited for her to answer.

"No, you can't be serious. You're getting desperate," she said.

"Sharon, come on!"

I pleaded with her as I sat down at my desk.

"If it matches the dogs at Lawson's house, it's no smoking gun, but it's something." I pleaded.

Sharon paused. I held my breath.

"Okay, Glen. You go get your search warrant for a dog," Sharon said, but added, "I am not going in front of the judge with you. And if the judge asks, you tell him this was your idea."

"Thanks, Sharon," I said. "Oh and by the way, I need two search warrants."

"Why, are there two dogs?" she asked.

"Yep" I said. I heard a click as she quickly hung up the phone.

I laughed knowing she was going to make me pay for it later.

I began to gather up my notes so I could take them over to the courthouse and get my dog search warrants. As I was grabbing the files I needed, I noticed the printed list.

It was the stack of phone records from the telephone used by Lawson and Branch Construction to take M Street rental calls. I sat back down for a moment. I stared at the records. Unlike people, records don't usually lie. Either a call was made or it wasn't. A person received a call or they didn't. With this phone list, I didn't have to try and figure out who was lying to me or why. I could just see the data and analyze it for what it was.

I grabbed a ruler and placed it horizontally on the sheet. Phone records are relatively easy to read, except that they are often in small type. It is important when you are reading them to try and keep the data all in rows so you are looking at the right records with the right times. I could see across the top of the page the call record headings. There was the date of the call, the call time, whether it was an incoming or outgoing number, the numbers dialed and the duration of the call. There was also another column of data that I had specifically requested which was called the Cell Tower Used.

Cellular telephones work like radios that send and receive signals between cell towers. Cell towers are spaced apart so their antennae can cover a certain amount of area. The closer to a tower you are, the stronger the signal. The stronger the signal from the tower, the more likely your call will be linked to that particular cell tower. With a cell phone, if you are stationary, you may be on a single tower for your entire phone conversation. If you are moving, say in a car, you may switch from one tower to the next without ever knowing it.

I had been playing with my department-issued cell phone for years and had used it to teach myself about the cell towers in and around Anchorage. I had even found a way to put my cell phone into a Service Mode. In this mode I could see on my phone display the strength of my cellular signal as well as the numeric number of the cell tower that my phone was using. I took my cell phone and drove around and observed when the cellular signal would begin to drop. I could see how it would then switch to another, stronger signal and its corresponding tower would show up on my screen.

Back then I even talked with Detective Huelskoetter, who is a licensed ham radio operator, about how we might someday use the towers to potentially place a person and their cell phone in a particular area of town. It wouldn't be as precise as a GPS, but could be helpful.

I wouldn't have the rest of the phone records until Monday, but since Branch had given us permission for his phone, this was the first batch of records that came in.

I scanned the columns and rows in the records looking for the weekend of Bethany's disappearance. I kept moving my ruler down the page until I found it. On the day of the fire there were twelve calls and based on their durations it looked like they were simply hang-ups.

Not very helpful.

There were seven phone calls the day before, on Saturday, May 3rd, the day Bethany went missing. There was only one outgoing call which was made to the cell phone's voicemail box at 12:29 P.M. and it lasted about a minute. Following the records, I scanned across the page. The cell tower used by the Branch Construction rental phone was referred to as Tower 302.

I wonder where cell tower 302 is?

I began flipping through the pages of the printouts given to us by the phone company. The telephone company gave us several pages with different headings and subheadings that included lots of technical information. On the last page I found a list of cellular tower locations. As was my luck, the list was not sorted by tower, but by the physical address. It took me a while to find the correct tower. According to the records, Tower 302 was situated on the 6th Avenue parking garage in downtown Anchorage. If the Branch rental cell phone made a call from the area of downtown around noon on Saturday then who was using it?

I looked at my watch and realized how late it was. I needed to get down to the courthouse if I was going to catch the judge before he left. I put the cell records in a stack for another time and headed out to see the judge about a dog.

Chapter 22   Hearing From Bethany

It was early Sunday morning when I went back into the station. I couldn't sleep again and I wanted to get caught up on my paperwork. There were no phones ringing, no supervisors to worry about and no one wanting to know what I was or wasn't doing.

I began looking through the five or six stacks of papers on my desk. The first document was a note containing all of the Police Auxiliary Search Team leader's names and phone numbers. This I set aside as it would later go into a binder with all of the information I had on the physical search for Bethany. I picked up each piece of paper in the pile and began to sort them into more binders. I got halfway through my first big stack when I saw the green notebook.

I put my feet up on my desk and opened it up. The notebook itself appeared to be a project Bethany was working on through a correspondence class for university credits. The white paper with the light blue colored lines reminded me of my days in school.

As I looked at the handwriting, I could see the soft gentle lines and curved letters that were unmistakably those of a female.

The first entry in the journal was from January. Bethany's name was at the top. It read:

1/24   Question: Do I look forward to writing? Yes or No? Why or why not?

If I'm in the right mood, which tends to be about one in the morning when I'm lying in bed, I love to write. It can be a way for me to clear my mind so that I can sleep. Sometimes I find it easier to write my thoughts than to speak them. I'm also a little shy about writing when I know that someone else will be reading it. It makes me feel somewhat vulnerable. I do look forward to writing when it's just for me or for someone close to me. I'm glad that I'm doing this as I know that writing will be very important for me later on down the road in my medical career. It'll be very important over the next eight years of college with the hundreds of papers that I will have to write.

I knew of Bethany's desire to help people, but this was the first time I had read it for myself. I turned the pages and read Bethany's thoughts about living in Nome, Alaska.

1/25 *God what a nice clear day in Nome. Wish I could get the rest of the day off and go flying. It seems weird that I'm working for an airline and have no idea where all of these little Alaskan villages are that we fly to every day. I would love to spend some time this summer out in a few of them. I'll bet that there is lots of good hiking to be had. I would like to go out toward White Mountain and do some camping. It's hard to stay active here in the cold and the dark. The gym gets old after awhile. I do love being near the ocean though. The waters are just too cold to surf or to snorkel. I guess I'll just have to take up sea kayaking until I can make it to warmer beaches. Wanting to be in a warmer climate makes sitting here in Nome really hard. I have to keep reminding myself why I am here and what my goals for the future are. It would be easy for me to be a sailing bum for the rest of my life, but I know my destiny is bigger than that. At least I want to believe that it is.*

As I read on I was surprised to read that Bethany wrote about her relationship with Ray Betner and her struggles with being in a relationship with him.

1/29 *I still can't believe that he would come knocking on my door at one in the morning to say that he has feelings for me. I don't see where he gets the nerve or even thinks I won't give him the time of day because he's older than I am. Yeah right, try the wife and kid.*

Bethany's words continued.

2/4 *My God what a crazy night. I didn't think that the weather could get so bad. One minute it starts snowing and blowing and in the next hour we've got four-foot snowdrifts. I can't believe that I let my friend talk me into getting out of bed and going for a drive. It took us two times around the block before we were completely buried in one of these huge snowdrifts. I didn't even think that we were still on the road. It was so frustrating pushing and digging for 2 hours and getting nowhere. I can't wait to get out of here and go to Spokane.*

2/6   Spokane, Washington. Crash and Burn. God what a bad way to start my 10 days off. I was hoping to get more snowboarding in but now I can't do much. Hell writing is a challenge. It was such a weird feeling when I landed on my shoulder. I could feel it give. When I tried to move it wouldn't budge. The Ski Patrol guys put my arm in a sling and wrapped gauze around it. I felt like a mummy. Then one of those guys wanted to put me on a stretcher board and bring me down the mountain. Yeah right. I'd have to be dead for them to carry me down in one of those things.

"This is one tough girl," I thought. I could actually see in my mind Bethany refusing be carried off the mountain in a stretcher. While on her trip to Spokane, Bethany continued to grapple with her ongoing relationship with Ray.

2/10   New relationships can be so difficult sometimes. I don't even know what way to take it with Ray. Should I be encouraging him to get back with his wife or try and make something serious with us? What he probably needs now is space. He needs time to think things over and get his ducks in a row. It's so difficult though. I can't tell him what I really feel. I think that it would change our relationship and just add more stress to it.

2/14   I can't believe that my 10 days off are over. It was hard to say goodbye to my sister, Havilah. I hope that I get a chance to see her again before she goes on her mission to Africa. I really wish that we could be closer sometimes. She seems so in need of a friend. I know I need her. She is so strong in her relationship with God.

2/16   First week back at work is over. I keep wondering what I'm doing here in Nome. I really need to save my money and get serious about school. I hate the feeling of just floating through things. I want so much more. I wonder if I'll always feel this way.

Maybe it's just a mindset and I need to change the way I think.

2/25   Went snowboarding and my shoulder feels better. It was great that my brother, Jamin and his friend Jason could join us. It's a lot more fun having a few boarders to go with. I like it when I'm challenged to keep up with the boys. It's fun to watch how the boys have to have these dumb little competitions amongst themselves. It makes me laugh.

3/4   I'm such a slacker. I finally have some days off and I haven't really done a single thing. I tried like three times yesterday to sit down and write a couple of essays for one of my classes. That's the thing about these essays. I can't seem to think of a decent topic. Maybe I can write about this upcoming crazy month with all of the Iditarod Race events going on. I've joined a basketball and a broom hockey team. I'm thinking about signing up for arm wrestling too.

By March it became apparent that Bethany had begun to seriously consider moving away from Nome.

3/10   I don't want to be here. I really need to move and get my own place. I love my brother, but I can't live with him anymore. I need to be my own person and do my own thing, but I don't want to disappoint him or anyone else.

3/17   I was able to have a few days off and get my stuff done finally. I cleaned and even gave my plants some much-needed care. They are finally looking alive. I guess that it's kinda like people here in Nome. Towards the end of the winter people's moods seem dark and down. Then we will get a couple of days of good sun and everyone is smiling and more upbeat. I know that I definitely am feeling better. That's why I need to move to a warmer and sunnier place.

3/22   The boys went out hunting today. I don't like it though as the smell of dead game makes me sick. The best part was that my friend Chris let me fly the plane back to Nome. It was incredible. It's been about three years since I've flown a plane. This made me want to take it up again.

I continued to slowly read each page. I had gotten out my marker to underline specific passages that might give me insights into this young woman however I soon became so engrossed in her words that I completely forgot about highlighting.

3/25   I've never discussed my future with anyone else. I've also never been with someone so much and have not gotten bored or tired of the relationship. It's so different with Ray. I like that he makes me think and that he wants to hear what I think. He won't take "I don't know" or "whatever" for an answer. I like that. We've been connected at the hip for three months now and I still can't get enough of him. He is so intelligent, caring and sensitive. But with all that being said it still scares me to be close to him. I don't like feeling vulnerable. Every time I do I get hurt.

3/31   I still don't know what happened. I was frustrated with Ray for being four hours late yesterday. We started talking and he said that he was going to try and work things out with his wife because he wants to be a part of his little girl's life. I can respect that but how come he could not realize that BEFORE I fell in love with him? I said okay and that I respected that and I left.

4/7   Have just about everything packed. It is incredible how much stuff I have here. In six months you really accumulate a bunch of stuff, even here in Nome. Ray says that he wants to stay in touch and be best friends, but I just need time and distance between us at least for right now. Just finished packing all of the last minute things and mailing off the rest. It's weird that this is really happening. I really am moving. I think I'll move to Anchorage and try going to summer school. It would be nice to get settled with a good job, take more classes and a decent monthly rent. I want to be totally on my own and not dependent on anyone. I'm not just someone's girlfriend. I want to be myself for a while. I want my own life and I want to try and figure out who I am.

4/9   It's so weird to be back home in Talkeetna. I walked into my old bedroom and it looked like I was stepping back into high school with all of the pictures, yearbooks, notes and awards. I feel like my life needs to go through a transition. I need to let go of the past and start living for the future.

4/17   I really want to find a place and a job in Anchorage. I'm going back to Anchorage on Monday. I hope to find an apartment. Then I will be able to get a job and things can fall into place. I feel a lot more confident. The longest that I have been in one place in the past four years is six months. I'm tired of it.

4/21   Went back to Anchorage with mom yesterday. It was so stinking early. I was up until 3am talking to Ray on the phone. I had to get up at 7:30 A.M. After driving and looking at apartments all day, I found one downtown right by the Coastal Trail. It has the most amazing view. I am so in love with it. While mom and I were checking it out the guy showing it asked if I wanted to work for him. Some summer cleanup and answering phones. What a perfect deal.

I even bought a car! It's so cute and it runs great. I had a perfect day. I think that God really answered my prayers.

4/22   I got approved to move into the apartment. Can't wait to get down there and start setting up!

Bethany ended her entry of April 22nd by drawing a simple smiley face. I turned the page and read Bethany's last journal entry. It was dated April 27th. I looked at my calendar. That was exactly one week before her disappearance.

4/27   Wow! I can't believe that this is the last time I'll be writing in my journal for English III. This was a class that I had put off for the past two years and now I am glad that I did because I would not have had you as my professor Mr. Creed. Although my spelling is still on the poor side I feel a lot more confident in my writing ability. Thank you very much Mr. Creed. It's been fun.

- Beth

On the last page I found a short note to Bethany from her professor. He had given her an A for her journal work. He finished by writing her a short note.

Nice job Bethany- And best of luck in your pursuit of higher education. May you reach your goals!

I sat there for a moment and just looked at this book lying in my lap. Its green cover was well-worn from its travels with Bethany. All I could think about was how Bethany came here to Anchorage to find herself.

I closed Bethany's journal. I managed to find one clean spot in the corner of my desk and there I placed Bethany's notebook. It would be the foundation for a new stack, one that was just about Bethany.

I continued sifting and organizing the rest of my papers until I had half a dozen binders full of documents. I stopped and decided I had done enough for one morning. As I walked out of police headquarters I could see the sun was coming up. The clear sky was becoming brighter and bluer as the sun rose over the Chugach Mountains.

I had no particular destination in mind as I drove my police car through the city. I always found that driving helps me to relax and think. On this Sunday morning, though, I was just driving around and watching the city beginning to stir. I was already halfway through the downtown area of Fairview when I realized I was again driving towards M Street.

I arrived on M Street to find it peaceful. The usual hustle and bustle of the volunteers was noticeably absent. Only a couple of people were standing around, enjoying the morning sun. As I parked my car, I saw another unusual sight. It was Linda Correira standing by herself. She was in the green belt between Bethany's fourplex and the burned out duplex. There was not much to see over at the duplex. The crime scene guys and the ATF had finished their work the day before and had boarded up the building. All was eerily quiet.

"Good morning, Linda," I said as I approached.

I looked at the orange-colored cup Linda held in both hands. The steam rose from the ceramic container.

"Coffee?" I asked.

"Green tea," Linda replied. "It helps me relax."

"How are you holding up?" I asked.

"Some days are better than others," she said with a slight smile, "Staying busy and prayer helps. Evenings are the most difficult. That is when I cry the most."

Linda Correira looked up and asked, "How are you doing? Really, are you getting enough rest? I'm a little worried about you Glen."

Enough rest?

Worried about me?

Who is this woman?

No one knew just how sick I became dealing with the missing Johnson brothers. I never told anyone I had been falling apart. Nobody knew how close I really came to being taken to the hospital for exhaustion.

"Do I look that bad?" I asked, trying to make a joke of it.

"No, Glen, you look fine," she said. "I just want to make sure you are not making yourself sick and that you are taking care of yourself."

"I'm doing well," I said. "Don't you worry about me. I'm in this for the long haul. I'm pacing myself."

There was a pause. Linda took another sip of tea and then said, "We've been talking. Billy and I just wanted to let you know how sorry we are about your sister."

I was stunned. I never talk about my sister.

"Thank you, Linda," I replied. "You and Billy know then, with my sister's murder I am a member of a terrible, awful club." I paused and added, "And I don't want you to ever be a member of my club.

The dues are way too high."

"I understand," Linda said. "Thank you for being here for us."

"You're welcome, Linda," I said.

As she took another sip of her tea I noticed a bracelet on her wrist. It was a handmade bracelet made with simple string and a few hand-painted green beads. The beads spelled out the word "Bethany".

"That's a cute bracelet," I said. "Is that something Bethany made for you?"

"No," Linda said, "little Joshua and his parents came by this morning. He wanted me to meet his mom and dad. I told them how brave he is and how wonderful their son was to help us look for Bethany."

"Joshua gave this to me," she said. "He said that because Bethany wasn't here he wanted to give me a present for Mother's Day."

Oh, my god, today is Mother's Day.

I didn't know what to say.

All I could muster was, "Linda, I'm going to find her you know."

"I know you are, Glen."

Together we looked out over the yard and toward the burned out duplex.

"Oh, I forgot," Linda said, "I have something for you."

Linda turned around and walked back to Bethany's apartment. She disappeared for a few minutes and then reappeared. She held a brown-colored file folder in her hand.

"We just got these," she explained as she handed me the folder. "It's from the dentist in Talkeetna. It's Bethany's x-rays."

I didn't open the folder. I didn't think it would be appropriate. I placed it under my arm. I said goodbye and headed for my car, leaving Linda to her tea.

I drove my police car away from M Street and I headed south towards the middle of town. As I did, I thought about a young boy and his very special gift to a mother he barely knows. I thought about Linda Correira who, on this Mother's day, is without her child. As I continued driving down the highway I realized I needed to stop and pick up something for my own mother. On this Mother's day I won't be able to give my mom a special handmade gift anything like what little Joshua gave to Linda Correira, but given the circumstances, some flowers and a hug from me will have to do.

Chapter 23   Executing Search Warrants

The briefing room was packed. "Good morning everyone, I said. "In a few hours we are going to serve simultaneous search warrants at two locations. Both warrants are regarding the disappearance of Bethany Correira."

All eyes and ears were on me. I explained that the first location, the Bram Auto Detail Shop, was important as it was likely one of the places where Lawson might have taken Bethany and it was where Lawson's SUV was detailed. I explained how we needed to look for hairs, fibers, items of clothing, anything that would indicate Bethany was ever in Lawson's car. It was not going to be easy or pretty as it had been five days since the car was detailed. The entire shop was going to have to be searched, including the garbage, both inside and outside of the shop.

When it came to the Lawsons' residence, I was clear that I wanted the entire house tossed. I wanted each and every piece of clothing belonging to either of the brothers to be checked for even the smallest drop of blood. I told the searchers I wanted them to examine every single piece of paper in the residence for anything that might tell me where they were on May 3rd and 4th. "We are going to be professional, but we are going to be thorough," I said. "We're not leaving until we've looked everywhere."

Then I held up a photo of Bethany.

"It has been ten days now. The city's been turned upside down looking for her. It's up to us to make sure we leave no stone unturned. Are there any questions?"

Seeing none I turned the briefing over to the team leaders. I walked across the hall to the APD computer crime unit and sat down at the video computer. I placed a VHS tape labeled "Tesoro - May 3" into the tape deck. I fired up the video software and rewound the tape. A black-and-white image appeared. It took a few minutes to adjust the picture but soon I was able to make out the interior of a convenience store. Most video-surveillance footage is not very good. I sped the video up and got it to around 8 o'clock in the morning. I kept moving the video until I spied a white male in dark sunglasses.

That has to be Lawson.

A large, man in a white t-shirt, black jacket, baseball cap and sunglasses could clearly be seen in the black-and-white footage. The male was at the counter purchasing what looked to be a pack of cigarettes. The time and date stamp on the video was 8:34 A.M. on Sunday, May 3rd. I grabbed a couple screen captures and saved the video.

I looked down at my watch. I was running late to meet Kristin Denning at the crime lab. I saved the video to a DVD and threw it on my desk on my way out the door and to the crime lab. I had already contacted the local Mercedes dealership to see if Lawson's SUV might have any kind of internal device we could use to figure out how many miles the car had gone. Other than a trip gauge, the dealer told me the Mercedes was not currently equipped with anything that might help us gauge its travel.

When I got to the Crime Lab I realized it had been three days since I had seen the white Mercedes. This time the car was not quite the same. The seats had been completely removed. Carpeting had been pulled up and in some places entire portions of the floor had been cut out. I met up with Kristin who told me they had found a few fingerprints here and there, mostly along the inner portions of the doors. Fingerprints are fine I thought, but seeing how Bethany had never been fingerprinted in her life, matching them to her was impossible. The other problem with fingerprints is they cannot be dated. That means a fingerprint from someone who has good reason to be there isn't helpful. If the prints came back to either of the Lawson brothers, I knew they'd be meaningless. Kristin pointed out a couple of spots along the seats where they looked at some residue but both areas turned out to be coffee stains.

On a table next to the car were personal items taken from the inside of the vehicle, mostly tools of various sizes and styles. The crime lab specialists were going over each of the tools with magnifying glasses and microscopes. On the other side of the table I saw a soft leather briefcase. Next to the briefcase there were papers and a set of Ray-Ban sunglasses like the ones Mike Lawson wore in the Tesoro station video. Going through the various papers in the briefcase I found a lease agreement with handwritten notes made out to Ted and Victoria Willette. I flipped to the second page. Where there was a space for the signatures I could see the name of Mike Lawson in the area allotted for the rental manager. The line where the Willettes were to sign was still blank. I asked the lab techs to make a copy of the paperwork and send it to me at the station.

I then turned my attention to Kristin who led me back to the inside of the Mercedes. In an area under the middle passenger seating area the lab technicians had removed a portion of the carpet. There they had discovered a large discolored area. It was suspicious enough that they took the whole section for additional testing. Kristin could see my hope and informed me that the suspect area had also been soaked with some sort of industrial cleaner containing bleach. The detail shop, she said, used so much solution that some areas were still sticky. Kristin told me that regrettably the chances of getting any DNA results were next to nil.

I thanked Kristin and asked her to have the techs put everything taken out of the car back when they were done.

"Why?" she asked.

"Because we're going to give his Mercedes back to him," I said.

"Why would you do that?" Kristin asked.

"Later today an ATF agent is coming over to see this Mercedes," I said. "He's going to install a Bird Dog inside of it."

Kristin's usual bright smile got even brighter. She knew that a Bird Dog is a GPS tracking device and that once it was installed I would be able to monitor Lawson's driving habits and pinpoint his location anywhere in the state. If Michael Lawson had anything to do with Bethany's disappearance then my plan was to see if we could force him to go to where she was.

Fifteen minutes later I arrived at Mike Lawson's house to find our large blue APD Crime Scene Van parked in front of the driveway. A dozen detective cars and a couple patrol vehicles were parked along the edge of the street, leaving little room to pass. As I approached the house I could see a few neighbors watching out their windows as the teams worked taking photographs and removing bags filled with various items of evidence from the house.

I walked into the residence and was greeted by Senior Patrol Officer John Daily. Officer Daily is a cop's cop. He has spent over 25 years as an Anchorage Police Officer. He is a SWAT team member, an instructor and is the best crime scene investigator I have ever worked with. He was once able to develop a palm print from a body at the scene of a sexual homicide. He and his partner, Lieutenant Gifford, built a makeshift plastic cover around the body. Using Cyanoacrylate or Super Glue and heat, John and the crime scene team were able to produce a palm print on the victim's inner thigh. They nearly caught the hillside around the body on fire trying to produce enough fumes to reveal the print. In the end, they developed an image that ultimately matched a suspect. As far as I was concerned, John Daily was my go-to guy.

"Hi, John, what's happening?" I asked.

"We found a body in the basement," he said.

I stopped and I looked straight at him. John then continued his joke in his normal deadpan style, "but it's not the one you're looking for."

Without missing a beat I replied, "Just leave it there then. I can only handle one homicide at a time."

I continued walking through the house. The other members of the crime scene team were busy taking photographs and searching. I walked out onto the back deck. It opened up to a large backyard. A big shed, painted red and trimmed in white, was located just

196

off the side of the house. I looked down and saw a propane grill. On the deck next to a grill was a red and silver can of Coleman fuel.

I motioned to one of the crime scene searchers and requested they photograph and seize the can. I walked back inside and found Officer Daily searching through the closets. He was going through every coat looking for blood, hairs, fibers or anything that might be of value.

Anything?" I asked.

"Not yet," Daily answered, "but we still have a long way to go."

"Where is Mr. Lawson?" I asked.

"I don't know," Daily answered, "nobody was here when we arrived."

"How did you get in?" I asked, "Did you kick the door in?"

"Nope." He answered, "A window on the second floor was unlocked. I just slid in."

"You slid in that tiny window?" I asked as I looked at Officer Daily and the thirty plus pounds of equipment that he carries on his person.

"Watch it, Klinkhart." Daily hit the switch on his flashlight and blasted my eyes with bright white light. I quickly turned away as I was momentarily blinded.

I started walking towards the front door while trying to fully regain my eyesight, trying not to show that he got me good that time.

"Thanks, John," I said. "Call me if you find anything."

"You got it, Klink," he responded with a chuckle.

Back in my car I called Huelskoetter at the auto detail shop. He reported they were not finding a lot of useful evidence, but they still had a lot more area to search. He said in an upstairs room there were old planters with dirt and various parts and pieces from lights and ballasts indicating it had once housed a marijuana grow operation. Anything illegal however had been long since been removed.

Several rags in the detail shop had tested positive for blood. Unfortunately, the testing we do on scene is often only presumptive and can sometimes produce a false positive result by other additives such as cleaning chemicals. Investigators were interviewing several of the employees to see which one of them detailed Lawson's Mercedes. They also seized a huge industrial vacuum cleaner that was so large they had to get a pickup truck to tow it back to police headquarters.

By the time I got to the station I was half an hour late for a two o'clock appointment with Christine Bennett, the newspaper delivery woman who'd reported the fire at M Street. I hate being late. I'd rather be five minutes early than five minutes late. Unfortunately, with everything happening at once, it was damn near impossible to keep my head on straight let alone make it anywhere on time. That bothered me.

I opened the interview room door and introduced myself

"Hello, Mrs. Bennett, I'm Detective Klinkhart," I said.

Christine Bennett sat in the interview room, her hands clenched together on the table. She was nervous. I tried to calm her by thanking her and asking if she wanted something to drink, a cup of coffee, water or a soda perhaps? She said "No, thank you" and asked if we had found the missing girl yet. I shook my head no and asked her if she had heard anything. Christine said that no, she hadn't. Christine worked for the state's largest newspaper, the Anchorage Daily News, as a delivery manager. I asked if anyone on the news side of her company had inquired about her reporting the fire to police. She indicated she had talked to some friends at work, but it didn't seem too important at the time. Christine asked me if the fire had anything to do with the missing girl. I deflected the question and told her we were still looking into it, but the Fire Department had stated it looked like the fire was accidental. I needed to keep any talk about arson on a need-to-know-basis.

I walked Christine through the same information that she had provided the 911 operator that Sunday morning when she called about the fire. I wanted to know more of the details of what she saw or didn't see. Once we had gotten through her basic rendition of the events I began to ask her more specific questions.

"So you were driving northbound on M street when you saw the fire, correct?"

"Yes. I looked at my cell phone as I called 911 and it was 6:39 A.M.," she said.

"Did you see anything or anyone unusual or was there anyone out and about that we need to talk to?"

"The only thing I thought was strange was there was this man, a single man... in a white... very immaculate white SUV. I don't know what kind of make it was 'cause I'm not that good with vehicles. It looked luxurious, 'cause I remember thinking that it was a Lincoln or something."

I bit my tongue. I couldn't act surprised or overly interested in what Christine had just said, but my stomach was doing flips.

"Where did you see this white SUV?"

"It was coming towards me from the south as I drove north in front of the fire and it was going really slow. The car drove past me and then turned around at the end of the road and parked. It was like he was watching the fire. But he wasn't on a cell or nothing. I remember that."

Christine went on to describe the SUV as "luxurious" and "white" but no matter how hard she tried she could not recall the specific make or model of the car. It is important and sometimes difficult for interviewers to keep from directing the witness in any one particular way. She was becoming a key witness and I knew I needed to be careful of how I asked my questions.

"Can you describe this man?" I asked. "Was he black? Hispanic?"

"He was white," she said. "He was older, maybe late 40s to mid-50s."

"Did he have a hat on?" I inquired.

"Nope, but he was wearing sunglasses," she recalled. "Which I thought was strange 'cause the sun was just coming up then." She paused and then continued, "He had dark hair... sideburns maybe."

"Anything else?" I asked.

"No, I didn't get a real good look at him," she replied.

"Tell me more about the white SUV..." I asked. "What did it do again after it passed you and the fire?"

"That was the strange part. He passed me and then backed the car up at the end of the street. He looked like he was just sitting there watching."

I pulled out a photo line-up sheet. I had prepared several photo lineup cards to show her. Each card had photos of different people on it except that one of them was an image of Mike Lawson. Given her description, I was hopeful Christine was going to be able to identify Lawson as the man behind the wheel of the white SUV.

I asked Christine to take her time and if she recognized the person she saw on M Street that morning to please circle that photo. If she could not identify anyone or if she were unsure I asked her to simply tell me so. The one thing I have learned about photo lineups is that witnesses want very much to be helpful. It is in most witnesses' nature to want to try and help the police, especially in a case like this one; however it's more important to the case that you not allow the witnesses to guess.

Christine signed the back of the photo lineup card and turned the images over. She carefully studied each photo, each face. I held my breath. She paused. She continued to look at each photograph carefully. Finally she spoke.

"I'm sorry," she said. "I don't know. I can't be sure."

"That's okay I'd rather you not guess," I said as disappointment washed over me. "I appreciate your coming in today, Mrs. Bennett."

"Well, I'm sorry I didn't help much," she said.

"Oh, no, you very much did."

The search of Mike and Bob Lawson's residence in south Anchorage.
Photo courtesy of the Anchorage Police Department.

Chapter 24   I Will Find You

I stared at the evidence paperwork listing the more than 120 items seized from the Lawson residence by Officer Daily and his crime scene team. They took towels from Mike Lawson's master bathroom that appeared to have bloodstains on them. They took raincoats spattered with "blood-like substances." They collected the gas can I saw on Lawson's deck, the one of the same brand and size found in the burned out M Street duplex. They grabbed hairs, fibers, guns and even another vacuum cleaner. In Bob's room they even found a small amount of marijuana and several handguns, but all the firearms checked out as legal. I still wanted to hold onto them and have them tested for DNA and fingerprints, just in case.

Detective Huelskoetter walked over and leaned on what little edge of my desk remained. I gestured to the paperwork.

"There is so much stuff to go through," I said. "Hell, I even got a search warrant for the hairs from his dog that we need to have processed."

Mark nodded his head, "How about I take the evidence sheets and start filling out the lab requests for you?"

"That would be a big help," I replied. "Also, could you please have someone bring Mr. Lawson's vehicle to the front of the police station? I think it's time that Mike got his Mercedes back."

"You got it," Mark replied with a grin.

I reached over and grabbed the file marked "Cell Phone Records – Mike Lawson." They showed Lawson's cell phone being used on the morning of Saturday, May 3rd to call Bethany. It was a short call, two minutes in length. I flipped back to Bethany's cell phone records. Listed was an incoming call from Lawson's phone. An hour later she spoke with her boyfriend Ray. And then nothing.

Lawson's records showed additional calls later on that morning.

Most of the calls were between the two Lawson brothers, Bob and Mike.

They told me they were together watching NASCAR that morning.

So why were they calling one another?

And what were they saying?

I added a note to my growing to do list on my large white board: "Get cell tower locations for both Lawson brothers' cell phones." Next I picked up the phone and dialed one of those very numbers.

"Mike Lawson please," I said.

"Speaking," the voice replied gruffly.

"Hi Mike, it's Detective Klinkhart here," I said in my nicest voice possible.

"Yes, sir," Mike said with equally fake sincerity.

"I just wanted to call and thank you for your cooperation the other day" I said.

"What's going on with my car and briefcase and stuff?" Lawson asked, his voice betraying a touch of anger.

"Oh, your car? I don't know about your car... hold on a second, I'll check." I put the phone on hold and waited for a few minutes to make it seem like I had to get permission. After a long pause, I took the phone off hold. "Yep, my boss said that we can release your SUV."

"And I want my commercial shop vacuums that you guys took from the detail shop" he said, getting more heated by the second.

"I think we can get that returned to you in a few days."

"Okay, fine. When can I get my car back?" he asked.

"I'll have it here in front of the police station at 4 P.M."

"Fine, I'll see you then," he said as he hung up the phone.

In the meantime, I spent my time listening to more recorded conversations we made between Franko and Lawson at both the Lawson residence and the Bayshore construction site.

Between mind-numbing shoptalk, blaring saws and pounding nails, Lawson's true personality emerged in a few telling exchanges. At one point Lawson tried to gain Franko's sympathy by saying once he was exonerated he didn't expect to ever hear the Anchorage Police Department say that they were sorry for putting him through this "witch hunt." Lawson continued to stay with his story that he only spoke with Bethany on the telephone that morning and she had gotten the problem with the keys fixed. At one point Franko pressed Lawson about Bethany and why the police took his car.

"She was never in your car though right?" Franko asked Lawson.

"I never had that fucking broad in my car," Lawson shot back. "Damn, fuck, I've met her twice! Just once to drop off cleaning supplies and the other time to fucking sign her lease."

I stopped the recording... I played Lawson's words back again. "I've never had that fucking broad in my car." I rewound it again and then again. Over and over I listened to Lawson describe Bethany as "that fucking broad."

I threw down my head phones and rubbed my eyes. I had been up since the crack of dawn. I picked up another file on my desk and began reading, when a few moments later a voice interrupted my thoughts.

"You getting any sleep?"

I looked up. It was Special Agent Rebecca Bobich. She was no longer dressed in her fire gear. She wore a black colored t-shirt with "ATF" imprinted on it and black cargo pants. She looked like a special agent, a gorgeous special agent, but a special agent

205

nonetheless.

"Not a lot," I admitted.

"Can I help?" Rebecca asked.

I handed her a new file that had just been tossed on my desk.

"This is the background file on Michael Lawson. Did you know that he is a convicted felon?"

Agent Bobich's eyes widened.

"What was he convicted of?"

"Well, they don't list all of the details, but he did five years in prison outta Chicago for aggravated sexual assault."

Rebecca flipped through the pages. "Do you realize what that means?"

"That he's a rapist?" I said.

Agent Bobich smiled at my attempt at a joke. "Yes, but didn't you guys get some guns and some dope out of the Lawson residence?"

"Just a couple of old handguns and a small amount of marijuana."

With that, Agent Bobich said, "But Mike's a felon and a felon can't be in possession of drugs or guns. You got his DNA didn't you?"

I nodded.

"Do you mind if I have the guns swabbed for DNA, fingerprints and have a gun purchasing trace done on them? If we can put Mike's prints or DNA on the guns found in the house then we might be able to charge him with something."

"That sounds like a perfect job for the Bureau of Alcohol, Tobacco and Firearms," I said.

Rebecca smiled and started to leave when I asked her for one more favor.

"What do you think about putting out a press release for me?" I asked.

Agent Bobich smiled.

That night I again arrived home late. It was getting to be a bad habit. It was now nearly midnight as I crept into Evan's bedroom to check on him. I looked over at Evan's bed. A smile and two tiny eyes greeted me.

With the lights still off I walked over and sat on the edge of his bed. Evan turned and he looked up at me with his blue eyes.

"Did you find Bethany today dad?"

"Not today buddy, but I'm still looking." I reached over and gave him a kiss on his forehead. "I love you buddy."

"Dad, can I ask you something?" Evan said in a sleepy voice.

I nodded and said, "Yes, you can ask me anything."

"If I got lost would you look for me?" he asked.

I wasn't quite sure what to say to that. I thought for a moment. I looked into his eyes and I stroked his blond hair. I leaned forward so he would be sure to hear me. I put my arms around him and I said, "Evan, if you were ever lost, I would never, ever stop looking for you."

He looked up at me. He smiled. I knew that he was listening.

I whispered, "And I will find you. Never forget that. No matter where you are, I will always come and I will find you."

Evan smiled again and then paused before asking, "Like finding Bethany, Dad?"

"Yes buddy, like finding Bethany. That's my job. Now go to sleep."

He closed his eyes completely and rolled over on his side. I pulled his covers up and I kissed him once more goodnight. I sat there on the edge of his bed for what seemed like the longest time. I just watched. I watched and I listened to him breathe as he slept.

Chapter 25   Better Living Through Technology

The next day the Anchorage Daily News front page headline said it all.

Fire next door to Correira's home is arson.

A Federal Fire Investigator concluded that someone intentionally set the blaze in the vacant duplex next to Bethany Correira's apartment the morning after she vanished, the Bureau of Alcohol, Tobacco, Firearms and Explosives announced Wednesday. The same day, Anchorage Police said that the arson may be linked to the young woman's disappearance on May 3rd.

Brad Earman, ATF Special Agent, wouldn't say how the fire at 622 M Street was ignited. But "we have an idea of who did this and why," he said on Wednesday.

It was the first time officials acknowledged they may know of someone connected to Corriera's disappearance. Earman said that some hairs, fibers and other debris were taken from the scene for testing. He said he is still waiting for results and did not know if the hairs were Correira's. Those results all will be passed on to the Anchorage Police.

Special Agent Earman would not say whether an arrest was imminent.

The rest of the article went on to say no more than what I asked Agent Bobich and the ATF to put out to the media. There was of course more conjecture from the press about where Bethany was and what, if anything, the police knew.

The press had been hounding me every day for the past two weeks. I gave them nothing. I continued to direct the media back to Bethany's parents to try and keep emphasis on the search for her. I wanted whoever was responsible to know that people were looking for her. I didn't want my investigation to be in the public eye.

Was Bethany dead? In my mind she was. But while I could prove arson I couldn't prove she was dead. Not yet. I wanted Lawson and his brother to know I knew it was arson, that I suspected them in Bethany's disappearance and that I was not going away. I wanted Lawson to read that article and be afraid. And then, hopefully, he might make a mistake.

I had recently obtained an additional search warrant, this time for Mike and Bob's watches. I'd recently heard of a case where a killer had cleaned up a scene and had taken care to destroy all of the evidence. He had destroyed or cleaned everything. Luckily the investigators had the idea to seize the suspect's wrist watch from him. Inside of the small nooks and crannies of the wristband they discovered human blood that came back to the victim. I had no such luck. Mike and Bob's watches were clean. Even the dog hair turned out to be a bust. There was no match between the hairs found on the gas can in the duplex and the dogs owned by Mike Lawson. A check of Bob and Mike Lawson's credit cards showed no charges during the weekend of Bethany's disappearance either.

My run of bad luck with evidence continued with the news that the State of Alaska Crime Lab had determined the blood on the towels from Lawson's bathroom was not Bethany's. It wasn't Lawson or Bob's either, but most importantly it wasn't Beth's. The blood detected on the raincoats found in the closet was not human. The crime lab techs thought it was most likely blood from salmon caught and cleaned while fishing.

My phone rang. Caller I.D. showed Franko's number.

"Hey Klink, its Franko" he said when I picked up. "Did you see the paper this morning?"

"I practically wrote the article myself," I said.

"Ah, you're good," he responded. "I thought you might like to know that Mike showed up at the construction site this morning with the newspaper in his hand. He was acting kinda nervous."

"Nervous how?"

"He was saying that the fire department said it was electrical and now the ATF idiots are saying its arson. He was pacing back and forth."

"Did Mike say anything about Bethany?"

"Nope." Franko said, "Not a word. He hung around for a few minutes and then made up some story that he had to leave."

"What was Mike driving?"

"His white Mercedes" Franko said. "I thought you guys seized it."

"We did, but we had to give it back."

"No evidence in it, huh?"

"Something like that. Thanks for calling Franko. Give me a ring if Mike shows up again."

"Will do," Franko said as I hung up the phone.

I leaned over and picked up the black tactical bag next to my desk. Detective Huelskoetter had dropped it off the night before. The black nylon case was heavier than I expected. The tactical straps and heavy duty zippers made it look like it was from our SWAT team. I unzipped the top of the bag and lifted up the cover. Everything looked like it was ready to go.

I opened up the laptop computer inside. I attached the various cables and the antenna and flipped the switch. The screen fired up. A moment later a map of Anchorage appeared on the monitor. The electronic map showed the roads going into and out of the Bayshore neighborhood. From there I could make out the construction site. A red line with a dot appeared on the map. The dot was moving away from Bayshore and was heading eastbound on Dimond Boulevard.

Now this is how you do surveillance.

We had tried to watch Mike Lawson using more traditional methods. For a week I had detectives tailing Lawson and any cars that he was associated with. We had dozens of detectives in civilian cars attempting to keep tabs on him.

Trying to do surveillance on a person is not like you see in the movies. It's not as easy as simply getting in your car and following them. To do it effectively you need at least three vehicles and each surveillance team needs to be trained in how to work with each other. It is sort of like a dance. Two cars will try and stay behind the suspect vehicle, while another car attempts to stay ahead of the bad guy. As the suspect moves or turns unexpectedly the lead car may miss the turn and can pull off thus giving the car behind him the eyes on the suspect. The car ahead will also be in position should either tailing car lose the suspect. Despite our best efforts, Lawson was able to figure out that he was indeed being followed.

The upside to our being so bad at following Lawson was that spotting us so often had made him paranoid.

During our last surveillance attempt Lawson and his brother Bob were seen by a spotter car leaving their house in south Anchorage. They were in Bob's white pickup truck. Bob was driving. The next surveillance car picked them up as they drove north on the Seward Highway. Within minutes the white truck had turned east into a residential area and then back out and onto the Seward Highway, this time going south. It was clear to the spotters that Bob was attempting counter measures to see if they were being followed. The truck then turned around again, this time almost hitting one of our spotter vehicles. The truck drove northbound again and pulled a fast turn into the parking lot of a Mexican restaurant. The surveillance team tried to follow but they were several blocks behind. By the time they got into position, the truck was already parked. It was empty. The surveillance teams backed off and waited. They kept the truck in sight and called me. I arrived a short time later.

As I watched from a distance, I could see two males leaving the restaurant. It was Bob and another male whom I did not recognize. They both were walking toward the truck. Bob was wearing a white t-shirt and jeans. The other male was wearing blue jeans, a denim jacket and a gray baseball cap. The two men got into the truck and began to head out of the area.

I listened as the spotter car announced over the radio, "the subject and his brother have exited the restaurant. The target is seated in the passenger side. They are heading westbound out of the parking lot."

As our surveillance cars began to move, I got out of my vehicle and walked into the restaurant.

It was a typical Mexican style restaurant. The walls were white with a stucco-like finish. You don't see much stucco in Alaska, except for in Mexican restaurants. Cinco De Mayo had been two weeks prior, but the restaurant's bar still had posters and decorations hung up celebrating the 5th of May.

The bar was relatively empty except for an elderly couple seated in one of the booths and the bartender standing behind the bar. I approached the bartender. He was an older white male in his 50s with white hair and a beard. He was wiping down the countertop as I approached.

"Did you see a couple of guys just leave here?" I asked.

"Yep." He said without looking up. He continued to wipe down the bar.

"Where were they sitting?"

The man looked up at me. He was irritated at my interruption. He pointed over to a table on the other side of the bar. There were three half full beer bottles on the table.

"I only saw two guys leave." I said to the bartender. "Where did the other guy go?"

"The big guy with the Elvis haircut? He went out the back."

The Bartender continued: "I thought they were going to stiff me on my tip."

"Why is that?"

"'Cuz the big guy traded coats with the little guy right before he ducked out," he said, then asked, "Hey, are you a cop?"

"Nope" I said. "They just took something from me."

I paused and added, "And I want it back."

I pulled out my cell phone as I walked back to my car.

"Tell the surveillance teams to pull off and go home. They got burned again."

It was that last failure that convinced the commanders upstairs to give me approval to have the GPS locator hidden in Lawson's vehicle.

Now I could sit at my desk and watch as Lawson's white Mercedes moved slowly across the computer screen. I pressed the history key and up popped a dialog box with the last twelve hours of tracking data. I could see that the SUV had been parked overnight at Lawson's residence in south Anchorage. The history showed that Lawson began to move only about an hour ago. He traveled north and then drove directly to the construction site in Bayshore. He made no stops and no deviations. I closed the history window and watched live as Lawson's car moved north and then east on Benson Boulevard. It finally stopped near the corner of Arctic Boulevard and Northern Lights. I recognized the location. It was Blues Central, a bar.

I watched for over an hour. The Mercedes didn't move. After another hour I pressed the notify button on the mapping software. I entered my cell phone number and pressed enter. This meant I would get a text message whenever Lawson's car moved.

While I waited at my desk, I flipped through my file of tips from "psychics." In every big case the media attention invariably generates calls from psychics and others who claim to have "visions." In the Johnson brothers case I logged over twenty-four separate psychic callers, all of whom claimed to have information. It always made me chuckle to think that twenty-four psychics all had visions that conflicted with each other.

That's not to say that I dismissed the psychics altogether. I always kept tips that came in from those who claim to have dreams or visions. If someone is able to provide such specific detail about a crime, the most likely explanation is that the tipster was actually there or that he got information from someone who was directly involved. I shook my head in amusement as I read through some of the more interesting "visions" that had come in from different people regarding Bethany's vanishing.

> "I see the number 14."
> "Her mouth is duct taped."
> "It's someone who lives in the neighborhood."
> "Look for the 5 houses or 5 blocks... the number 5."
> "The initials B.C. - Bethany Correira, Bootleggers Cove."
> "You missed it... Look in the numbers."

It was all so much bullshit. I threw the file down on the floor.

I thumbed through the rest of my files again. I kept looking for something that I could use. I kept coming back to the phone records. Those calls from Lawson to his brother Bob on the day that Bethany's cell phone went silent were bugging me. The brothers had told me they were together that morning.

So why were they calling each other?

Did I miss another pond?

Chapter 26   The Devil Is In The Details

I grabbed my laptop and a handful of my files. I carried everything into the Homicide Lounge so I could spread the records out. I laid out the phone records belonging to Lawson onto the conference room table. Next I laid out his brother Bob's records. Next I taped Bethany's cell phone bills up on the wall. By hand I went through each set of records line by line, comparing them and entering data into my computer. I then took all of the information I entered on the laptop and overlaid the data on top of the mapping software. Once the map appeared I began to step myself through the progression of calls on Saturday, May 3rd.

At 8:05 A.M. Lawson's cell phone called Bethany's. The data showed his phone was hitting a cell tower in south Anchorage near his residence. The call lasted only 49 seconds.

I stopped and pulled up the videotape of Mike Lawson on my computer. It showed that Mike Lawson was at the convenience store buying cigarettes. The time on the tape was 8:34 A.M. I added that to the map.

Mike Lawson caught on convenience store surveillance footage on the morning of May 3rd. *Photo courtesy of the Anchorage Police Department.*

The next entry was from Beth's cell phone bill. At 8:58 A.M. she had a phone conversation with her boyfriend, Ray. Their conversation lasted only two minutes. Bethany disappeared soon after.

I scrolled forward to the next series of calls, which originated from Lawson's phone beginning at 10:51 A.M., about two hours after Bethany talked to Ray. Lawson's phone was no longer hitting the tower near his residence in south Anchorage. Instead, the map clearly showed that Mike Lawson's cell phone was hitting a tower only five blocks east of Bethany's M Street apartment.

"He was fucking downtown!" I exclaimed.

I pressed a key on the computer to enlarge the map. The computer screen showed the tower east of the apartment. I entered the cell tower number "302Z". The computer displayed the tower signal broken down into three quadrants with a red cone emanating from the cell site, indicating that Lawson's phone at the time of the calls was located somewhere west of the tower, in or near Bootleggers Cove. I pulled up Bethany's apartment on the map. Beth's fourplex apartment and the burned-out duplex next door were smack in the middle of the signal.

Lawson said he'd been home all day but his cell phone was a stone's throw away from Beth's house only two hours after she was last heard from.

I looked at the records again. Who was Lawson trying to call? The number appeared on the screen. It was his brother, Bob. The call had gone to voice mail. Bob hadn't picked up. The records showed 30 seconds later, Lawson, still near Bethany's apartment, tried to call the home number for the south Anchorage residence he and Bob shared. No one answered.

Thirty seconds later Lawson called his brother's cell phone again. Again, there was no answer. Next Lawson tried to call the fax line at the south Anchorage house. No answer. Again, he tried his brother's mobile phone. Again, Bob did not answer. Twenty seconds later, Lawson called the house line once more.

Bob must be a heavy sleeper.

Finally, at 10:54 A.M. Lawson called his brother's mobile phone and it was picked up. The records showed Bob's phone hitting the cell tower closest to their residence. The phone call terminated at 10:56 A.M.

I stared at the computer screen.

Seven calls in three minutes.

Mike really wanted to talk to Bob in a very bad way.

Adrenaline rushed through my body. I had trouble focusing. This was more than just a hunch. This was the first real evidence that Lawson and Bob were lying about their whereabouts on the day Bethany went missing. Lawson or at least his cell phone, had in fact been within blocks of Beth's apartment.

Lawson obviously had tried desperately to reach out to his brother. They talked for two whole minutes.

If I knew what was said in those two minutes could I find Bethany?

I looked around. There was no one to talk to, no one to share this with. The room was empty. I looked back at my computer and pressed on, tracking the brothers through the phone records.

Nearly an hour after the initial flurry of calls, Lawson's cell phone moved south to the central part of town as Lawson called his voice mail. Lawson and his cell phone stayed in the area for less than an hour and then returned to the area of M Street. He made one more call to an unknown phone number and then his phone went dark for three hours.

By mid-afternoon, according to the records, Lawson was back at his house in south Anchorage. He stayed there for the rest of the day.

Where was Bethany?

Did he kill her and then take her to his place?

If so, why did we not find any evidence in his house?

I took a deep breath, picked up the phone and called the sergeant.

Soon the Homicide Lounge was packed with detectives, crime scene officers and supervisors. I displayed the computer map on the wall as I walked everyone through my analysis.

"So as you can see, there was a flurry of calls from Lawson's cell phone beginning at 10:51 A.M.," I said. The small chart showed just how close Lawson's phone was to Bethany's apartment complex.

"Lawson then made a few more calls and was in the midtown area of Anchorage before going back up to M Street again."

"Isn't Bram Auto in that area of midtown?" Detective Huelskoetter asked.

"Yes it is," I answered with a smile. "After going back to M Street Lawson then returned to his house way down here in south Anchorage."

I pointed to the Lawson house on the map.

"It appears that he stayed there for several hours."

"So where the hell is the girl?" the sergeant bellowed.

That's the million-dollar question, you dumbass.

"We've searched Bethany's apartment and come up with nothing. We also got nothing from the burned out duplex next door and nothing from Mike and Bob's house," I said. "Given that Lawson was so good about cleaning up his vehicle I am going with the theory that he put Bethany in the white SUV."

Everyone nodded. I continued to explain that if we assumed that Lawson killed Bethany at M Street Saturday morning, then called his brother while still there, he might have next gone to Bram Auto Detail for cleaning supplies, which would explain his short trip to midtown before returning to Bootleggers Cove, presumably to clean up the murder scene.

"When are you going to tell us where she is Klinkhart?" the sergeant interrupted.

"I'm getting to that," I answered.

The normally vocal group of cops seated around the large conference table sat quietly. I pressed a button on the computer to display a map of Eagle River, a town just 20 minutes north of Anchorage.

"Analysis of Lawson's and Bob's cell phones shows that later that evening, at approximately 5:17 P.M., Lawson's cell phone hit a cell tower traveling between Anchorage and Eagle River."

I told the group that thirty minutes later Lawson took a call from an unknown phone number that was just enough to give us his new location.

I pressed a key and the image of another map appeared on the wall.

"By then Mike's cell phone was in Wasilla, about 45 miles farther north of Anchorage. Mike talked to someone for four minutes and by the time he hung up, his cell phone had switched to another tower here along the Parks Highway."

"He's driving north," a detective noted.

"Exactly," I said. "The times between the calls and the location of the phone when the calls were made, show clearly that Mike was driving a vehicle northbound out of Anchorage past Eagle River and then north out of Wasilla on Saturday night. All of this during the time when Mike and his brother swear they were both at home."

"Where was Bob during this time?" Huelskoetter asked.

"I don't have proof, but Bob's cell phone records show absolutely no activity during the time of Lawson's trip north out of Anchorage. Mike and Bob call each other all the time. It was Mike who called looking for Bob in a panic Saturday morning. The fact that Bob and Mike didn't call one another even once during this period tells me that the two brothers were together during this little trip north Saturday night."

"It's possible, but it's still only a hunch," the sergeant growled.

For once I had to agree with him.

"You're correct, sir," I said. "But it's better than anything we've had so far."

"So where is she?" Detective Perrenoud asked.

"They took her somewhere north," I said as I forwarded the presentation slide once more.

This time a larger map appeared. It covered all of south central Alaska from Anchorage north to Fairbanks, some 360 miles away. I explained to the group that the next time Lawson's phone was active was approximately four hours later. By that time he was back in Anchorage. I pulled out my copy of the thick Alaska Milepost map book and set it on the table.

"If you assume that these guys were driving with a body in the back seat then it's reasonable to assume that they were staying close to the speed limit. I went through the mileage records for the Parks Highway north of Wasilla and factored in the posted speed limits."

"If they were last tagged by Mike's phone in North Wasilla and then they arrived back in Anchorage four hours and seventeen minutes later how far could they have traveled?"

I posed the question out loud to no one in particular.

"This all sounds like one of those god-awful math problems," one of the officers said. "Like if a train leaves the station at noon and travels 38 miles..."

"You got it," I said. "Based on this math problem, Mike and Bob could have traveled as far as 135 miles north, dumped Bethany's body and then returned in time to hit the Anchorage phone tower at 10 P.M."

"So she could be anywhere 135 miles up or down the highway," Detective Huelskoetter said. "That's a hell of a lot of area for us to be looking for a body."

Mark was the math wizard of the group. He could recall numbers, license plates, case numbers and even dates like no one else I had ever met.

Huelskoetter paused for a moment and then announced, "That's as much as 2600 square miles. That's about the size of Connecticut."

"How the hell are we going to search an area the size of Connecticut?" the sergeant barked.

After several hours of heated discussion it became painfully obvious that it was going to be too difficult to even try and search such an enormous area. We needed more to go on if we were going to find Bethany. My initial high of finding the cell phone tower data began to fade into a familiar sense of disappointment and frustration.

Chapter 27   Life and Death, Goes On

Homicides in Anchorage didn't just stop because a 21-year-old-girl was missing, no matter how many posters went up. The rest of the summer brought more murder cases to our fair city.

Cases like the murder of Dennis Kane. Found by coworkers in his house after he failed to show up for work, Kane had been brutally murdered by one or more possible assailants. He put up a fight, even managing to knock out a six-foot window in the process before finally succumbing to his injuries. Detective Huelskoetter took the lead on the Kane murder case. He spent several years following up the case and every lead that he could. Huelskoetter even traveled to several other "Lower 48" states trying to find witnesses who would talk to him about the case. Eventually Huelskoetter put together a well-constructed case using interviews, DNA and blood patterns left at the scene. All of the evidence tied Kane's stepson to the murder.

The case of Kiva Freidman was a particularly terrible domestic violence homicide. Kiva was about to break off her relationship with her boyfriend when a simple, unassuming, message left on her answering machine by a male friend set off her killer, Jerry McClain. He tied Kiva up, bound and gagged her. Jerry placed a large mirror in front of her and forced her to watch as he repeatedly raped and sodomized her throughout the night. He beat her so many times with a baseball bat, an Alex Rodriguez Louisville Slugger, that the medical examiner and I stopped counting the hits just to one leg after we reached thirty-two strikes. McClain hit her legs with the bat so hard and so many times that it liquefied the muscle and fat tissues inside. By morning Kiva was dead. It was only then that McClain dialed 911. He was convicted of murder in the first degree.

Another case involved a young girl, about Bethany's age, who was found stabbed to death in an apartment complex in north Anchorage. Her blood was spattered inside the apartment corridors, indicating that she had been chased down and stabbed by her killer. Twenty-two year old Megan Maxwell was found at the bottom of the stairs just feet from an exit door and possible safety. It wasn't CSI evidence that located her killer, Earl Voyles. Instead it was talking with people in the apartment complex where the murder occurred. I was on "knock and talk" duty for the second day in a row with Detective Kristie Ratcliff when I suggested that we go back to one specific apartment. I couldn't put my finger on what it was exactly but the guy and his wife who lived there had seemed a bit odd when I spoke with them the day before.

The man, Martin Wayne, answered the door wearing a stained white tank-top shirt over his impressively large belly. He'd told me he and his wife were in their apartment watching TV at the time of the murder, but hadn't seen or heard a thing.

I'm not sure why I wanted to go speak with him again; perhaps it was just to have Detective Ratcliff see the apartment and its interesting residents. When we knocked on the door Mr. Wayne was home, wearing the same clothes as the day before and again watching television. As I asked him to again describe what he was doing the night of the murder, he again told me about watching television and drinking some beers with his wife and his brother.

"Your brother was with you?" I asked.

"Yeah, he left out the back when all those cops showed up," Wayne said. "I think my brother might have an outstanding traffic ticket or something. "

"Was your brother ever outside of the apartment that night?" I asked.

"Yeah, didn't I tell you? He was gone for some cigarettes but he came back," Wayne said.

"What is your brother's name?" Ratcliff asked as she got out her notepad.

"Earl Voyles," he replied.

We took the name back to headquarters and when Voyles was finally located and brought in for questioning he denied ever being at the apartment and seeing or even knowing anything about the victim. Despite his denials during the interview, Detective Huelskoetter noticed small stains on the shoes Voyles was wearing. Those stains turned out to be blood. Megan Maxwell's blood.

Voyles was eventually convicted of second-degree murder for Megan's death. Near as we could figure, Megan was simply trying to get to her apartment when Voyles decided to approach her in the hallway. When she rebuffed his advances, Earl Voyles attacked her.

Every murder that summer placed further demands on our department as investigators worked each case to its conclusion.

I was lucky. The rest of the homicide team showed a lot of honor and loyalty to the Correira family and to me, by taking up some of my slack. Normally each of the homicide detectives rotates as case officer or lead investigator, on new murder cases. If it's not your turn to run a case then you help by playing a supporting investigative role. In any given year a detective might be the case officer on three or four homicides. During that summer and fall, the other detectives took over my work load to allow me to concentrate on Bethany's case almost exclusively. I was grateful for this and in return I tried to help out on other cases as time permitted, which was not very often.

With my growing admiration for the Correira family, Linda Correira in particular, I was very concerned about losing my focus or worse, getting target lock on one theory, one piece of evidence or even one suspect. If Lawson was involved and I firmly believed that he was, I still knew that everyone connected with the case was likely to show up later as a suspect for the defense.

There are three typical defenses at a murder trial. The first is the "it was an accident" defense. The second is "I wasn't there, it wasn't me" and the last is what cops and prosecutors call, SODDIT or "Some Other Dude Did It."

Given Lawson's large ego, I was convinced that he would try and point the finger at anyone else but himself. That meant I needed to make sure that all of the other dozens upon dozens of people that potentially could be considered suspects were interviewed and definitively ruled out.

I couldn't tell Bethany's family that I strongly suspected she was somewhere within 135 miles north of Anchorage. I knew by this time that their search efforts in and around the city were almost certainly going to be unsuccessful.

I don't know if it was her spirituality or her strong New England upbringing or her belief in me, but to my continuing surprise Linda Correira seemed to have faith that we were doing everything that we could for her daughter. She often stood up for me and our investigation when her friends, neighbors, searchers, the press and even other family members would come to her out of frustration and anger over the lack of perceived progress.

"The police are doing their job," she told the critics. "Glen is working hard and he is going to find her."

This was a woman who believed in me, even if I didn't always believe in myself. Despite my ability to outwardly appear to be large and in charge of her daughter's case, I was often tired, frustrated and constantly doubting myself. I was so afraid to fail.

I wanted to tell Linda Correira that we had our suspicions about Mike Lawson. I wanted to tell her about all of the circumstantial information, such as the cell phone and cell tower data. I wanted to tell her about Lawson's past and all of his suspicious activities. Unfortunately, I knew that even if the information I had added up to something or some place to go look for her daughter, it was not the time to do so.

It wouldn't have been appropriate to tell her about the conversations with Lawson's ex-wives either. At last count we found that Lawson had been married at least four times, possibly five.

One of Lawson's ex-wives I spoke with was Renée Lawson. Renée was Lawson's fourth wife and had been divorced from him for several years by the time I tracked her down. We in law enforcement come to appreciate that ex-wives and ex-girlfriends of suspects can be very helpful as they are often willing to spill the goods, especially if things ended badly.

I located Renée Lawson in California. She'd not heard about the missing girl but the fact Lawson was in the mix did not surprise her.

Married to Lawson for eight years, Renée had witnessed first-hand his rise to success in the roofing industry as well as the demise of the company. Renée said that Lawson's favorite pastime was snorting cocaine and drinking heavily. She said he'd once told her he'd been in jail on a rape charge brought against him by a hitchhiker, but that the alleged victim had fabricated her story and that whatever had occurred, he'd been high on cocaine and therefore felt that he wasn't responsible for his actions.

Renée described Lawson as "manipulative" and "controlling," and said he frequented prostitutes while they were together. She admitted that she and Lawson, as well as his brother Bob, would party until the money ran out and said that Lawson developed a lot of paranoia from his cocaine addiction.

As Renée spoke about her ex, it was evident she pretty much hated him. Things changed, albeit slightly, when she spoke of Lawson's brother, Bob. Renée said that during her marriage to Lawson, she and Bob had an ongoing affair. She said that Bob was often "weak" and "submissive" to his brother. This seemed consistent with the interactions I observed between the two brothers when Officer Ritala and I first met them at their house.

"Bob would do anything for his brother," she said.

Renée described Bob as a hard worker who wasn't afraid to get his hands dirty, while Lawson didn't like to work, preferring to portray himself as the "businessman" always at the center of attention. Renée said it was Lawson who pushed Bob towards her. Lawson not only knew about the affair between her and Bob, he actually encouraged it, she said. According to Renée, Lawson would often use her affair with Bob as an excuse to go out and "do his own thing."

I wanted to find out what made Lawson tick or more importantly, what set him off. I figured it might come in handy to know his potential weaknesses so I asked her if there was anything in particular that bugged him.

"Mike's biggest fear was that people would learn he was a sex offender," she said without hesitation. I made a note of it and asked her about the business, Lawson Roofing.

Renée told me how as the business took off, the use of drugs and the money to support the partying also increased. Renée often worked on the books and she saw the shambles the finances became as Lawson put the profits up his nose and racked up huge credit card bills. The company began to collapse under Lawson's insatiable appetite for sex and drugs. He would invite prostitutes back to the house and in some cases convince his wife to join in. The booze, the coke and the deviant sex never seemed to stop where Lawson was concerned.

Renée also told me of a time when Lawson was accused of rape a number of years ago by the sixteen-year old daughter of one of his employees. She'd heard from one of the other roofing company employees up in Fairbanks that Lawson had hired a young girl to clean the office. The rumor was Lawson gave the girl drugs and then forced her to have sex with him. When the girl told her parents, they confronted the brothers, but that Bob backed up Lawson's side of the story by saying he was there at the time of the alleged rape and that nothing happened.

Renée said that at the time she'd supported Lawson as he cried to her saying he was innocent. Looking back, though, Renée said she doubted Lawson's story. She agreed to give me the name of the girl.

I also gained valuable information about Lawson from his current wife, Patty, who'd left him shortly before Bethany vanished.

When we first spoke, Patty wasn't willing to tell me what really happened between her and Lawson. She initially told us that he wasn't violent and that nothing serious happened.

As I continued to speak with Patty Lawson and I began to gain her trust. I came to realize she was in a situation not unlike millions of other abused women. She had fallen for this smooth-talking man. They met and quickly married right after she moved to Alaska. I suspected after a short time Lawson became increasingly domineering and controlling. She had fallen into a potentially violent situation and although she continued to deny it, I could tell Patty was afraid of Lawson and for good reason.

As Patty and I talked in separate phone conversations spaced over several months she eventually began to reveal more information. As I suspected, she had no relevant information specifically about Bethany, but she did provide even more insight into her estranged husband.

I asked Patty Lawson about her dogs, the two small, black and white Lhasa Apsos she had taken to the pound. Patty told me that after the fight with Lawson, she and her son took whatever they could carry and got onto the next plane out of town. This was not before she took their two dogs from the house and dropped them off at the Humane Society. I could understand a woman fleeing with her son and even taking her dogs with her, but taking the dogs to the pound where they were likely to be euthanized struck me as odd. Patty admitted to me she was more concerned for the dog's safety if she left them with Lawson.

She confirmed that Lawson still had a cocaine problem. According to Patty, it was Lawson's exorbitant spending and wanton drug use that had brought down the company.

Like Renée, Patty told me Lawson had admitted to being arrested for sexual assault in Illinois although in the version he told Patty, the alleged victim was his girlfriend, not a hitchhiker. Otherwise the story was the same: Lawson said he was on drugs at the time, but swore to her the allegation was totally fabricated and that he'd never raped anyone.

Finally one day Patty confided in me she left only after Lawson and her adult son, Sam, had gotten into an "explosive" argument that devolved into each threatening the other with violence. Lawson was on drugs and Patty knew he kept a gun close at hand. He had started keeping the gun with him after his biological son was arrested in another case more than a year before Bethany's disappearance. Lawson's son, Michael Jr., was in jail for being involved in the beating and a shooting of a man in downtown Anchorage, just a few blocks from M Street.

Allegedly, Mike Jr. and a friend had been hired to beat up the victim over a drug debt. To hear the younger Lawson's rendition of the story, he brought a baseball bat to simply rough the guy up. His friend pulled out a gun and shot the victim instead. Fortunately for both of them, the victim survived. Patty said Lawson tried to minimize his son's role in the shooting by claiming he was set up.

According to Patty, Lawson visited his son in prison down in Seward, Alaska from time to time. Located 126 miles south of Anchorage, Seward is a small coastal town that houses the State's largest prison, Spring Creek Correctional Facility. Spring Creek is a maximum-security prison in one of the most picturesque locations of Alaska. Built into a valley situated against the mountains just outside of Seward, the prison offers a view of the waters of beautiful Resurrection Bay on one side and mountains and glaciers on the other. Its location also serves to make the prison relatively isolated and protected.

I was very familiar with Spring Creek Correctional Facility as several people I arrested for murder were serving time there, including Alexander Eckhardt for killing Denise Payne.

There was also another prisoner at Spring Creek with whom I had a close connection: Alan Chase Jr. had served out a portion of his 75 year sentence for my sister's murder there before being transferred out of state to a contract prison in Arizona. Every so often I would travel down to Seward with my father to go fishing. Seward is a wonderful small town. Its tourist boats take people out on Resurrection Bay to see the abundant wildlife such as porpoise, whales, puffins and sea otters.

For years my family has owned a cabin just south of Seward. After a good day of sport fishing for silver salmon, my dad and I would sit on the cabin deck, overlooking the bay. We would sometimes share a beer and eat peanuts. It was our tradition. Although we never discussed the prison nearby, I would at times sit in my chair with the smell of the sea in the air and salt from the peanuts on my lips, look over and see the lights of Spring Creek prison. I would think about this man, Alan Chase Jr. He was a man whom I didn't really know, but whom I had spent the last 20 years of my life trying to understand. I didn't think I would ever be able to know why he did what he did to Dawn, but I was trying. Perhaps someday I will understand.

Chapter 28   Let's Get A Drink

Agent Rebecca Bobich and I had spent most of the evening around the table in the Homicide Lounge going through the new reports and double checking the old files. Still I hoped we would find something useful that we missed.

"This background report shows Mike's conviction in Illinois for the sex assault," she said, as she continued to read the report in her hand.

"That's right. Did we ever get the full police report on his arrest that night?" I asked.

"I think so," she said, as she began looking for it in another file.

She pulled out a stack of papers. The blurry and dark images on the pages told me they were either photocopied many times over, were old or perhaps both.

Rebecca started to read through the files.

"It was over 20 years ago," she read. "It was a six-count indictment against Michael A. Lawson, for Aggravated Criminal Sexual Assault from the State of Illinois."

I leaned forward as Rebecca continued reading.

"Michael A. Lawson was found guilty in a jury trial. He was sentenced to seven years with the Illinois Department of Corrections."

"Where is the initial police report?" I asked.

Rebecca shuffled through the stack some more. She found the report and then handed it to me.

It was a copy of a report from the Naperville, Illinois Police Department. The report had been filled out by hand, likely by the initial police officer. The rest of the report looked as if it had been typed on a typewriter. The photocopy made it difficult to make out but I managed to locate the initial narrative I wanted to see.

I read the report aloud to Rebecca. According to the old report the police received an early morning 911 call from Michael Lawson himself. He asked police dispatchers if they had received a telephone call yet from a Tricia Baker. When the 911 operator asked why he was calling, Lawson said, quote, "You'll find out," and then he added, "I'm going to die. Bye."

Police traced the call to an address associated with Michael Lawson.

At the same time, a neighbor of Baker's called into 911 and stated that a woman named Tricia Baker was with them. The neighbor told police that the girl was hysterical. She reported being beaten and raped.

Upon arrival at Lawson's residence the police soon discovered Mike seated in a car nearby with his wrists slashed. He was semi-conscious and unresponsive due to blood loss. Lawson was taken to the hospital and was later arrested.

The officers also entered his apartment after observing blood on the front door. More blood was located on the floor in the dining room and in the living room. In the kitchen the officers found large amounts of blood on the counter area. In the master bedroom the police noted a suitcase full of clothes on the bed.

In another bedroom they saw a bloody tampon in the middle of an unmade bed. On the floor was an open jar of Vaseline, two pieces of duct tape and two strands of rope. The officers secured the apartment and called a crime scene team.

Neighbors reported seeing Lawson running up and down the stairs three or four different times prior to the police arriving.

The victim reported she and Lawson had been dating. They had gotten into a verbal altercation and Lawson had brandished a large kitchen knife. He took her to a bedroom where he tied her wrists and duct-taped her mouth. She told officers Lawson raped her repeatedly both vaginally and anally. After hours of being assaulted, she managed to untie herself and run to a friend's house.

Her physical injuries included a cut lip, swollen arms and jaw. Her wrists showed signs of abrasions consistent with being bound with rope.

Lawson was convicted and the various counts against him were consolidated. He served only five years. I looked up at Rebecca. She shook her head in disbelief.

"There's more," I said.

Behind that police report was another case from five years earlier.

In that earlier report, the victim, a Mary Lemski, reported she was at a girlfriend's home when they were invited over to a party in a neighbor's apartment. Several people were present in the home, including Mike Lawson. After a large amount of drinking, the victim reported she and Mike Lawson left the party to get cigarettes. While in the car, Lawson grabbed her by the arm and brandished a bottle of Jack Daniels. He threatened to hit her with it if she did not do as she was told. He took her to his apartment where he told her to get undressed. When she refused, he tore her clothes off of her and forced her onto a bed where he raped her. Knowing and fearing DNA evidence, Lawson made the victim go into the bathroom to "clean up" and he watched to make sure she "did it right."

Lawson was contacted by law enforcement and immediately told the police he did not rape the woman and he wanted to "cooperate." For some reason, according to the report, Lawson then went into some sort of "convulsions" that led the officers to take him to a hospital. Once there, Lawson told them that, on the advice of his attorney, he would not answer any further questions.

"That sure sounds familiar," Rebecca said. I nodded and

continued reading.

According to the report, two days later, Lawson and his attorney came into the police station to make a statement. According to Lawson, the victim was "flirting" with him at the party. After leaving to get cigarettes, he asked if she wanted to go to his place to play "backgammon." He said they went to his apartment where after playing a couple games of backgammon, they had consensual sex. Afterward he asked her if she wanted to go out to dinner and a movie sometime. Lawson denied he forced the victim to do anything. Lawson told the police that according to his doctors at the time, he could not lift more than a "gallon" of milk due to a spinal-fusion surgery he'd had several weeks earlier.

"And did the police follow up on his medical condition?" Rebecca asked.

"Yep," I answered. "According to the investigators, they spoke with Lawson's doctor who said Lawson cannot lift more than eight pounds. The doctor at the time also said he did not think Mr. Lawson could have enough strength to restrain anyone."

Rebecca shook her head again. "Let me guess... they dropped the charges."

"Yep," I said. "The victim was too intoxicated to give a good statement and Lawson was able to talk his way out of it."

I threw the old police reports back into the file. My head hurt. I rubbed my face with my hands and tried to wake up.

"You okay?" Rebecca asked. She removed one of the case binders from her lap and set it on the table. She leaned forward and looked at me with her big brown eyes.

"I mean, how are you really?" she asked again.

Agent Bobich and I had been working closely together on this case for past several months. I was struck by her drive to help and her attention to detail. As we spent more and more time together I learned that she was not only a top ATF agent, but also a trained firearms handler, an arson investigator and a certified medic. On top of that she was a wife and a mother working hard to raise two small children.

"Klink?" Rebecca said as she leaned forward over the table. "Hello? Earth to Klink. You okay?"

"Yes, I'm fine, thanks. I'm just tired," I said as I grabbed another file and pretended to read.

"What are we missing?" I said

Rebecca sat back down and closed the file in front of her. "I've gone through this thing as many times as you have and you've done everything you can to connect the dots. There doesn't seem to be any physical evidence connecting Lawson to Bethany."

"According to my tally we have collected nearly four hundred pieces of individual evidence from Bethany's apartment, the burned out duplex, Mike's car, Mike's house and even from his person," I said. "Nothing matches up."

"But doesn't that tell us something?" Rebecca said.

"It tells me he did a good job of cleaning up."

"What else is there?"

I paused and looked at her.

"I think we need to change tracks," I said. "Let's stop investigating Bethany's disappearance for a while."

"What?" Rebecca looked at me as if I had lost my mind.

"I think we need to learn more about Lawson," I said. "I want to know what's inside his head."

"So... now what?"

"Let's go get a drink," I said.

I could tell by the look on her face Rebecca thought I was crazy. I winked and grabbed my coat. I walked out of the conference room thinking she might not even follow me. I turned and headed out of the homicide unit. I was approaching the door to the parking lot when I heard Rebecca's footsteps catching up.

Twenty minutes later, the music was blaring as we entered the darkened bar. I stopped for a moment. Rebecca stopped next to me. I had learned as a young patrol officer working in the bar scene along 4th Avenue in downtown Anchorage that you need to give your eyes time to adjust when entering a bar. It's a safety thing. As my pupils began to open up I could see that Blues Central was like most bars in Anchorage. The place was small, loud and smelled like stale beer.

"You sure do know how to show a girl a good time," Rebecca quipped.

We sat down. The bar was practically empty except for a bartender and a female waitress. The waitress, a blonde with streaks of black in her hair, looked up and acknowledged us. Her short cut-off jeans and low cut white-colored blouse told me she likely made pretty good tips when the bar was crowded.

"I'll be with you guys in a minute," she said.

After scanning the room again for anyone who might overhear our conversation, I told Rebecca that according to his ex-wives, Lawson liked to hang out here. Also, our GPS device in his car had confirmed Lawson would often come here for the day rather than be at the job site. Other informants had put him at Blues Central on multiple occasions drinking and hitting on the waitresses and any other women who happened to wander into the bar. Although I couldn't be sure the people here would actually talk with me, I figured this was as good a place as any to start.

"What'll it be?" the waitress asked.

"Two Diet Cokes," I said.

The waitress looked us over: a man and a woman in business suits ordering diet sodas in the middle of the afternoon.

"Anything else I can get for you?" she asked, suddenly wary.

I pulled out a photo of Mike Lawson from my coat pocket and slid it toward her. She looked at it briefly and then shook her head no. I pulled out my badge and slid it next to the image of Lawson.

"I'm Detective Klinkhart," I said. "This is Special Agent Rebecca Bobich, ATF. Are you sure you don't know Mr. Lawson? We heard he comes here frequently."

The waitress looked around nervously.

"Yeah, I know Mike," she admitted. "He's a regular."

I took out a photo of Bethany. I handed it to the waitress. The look on her face told me she recognized Bethany from all of the posters around town. I went on to explain that Lawson wasn't in any trouble but that he was Bethany's apartment manager and for that reason we were doing a background check on him. This seemed to relax the waitress. She left and returned with our drinks a short time later.

As she set down the sodas, she explained that Lawson was one of many regulars at Blues Central. He came in a couple of times a week and sometimes at night when a band was playing. I asked her if Lawson was a good tipper and she responded that yes, he was a good tipper and that "he should be."

I asked her what she meant.

She turned and looked around. She paused and then said, "Mike is a talker... he thinks he is a real ladies' man... always talking up the girls here, especially the waitresses. He likes to come on strong... but it's not unusual... I get it a lot from guys around here."

As I looked around the bar with its neon-beer signs on the walls and the ceiling painted black I replied, "I guess it comes with the territory, huh?"

She smiled. "I don't have a problem with Mike. I can handle him in small bits, for the most part."

"Is there anything about Lawson that is unusual or that makes him different from the other customers?" Rebecca asked.

The waitress turned to Rebecca and lowered her voice slightly, "I heard from another waitress that the other night Mike was in here with his friend, Big Al, drinking and carrying on."

"What's so unusual about that?" Rebecca asked.

Alvin Jackson or Big Al as he was called, was one of the people Lawson told us he was out with the night of Bethany's disappearance. Lawson and Big Al seemed to spend a lot of time together, even working together as partners at the car detail shop, Bram Auto. Investigators had already spoken with Big Al about the day Bethany disappeared. Big Al told us Lawson stopped by late that morning. He didn't hang around long. Al didn't see Lawson again until late that night when he met Lawson and his brother for drinks at Blues Central.

The waitress continued, "Well, I heard from another waitress, Jackie, that Mike was going around to all of the women in the bar last week asking for a lock of their hair."

I looked at Rebecca. Her eyes were as big as saucers and her mouth was open. I turned back to the waitress.

"Did you say that he was asking for their hair?" I asked.

"Yeah he did and the way I heard it, lots of women gave him some."

Rebecca asked, "Any idea why he was asking for woman's hair?"

"Nope, I didn't work that night," she replied.

"Can I have Jackie's phone number please?" I asked.

242

The waitress looked concerned. She didn't realize she had inadvertently given us Jackie's name.

"Don't worry, I'm not going to tell her who told us..." I explained. "If I did that, no one would ever talk to me, right?" The waitress nodded and proceeded to write down Jackie's phone number on a napkin.

"Is Mike a suspect in that girl's disappearance?" she asked.

I dropped twenty bucks on the table and Agent Bobich and I got up from our seats.

"Everyone is a suspect," I said.

Rebecca and I stepped out of the dark cave of Blues Central. The light of the afternoon sun caused my pupils to constrict. It hurt a bit and I reached in my pocket for my sunglasses.

"He's taking hair samples from women?" Rebecca said to me as we walked to my car. "How creepy is that?"

"Very," I said. "I suspect we'll be seeing those hair clippings again."

"You think Lawson is smart enough to plant girls' hair and throw us off the trail?"

"I think he is capable of a lot of things," I said as I shut the car door. As I started to put the key in the ignition, I glanced up.

"Look, Rebecca," I said motioning towards the large strip mall that housed the Blues Central bar and several other small businesses.

"I'll be damned... would you look at that," she remarked.

Taped on the doors and the windows of each of the businesses was a poster. Not just any poster, but *the poster*. Bethany's missing poster hung on each of the businesses in the complex. All of them had a poster of Bethany prominently displayed on their storefront... all of them except for one... Blues Central.

Chapter 29   Hair

I knew someone was in the apartment because the sound of the television died immediately after I first knocked. I pounded several times on the door before she answered. Jackie was in her twenties, thin with dark eyes. Her brown hair had a thin streak of magenta dyed along one side. It was three o'clock in the afternoon but she looked like she had just gotten up.

"I'm looking for Jackie," I asked.

"That's me."

"I'm Detective Klinkhart, Anchorage Police Department," I said as I showed her my badge. Jackie hesitated. She clearly did not want to speak with me.

Quickly I added, "You're not in any trouble, I just want to ask you a couple of questions."

Reluctantly she opened the door and I walked in.

Her sparse apartment was messy but not the worst I've seen. I noted the odor of cats and dirty litter box. Jackie moved a pile of old newspapers from the worn sofa and picked up a black Siamese cat that was nestling around her feet. She placed the cat on her lap like a shield between her and me.

"I want to talk to you about Mike Lawson," I said.

Jackie pulled the cat tight. She shook her head, "I don't know any Mike Lawson."

Clearly Jackie was scared. I really wasn't in the mood for a round of "yes, you do," "no, I don't" so I went right to the point.

"Jackie, you and I both know Mike Lawson," I said. "I believe he is capable of a lot of things, bad things and I need to know what you know about Mike and about his asking around the bar for women's hair."

Jackie looked at me but did not speak. Purposely I stayed silent. Sometimes silence can be as powerful as shouting. I simply stared at Jackie and waited. She continued to hold her cat closely to her chest. A few minutes later and without making eye contact, she finally spoke.

"Mike Lawson had a pair of scissors. He was going around the bar asking for bits of hair from all of the girls. He told everyone it was for a joke."

"Did you give him some of your hair?" I asked.

"Yes," Jackie replied.

"How much hair did Lawson get?"

"A handful," Jackie said. "He tied it up in a bow with a piece of fabric someone gave him.

"Is that it?"

Jackie said nothing. She continued to stare across the room. I could see she knew more than she was saying.

"What else do you want to tell me?"

Jackie stayed frozen, holding her cat and looking like a scared little girl.

"Jackie," I said. "I'm going to tell you a secret."

Jackie looked straight ahead.

I needed to get her to talk. I could tell that this woman had been through a lot in her young life. Jackie had probably heard it all from people before, especially from men. I also sensed that Jackie had likely been interviewed by cops like me before. If I wanted to get her to talk to me I was going to have to try something other than scaring or confronting her. Perhaps telling this woman the truth might be a good place to start.

"Jackie, Mike Lawson had something to do with the missing girl that everyone is talking about," I told her. "Lawson is a very bad man. This girl, Bethany, is out there somewhere. We need to find her. I need to find out what he did with her."

Soon I could see a tear running down the side of her face. A minute passed.

I put away my notebook and stood up. I thanked Jackie for her time and made for the door. As I did, there was a sound from behind me.

"He tried to rape me and my friend," Jackie said.

I turned around, took out my notepad and sat back down on the couch. Jackie began to tell me her story of how months before the hair incident and even before Bethany disappeared, she and another waitress at Blues Central had been preparing to get off work when Lawson came into the bar. He was boisterous yet charming. Before long Lawson asked both women to go bowling with him and they agreed. Lawson drove them away in his white Mercedes. But along the way Lawson said he needed to stop by his Roofing Company offices to get something. He seemed really interested in showing them around his offices. As they walked around the office and through the warehouse, Lawson directed the girls down one of the office corridors. With Lawson behind them the girls walked down the hallway towards an open conference room. As they entered, Jackie heard Lawson say, "Turn around." When Jackie and her friend turned around, he was standing in the doorway with a gun, pointed in their direction. Jackie could not believe what she was seeing.

"Mike, what the fuck?" Jackie said.

Lawson pulled back the hammer of the gun and pointed it at Jackie and said, "Get on your fucking knees." Jackie's coworker reluctantly got down on her knees. Jackie froze. She knew what Lawson wanted. There was no way she was going to get on her knees for him or anyone else.

"No, Mike, you'll have to shoot me," Jackie said.

Lawson took two steps towards her.

"I said get on your fucking knees, bitch," he demanded as he placed the gun within inches of Jackie's forehead.

Jackie closed her eyes and waited for the gunshot. Suddenly she heard a door behind Lawson open. Jackie opened her eyes and saw him quickly stuff the handgun into his waistband and turn towards the sound. One of Lawson's employees walked into the hallway. He waved at Lawson, who waved back like nothing was out of the ordinary.

After the man left their view, Lawson turned around and said, "I was just joking ladies, it's not even a real gun." Jackie knew he was lying. She had seen the gun, up close. She had felt the metal on her forehead. It was real.

"You two ready to go bowling?" Lawson said with a smile.

Jackie lifted her friend up off the floor. Her friend was crying. Without saying a word, Jackie pulled her friend along the hallway and past Lawson. Jackie walked herself and her friend out of the building.

When Jackie had finished telling me her story, I put away my notebook. I stood up, I reached over and I touched her shoulder.

I said, "Thank you. I can't tell you how much I appreciate your talking to me. I promise I will do what I can to make sure he never hurts you or anyone else again."

Jackie said nothing. As I shut the door behind me, the woman stayed seated, holding her cat in her arms and staring into the empty space of her apartment.

Chapter 30   Beluga Point

"Glen... the body of a girl just washed up at Beluga Point."

The voice on the phone belonged to Detective Joe Hoffbeck. I had just gotten home and was in the process of changing out of my work clothes when he called.

"I'm on my way," I said as I reopened my gun safe and grabbed my handgun.

The drive south from Anchorage to Beluga Point was relatively short. The flats of Turnagain Arm stretched out across the bay as I followed the Seward Highway out of Anchorage. The tall gray mountain cliffs on my left were reflected in the water to my right. Beluga Point is a small rest stop along the highway. Tourists and locals visit the lookout trying to catch a glance of wildlife such as Dall sheep or beluga whales. There is a large run of salmon that comes up Turnagain Arm each year to spawn. The belugas follow the fish looking for an easy meal. As I drove the winding highway my mind churned like the turbulent waters of the inlet.

A girl's body?

It can't be Bethany.

There is no way.

They took her north, not south.

I slowed down as I approached a large Chugach State Park sign which read, "Beluga Point Turnout". I pulled off the highway and into the parking lot. Several emergency vehicles were already on scene. As I opened my car door I could smell the fresh sea air. The normally windy area was unusually calm that evening. It was nine o'clock at night but the sun was still high in the sky. The Anchorage Fire Department water rescue crew was down by the water. I stepped over the guardrail and carefully walked down the rocky cliff. Hoffbeck was already there. He was standing next to an Alaska State Trooper.

"What do we got Joe?" I asked as I pulled on my rubber gloves and quickly stuck my tie into my front pocket.

"Some guy and his kids were playing near the water when they spotted what they thought was a dead sheep," he said. "When the dad got a closer look he saw it was a human torso."

"A torso?"

"Yep. The legs, arms and the head are gone," the seasoned detective said calmly. "Looks like it's been in the water for a while too."

He directed me to a large red plastic bag. A label on it read "BIOHAZARD". The rescue crew who arrived first had placed the body in the bag after retrieving it from the water. I bent down and looked inside. Joe was right. In the bottom of the bag was the torso of a female. It was gray, nearly white. The skin was wrinkled and bleached indicating it had been in the water for several weeks, if not months. My mind flashed back to how Isaiah Johnson's little hands had begun to look white after being in the ice cold pond for those three weeks.

I opened the bag some more so I could examine the injuries. The top of both femurs was cut clean through. It looked as if a knife or similar object had been used to cut the skin and the underlying flesh. Whoever had dismembered and decapitated this woman had used some kind of saw on the larger bones. The ends of the bones were worn smooth, likely from the water, sand and tidal action rubbing against them.

"I need to check something," I said. "Joe, help me roll her over."

Hoffbeck reached into the bag with me and grabbed the shoulders of the torso. I held the bottom half as we flipped her over. I held my breath expecting the familiar rancid stench of a body. Instead I smelled nothing but sea salt. The ice cold waters of Turnagain Arm had preserved the body like a refrigerator. I looked at the torso again, checking for a certain small, sea turtle tattoo. That's when I saw it. There, on the lower portion of the back, just above the tail bone there was a patch of rough cuts. A section of skin had been removed by some sort of knife.

"Looks like someone cut out a tattoo," Joe said. I looked at him and nodded my head "yes" as I ripped off my rubber gloves.

The drive back to Anchorage was not an easy one. I could not understand how the corpse in that red bag could be Bethany. The timeline for the body to be in the water was, however, consistent. The shape and the size of the torso could be the same as Bethany and a missing tattoo on the small of the back was very compelling. Still I could not shake the thought it just didn't seem right.

"They took her north, not south," I muttered to myself.

Taking apart a body is not an easy task. Alaska is known for its hunting and fishing opportunities and thus there are lots of outdoorsmen here who can field dress a moose, caribou or even a bear. But to dismember a human being requires a secure place to work, time to do the job and a stomach to handle the gore. Mike Lawson did not strike me as that kind of guy. His brother Bob was a hard worker, but I wasn't sure if Bob would be able to stomach such a bloody proposition. Also, if this was Bethany, where did they dismember her body? The duplex on M Street? We had searched that apartment three times and found nothing. If they took her home to their house or the auto detailing shop, then why didn't we find any blood? Cutting up a body makes a huge mess. Nothing indicated to me there was any serious bloodletting in any of those places. As I drove back into Anchorage, I looked down at my cell phone. Someone else needed to know what we just found. I pressed the buttons to one of the few phone numbers I knew by heart, Bethany's mom.

"Hello, Linda, it's Glen. I need to talk to you."

The body discovered at Beluga Point, southeast of Anchorage.
Photo courtesy of the Anchorage Police Department.

Detective Klinkhart takes measurements at Beluga Point along
Turnagain Arm. *Photo courtesy of the Anchorage Police Department.*

Chapter 31   What About Bob?

It took two months for DNA testing to be completed, but in the end I was right about the torso. It wasn't Bethany. Rebecca and the ATF were kind enough to foot the $10,000 bill for the mitochondrial DNA tests. In the end, there was no genetic link between the torso and the Correira family. I was glad to know that at least for now, I know what I am doing.

Two days later I was back in Sharon's office arguing with her.

"We don't have enough to arrest them," Sharon said as she scanned through the files I brought her. "And now you tell me the torso found in Turnagain Arm isn't Bethany."

"No, the torso isn't Bethany, but your boss said we didn't need a body," I reminded her.

"Well, he changed his mind," she said, furrowing her brow and looking at me over her glasses.

Sharon was my friend as well as my legal and moral compass. I wanted her to tell me we had enough to arrest Mike Lawson for the murder of Bethany Correira. We had lots of circumstantial evidence: We had Lance Hart from ATF finding the duplex fire was arson. We had Mike Lawson lying about his and his brother's whereabouts on May 3rd. We had Lawson's cell phone in Bethany's neighborhood the morning of her disappearance. We had a white luxury SUV seen by a newspaper carrier near M Street at the time of the fire. We had Lawson's strange activity of cutting off women's hair at the bar. We had Lawson's criminal history of rape in Chicago along with accounts of his trying to sexually assault women in Alaska.

"What else do we need, Sharon?"

"Glen, I know and you know, that Mike Lawson did something to Bethany but I have to prove it. Give me something I can prove."

253

"Like what?"

"What about Bob?" Sharon asked.

"What about Bob?" I replied.

"Any chance we can get Bob in and get him to roll on Mike?"

"Bob and Mike are tight, really tight," I said.

From what I could determine, the brothers were inseparable. They had been very, very close ever since their parents died when they were just teenagers. Lawson and Bob built up their roofing company together. Lawson was the ringleader and Bob the worker. Lawson made promises and Brother Bob made them happen. They worked, lived and partied together.

Sharon continued to look over the stack of reports. By now the Bethany Correira case filled over ten three-inch binders.

"Glen, we have enough to arrest Mike Lawson, but not enough to get a conviction. You and I have worked together long enough that you know we can't arrest him without something more."

I rubbed my eyes with my hands. I looked up at Sharon hoping she was going to have another one of her moments of brilliance.

"What do I need for a conviction?" I asked.

Still looking down at the report in front of her Sharon replied, "Find Bethany."

Chapter 32   Planting Seeds

Two chairs and a single, folding table were all that occupied the interview room. Bob Lawson stepped inside. I asked him to take a seat in the folding chair. I set my notebook on the table and turned on my small audio recorder. I asked if he wanted anything to drink. He adjusted his worn baseball cap and shook his head, "no."

I read Bob his Miranda Rights. He indicated he understood each of his rights and he agreed to speak with me.

Rather than asking him a lot of questions, I went through everything he had already told investigators. He told us he was with his brother all day when Bethany disappeared. Both of them were at their house that morning watching the NASCAR races on television. Afterward they went to the Blues Central bar for drinks and later they drove to another bar, Al's Alaskan Inn. Bob said he took a cab home late that night. I pulled out a piece of paper with a timeline printed on it just for his review. Bob nodded his head and said it looked right to him.

"Now Bob, I'm not trying to trick you or put words in your mouth, you understand that?"

He nodded "Yes."

"Does all of this sound accurate as to what you have told me or other investigators in the past several months?"

"Yes, sir, it does," he said nervously.

"Okay, Bob, that's good," I said as I put the timeline back into my stack of papers. Leaning forward in my chair I lowered my voice and said, "I'm going to tell you a secret." Bob looked up at me. "Your brother was involved in Bethany's disappearance," I said softly, but firmly.

"So, you're saying that you think Mike was involved?"

"No, I'm not saying I think he was involved, I'm saying that I know he was involved."

"I don't believe it," Bob said. He leaned back in his chair. I could see he was not going to bend easily to my opinion, but that was not my intent. My goal was to get him to listen, not to talk.

"Bob, I was able to verify several of the things you said," I explained. Bob again leaned back against his chair and this time he crossed his arms, which telegraphed to me he was going to be defiant to whatever I was telling him.

"I am not going to be able to verify other things you told police because they simply aren't true," I said. Bob started to open his mouth as if to say something. I put my hand up and like an obedient dog, he closed his mouth. I told him I knew when he woke up at 10:00 A.M. on the morning of Bethany's disappearance, his brother was not at the house with him. Bob stared at me and began shaking his head, "No". I told him we were aware his brother called him from his cell phone and that he called from Bootleggers Cove. Bob continued to stare at me, but now his head had stopped shaking altogether.

"We know your brother was trying desperately to reach you," I said. "He tried calling you at the house. He tried calling your cell phone. He tried calling the house again. He even called the fax line for God's sake. He finally got you on your cell phone. And that is when you guys had a two-minute conversation. Didn't you?"

Bob's eyes were locked on mine. He didn't move. I kept going, "Mike called you in a panic. He called you because he was in trouble, didn't he?" Bob resumed slowly shaking his head back and forth, "No."

"Your brother got himself into some trouble and he was calling you to save him. We know that," I said. Bob lifted his small, calloused hands and rubbed his face. His scruffy facial hair, his wrinkles and the bags under his eyes made him appear many years older than forty-seven. I watched as he looked down at the floor and again crossed his arms in a defensive pose.

"Nope," Bob said. "He never called me... you're trying to put words in my mouth now."

"No, no, I'm not trying to put words in your mouth," I replied.

"That's my statement," he said as he pointed to the timeline in my notebook. "That's my statement and I'm sticking with that. You're trying to twist stuff now."

"No, Bob. I know you were at home that day. Okay? But your brother wasn't home... he knows he wasn't at home, I know he wasn't at home and you know he wasn't at home."

"I'm sticking with my statement," he replied as he leaned back in his chair, his head touching the wall behind him. Inside the small interview room he was trying to pull himself as far away from me as he could. I turned up the heat.

"Bob, you've lied to protect your brother before, I know that," I said as I pulled out a stack of paper. I tossed it in front of him. It was a transcript of an interview of a young girl named Britney, the daughter of one of the brother's bookkeepers. Six years ago the two brothers had hired the then 16-year-old to clean up around their offices in Fairbanks. After getting her name and phone number from Lawson's ex-wife, Renée, I called Britney. She told me she was just a teenager when she had been sent to Fairbanks to stay with her father and step-mom. She said she been fighting with her mother in Anchorage and having discipline problems in school. She admitted she even spent time in the McLaughlin Youth Detention Center. Britney described herself as being a "wild child" who had been experimenting with drugs at the time.

It was at the brother's roofing business in Fairbanks where she met Lawson and his brother, Bob. She said Lawson offered her cocaine and she accepted. All of them used the coke. After she had ingested the drug, Lawson walked her into a back room. He stood behind her and began kissing her softly on the back of the neck. Britney said, "No!" and told him to stop. He continued as if he never ever heard her. He began to grab her breasts under her shirt. She tried to pull away. As she did, he pushed her face down

257

onto the couch. The young teenager continued to beg for him to stop, even as he pulled down her sweat pants. He held her arms behind her back and began to rape her from behind.

Afterward he released his hold on the girl. Red colored finger marks remained on the back of her arms. He told her to get dressed and to not tell anyone or he would say that she came onto him. Her mother worked for him and she would lose her job. Crying and embarrassed, Britney gathered up her clothes and ran out of the room. She ran past Bob, who was seated just outside watching television.

Despite Lawson's threats, she told her parents, who later confronted Mike. He told them their daughter was making up the story and he only wanted to help her out by giving her a job. He told them that if they didn't believe him to ask his brother. When they questioned Bob, he told them nothing happened. He said Britney simply came in and cleaned up around the place while he and his brother sat and watched television. Britney's parents believed them. She was immediately flown back to Anchorage where she continued to get into problems, eventually dropping out of school.

Now it was my turn to stare at Bob and wait for a reaction.

"No way," he said. "That's false. It never happened. Maybe I should have an attorney present; you guys are trying to put words in my mouth."

I leaned forward and said softly, "I told you before, I'm not trying to put words in your mouth. I'm trying to give you an opportunity to do the right thing." I continued, "This is about Bethany. Your brother is looking at some serious charges. I'm talking about murder... kidnapping... and arson." When I said the word "arson", Bob's body posture changed. He tensed up and he shifted nervously in his seat. That word clearly bothered him, but he refused to speak. I tried another tactic.

"I think an attorney is a great idea. You need your own attorney."

Surprised, Bob looked up at me. Telling a suspect he needs to talk to an attorney was not something a good detective does. In this case it might be helpful, but there was a risk. If Bob told an attorney the entire truth of what he knew, the lawyer might tell him to stop talking to us. On the other hand, I wanted him to feel even more pressure and this might just do the trick.

"I think you should find an attorney and I want the name of that attorney. It's going to be important that your lawyer call me... I need to talk to him." I explained to him when he meets with his attorney he needed to do one thing: tell the truth, the whole truth and not what he was telling me now.

Bob was no longer leaning back with his arms crossed. He was now sitting forward, his hands on his knees. I told him he needed to tell his lawyer about the phone calls to the house that morning and that his brother's constant calling woke him up. His attorney needed to know what Mike told him. He also needed to tell his lawyer about their little trip up north and out of town. As I spoke, Bob's eyes widened and his face turned pale.

"You need to tell that attorney the entire truth," I said. "You need to tell him about going back to the duplex to start the fire." Bob tried to give me a look of disbelief but his eyes told me a different story, he looked scared.

"Let me warn you, if you tell your attorney the same crap you are telling me here, then he can't help you... Do you understand?"

All he could get out was a simple, "Yeah."

"And this needs to happen sooner than later. Can you contact an attorney today?"

"Yeah," he said looking down.

"And I would suggest getting your own attorney, not your brother's lawyer. You need someone who has your best interests in mind." He looked up at me again. I reached once more into my notebook. I pulled out a copy of Bob's personal cell phone records and I handed the printouts to him.

259

"Make sure you show this to your attorney," I said as he stared at the records. I just stared at him and waited for his next move.

After a few minutes of sitting in silence, Bob folded the papers in half and slid them into the inside pocket of his jacket. He stood up without saying a word. I reached out and shook his hand. I turned off the audio recorder and escorted him out of the interview room.

A few minutes later I returned to gather up my papers and my recorder. Rebecca came around from the back of the interview room. She had been watching the entire time from behind the two way mirror.

"What do you think?" she asked.

"I think we planted the seeds," I said, "But let's hope I didn't just fuck this whole thing up."

Chapter 33   Linda, Bethany and Me

Whenever I talked with Linda Correira, which was nearly every day, I never referred to Bethany in the past tense, even though I knew, based on my years of training and experience, as the days turned into weeks and the weeks turned to months, Bethany was almost certainly dead. Unfortunately, I had no proof of it and her mother's heart told her the exact opposite.

Every word from Linda, every gesture from her hands, every action from her small frame said that she knew that Bethany was alive.

"Bethany is strong," she told me, "She is a fighter."

At first the talks between Linda Correira and me were pretty formal. But soon our discussions became more and more open. We talked about her other children, Brian, Jamin and Havilah. I had yet to meet Havilah, Bethany's younger sister and best friend. Havilah was in Africa helping feed and educate the impoverished.

I often complimented Linda and the searchers on the vast number of posters of Bethany that blanketed the city. I reminded Linda to keep Bethany in the public eye because someone had to know something. Soon enough Bethany's posters were on nearly every light pole and building in the city.

One afternoon on a rare day off about a month into the investigation I was driving around with Evan in the back seat of my car. We were just driving along, him in his car seat and me upfront listening to some Jimmy Buffet music through the car stereo. All of a sudden I heard Evan exclaim from the back seat, "Dad, there's Bethany!"

For a moment my heart nearly came out of my chest. I turned to my right just in time to see a poster with Bethany's face on it attached to the corner light pole. I looked behind me and I could see Evan pointing at the poster and smiling from ear to ear. He was so very cute. From that time on Evan and I often played a game we called "Find Bethany," seeing who could spot the next Bethany poster first. Evan got pretty good at it.

Seeing those posters reminded me that I had been trying really hard to figure out what Bethany was wearing the day she disappeared. Despite going through her clothes in her apartment on M Street, talking with her boyfriend, Ray and having her mother check to see what of Beth's clothes might be missing, we still did not have enough to release a clothing description to the public.

We knew that Bethany had a tattoo on the small of her back in the shape of a sea turtle and Linda Correira described the jewelry that Beth was likely wearing when she went missing. On Bethany's toes she had several silver toe rings. On one hand she had a diamond-studded ring. On her other hand was a gold ring with the letters "MC" which stood for Masters Commission, a youth ministry program that had awarded Bethany the ring after she completed a yearlong program. It was one of Beth's favorite items and it was missing from her apartment. Two other pieces of jewelry that we did not find in Bethany's apartment or car were the white puka shell necklace and matching ankle bracelet that Ray had given to Bethany just days before she disappeared.

I decided to keep the information about Bethany's jewelry a secret from the public. I had no clothing description to go on and since it was likely Bethany was wearing her jewelry when she disappeared it may be the only way I could ever know for certain if someone was telling me the truth about her.

By the end of the summer, Bethany's apartment building on M Street was empty of all of the renters as well as the search teams. The entire complex was destined to be vacated and eventually demolished to make room for new condominiums. The burned-out duplex next door had already been bulldozed. The ATF had been in and out of it a half dozen times. We took hundreds of bits and pieces from the duplex. We took sections of the floors, doors and even entire bathrooms including tubs, tiles, pipes and sinks. Some of it was helpful in determining the origin of the fire and the arson, but most of the items failed to help me figure out what happened to Bethany.

By September the short summer of Alaska had given way to the cool, rainy, fall. The Correira family had called off the search for Bethany within the city limits. Searchers had covered all of Anchorage, walking some areas multiple times.

Down at M Street the only clues I could uncover were the yellow leaves on the trees telling me winter was right around the corner. I'd made a habit of stopping by M Street all by myself. At least once a week I would drive to M Street, get out of my car and walk around the scene. The search tents had been removed and the searchers were all gone. I was alone.

I would walk and look around the property if for no other reason than to simply look around and go through the case again in my head. I would think about the case and I would think about Bethany.

I also began thinking about Dawn. It began slowly at first, almost without any warning or understanding. I didn't mean to and I didn't even try to. Maybe it was the burned out duplex. The look and the smell of the charred ruins on M Street took me back, fleetingly, to my parents' house and to our fire.

I wondered if Bethany and Dawn were somewhere together. If they were together, what would Bethany and Dawn say to each other? Would Dawn tell Bethany that her dorky brother was the one who was looking for her? Were they laughing at the thought of this fifteen-year old kid who couldn't save Dawn, being the person now solely responsible for finding Bethany?

I wondered if Bethany could see me standing there.

Did Bethany want to be found?

Was she going to help me find her?

Often I found myself saying the words aloud, although I always made doubly sure I was alone when I did. I always asked her the same question: "Where are you, Bethany?"

Then I would wait. I would wait for a minute or two. Sometimes I felt the wind begin to blow through the trees around me. Other times the sounds of the birds would let me know I was being heard.

On this particular fall day I was there on M Street thinking about Mike Lawson. He was never going to talk to me. His brother Bob wasn't exactly hiding from me, but he wasn't being helpful either. If Bob didn't develop a conscience soon, I knew he probably never would. Bob might just as likely become convinced by his brother to simply keep his mouth shut. Mike Lawson was a master manipulator. He used everyone in order to get what he wanted, even his own brother. I thought back to Renée telling me how she was convinced that Lawson purposefully maneuvered her and Bob into having an affair, then using the affair to make Bob feel beholden to him. Renée told me that Mike Lawson, for his final manipulative touch, even bought a Bible engraved with Bob's name and gave it to his brother as a "token of forgiveness."

The more I thought about it, the more I realized that although I believed Bob had a conscience, something I was sure his brother lacked, it really did not matter. Bob was beholden to his brother, whether out of guilt, loyalty or both. He always had been and always would be.

"Bethany? What if I can't win?" I said out loud.

A moment later I heard the wind begin to rustle through the trees, slowly at first and then faster. I closed my eyes for a moment. Soon I could feel the cool breeze running along the side of my face. I opened my eyes. I pulled my keys out from my coat pocket. I looked at my watch. I had to get home. It was time to say goodnight to Evan.

Chapter 34   Asking For Help

For all the vast size of Alaska, the U.S. Government only has two Secret Service Agents who cover the entire state. Their office occupies one small corner of the federal building in downtown Anchorage.

I knocked on the bulletproof glass in front of their main office doors. The two-inch thick Plexiglas had a small speaker mounted in the middle of it. The front office was large enough that I could see no one was present and the muffled sound of my rapping on the window was not likely to carry very far. I looked around and found the speaker button. I pressed it. An audible tone echoed on the other side. A moment later, a tall, thin man with light-colored hair and a dark blue shirt appeared from around the corner.

"Hi, Klink," he said as he approached.

"Good morning, Mac."

Timothy "Mac" Whisler and I had met only a couple of times before. We had worked several smaller cases together, mostly counterfeiting rings.

The seal of the large metal door next to me opened with a loud crack. We shook hands and he led me into his office. It seemed even smaller than the front lobby. It was filled with items from his various cases. Images of Washington D.C., New York and San Francisco adorned the walls. The photos showed Mac with the kind of important people I had only read about in newspapers and magazines. A photo of Mac alongside the President was hanging on a wall behind him. Next to the various mementos on his desk was a photo of Mac and his family. It clearly held a place of honor on his desk.

I sat down and reached into my bag to get my laptop. Mac sat down and waited patiently while I fumbled around with my computer. I had spent most of the night putting together a presentation of Bethany's case. I had brought with me dozens of photos and exhibits.

"Thanks for seeing me, Mac. I know how busy you are."

"No worries," Mac replied.

I turned my laptop towards him so he could see the screen. I started by showing him a slide which said, "Case File: Bethany Correira – Law Enforcement Eyes Only."

"I'm sure you are aware I'm looking for Bethany Correira," I said as I showed him a slide with a photograph of Bethany. She was smiling, wearing a green and yellow summer dress and a puka shell necklace around her neck—the same puka shell necklace I suspected she was still wearing, somewhere.

I had only just started my presentation, when Agent Whisler interrupted me.

"Glen, are you asking us to help you on this case?" he asked.

"Yes," I answered. "I'm not sure how you guys can help yet, but I wanted to ask."

Mac looked at me and said, "Glen, you can stop right there."

I waited to hear what Mac had to say next.

"I already have approval from D.C. to assist you in any way you need. You ask for something, anything and we will get it for you."

Well, that was easy.

A short time later and a few blocks away, I met with FBI Special Agent Colton Seale. Colton was stationed in one of the many cubicles on the second floor, each with its own matching gray fabric walls and equally gray countertops.

Colton looked nothing like any other FBI agent I had ever seen or worked with before. His thin face held a pair of small eyeglasses perched on the top of his nose. He had an untrimmed graying goatee, which, although unkempt, was nothing compared to his wild hair, much of which often stood straight up in various places. He looked more like a mad scientist than a trained Special Agent for the FBI.

I had worked several fraud and computer cases with Colton. His ability to analyze and to dig into people's financial records was second to none. It was that expertise that I needed if I were to carry out my plan. Colton slowly and deliberately read each page of the paperwork I gave him. What some might mistake as a person who was a slow reader was in fact a perfect example of the deliberate way he worked. After half an hour however, even I was getting impatient as I had more places to go and more people to see.

"Colton, are you in?" I asked.

"Absolutely," he replied.

"Great," I said. "Can you get started right away?"

"Absolutely," he repeated, still slowly, methodically, reading each line of the report.

I collected my files and let myself out of the cubicle, leaving Colton to digest the rest of his paperwork. I needed to get over to the U.S. Attorney's office and speak with Assistant U.S. Attorney, Tom Bradley, about getting more help with Bethany's case.

After meeting with the U.S. Attorney, I went back to the homicide unit. Huelskoetter met me in the Homicide Lounge to go through the case files and see what copies of which files the Feds might need. We were moving along well until Sarge walked in. I offered him a chair. He refused and chose to stand.

"It's been six months... what are we doing with this case?" Sarge asked. He used the word "we" as if it actually included him. I could not think of anything Sarge had done in the past several weeks to help me in this case except to stay mostly out of my way.

"The media is on us bad," he complained. "They think we're clueless."

Some of us are.

"Are you two going to go outside and actually do some police work today?" Sarge said with a crooked smile.

"If you need to know, we've changed gears," I said.

Sarge gave me his most displeased look and wanted to know what the hell I was talking about. Sarge always wanted to know, even when he really didn't need to know. It had nothing to do with wanting to help or even understanding what was going on. He just wanted to be in charge.

Knowing I was going to have to tell him, I proceeded to explain I felt we needed a different tack. The plan to use a GPS and the media to see if Lawson would lead us to Bethany clearly had not worked.

Sarge chimed in: "What the fuck about Bob? I thought you interrogated him."

I tried to explain to the sergeant that it was clear to me that Bob was simply not going to turn his brother in. We had tried other ways to get to Lawson. We had tried to get to him through his friends, most of whom had told us to go fuck ourselves. The rest were too afraid of Lawson to help. I explained that I wanted to begin a process of severely ratcheting up the pressure on Lawson. I wanted to make his life miserable.

"So you're gonna fuck with Lawson to make him confess then huh?" Sarge asked.

"No," I said smugly. "Pissing off Lawson is only a benefit. The real target is Bob."

The baffled look on Sarge's face not only expressed to me his inability to process what I had just said, but it also gave me my first really happy moment in the Homicide Lounge in a very long time.

"Mike thinks it's all about Mike," I said. "As we begin to increase his stress level, he will dig in his heels. He will be able to justify in his mind and to his friends, that the police are harassing him."

I continued: "But in reality it will be Bob, whom I believe actually has a conscience, who will feel the pressure. Mike Lawson will see the police as a bunch of dumb fucks that don't have a clue. Bob on the other hand is going to see we are not going to go away. Not ever."

Sarge argued back, "You're making a big fucking jump that Brother Bob has a goddamn conscience, Klink."

"I believe that Brother Bob does have a conscience... I just have to find it," I said.

I then gave the sergeant an out.

"If it doesn't work you can blame me."

"Damn straight," Sarge said. "Now get back to work." He stomped out.

Huelskoetter and I waited until he was well gone before speaking a single word. I watched as Huelskoetter rolled his eyes and said, "He has no clue."

"What about the Internal Revenue Service?" Mark said.

"The IRS? Great idea," I said. "Do you know anyone over there?"

"I've worked with Special Agent Larry Caldrone," Mark replied. "Do you want me to go see him and see if he wants to play?"

"You'd better believe it," I said, "Brother Bob and Creepy Mike may not be afraid of us, but maybe they will be scared of having the Feds on their ass. Oh and have the IRS get with Mac and Colton over at FBI. I want this to be a joint effort."

"It's almost like we have our own task force," Mark said. "We might need a cool federal task force name... like Operation Nutcracker!"

I had a different suggestion. "How about, Operation Lets-Not-Fuck-This-Up?"

Chapter 35   A Registered Sex Offender

"Hello," Lawson answered.

"Yeah, Mike Lawson please," I said.

"Speaking."

"Hi Mike! This is Detective Klinkhart!" I said it like I was talking with an old friend, a best buddy.

"Uh, huh," was all Lawson could say.

"Mike, I know you and your attorney wanted to get some more of your personal items back," I explained, "and it took a lot to get your car back to you."

"I have some more items to give back to you, sunglasses, papers, etcetera," I said, "I have them all packaged up here for you at the police station."

"I'll have my brother come pick them up," he said curtly.

"No problem," I said, thinking I would love another chance to talk with Brother Bob.

"Oh, one more thing Mike," I said.

"Yeah?"

"Do you know where the Department of Public Safety is, Mike? The Alaska State Trooper Building on Tudor Road?"

"Yeah, I know where it is," he growled.

"Well, Mike, you see the reason I ask is because I've been doing some research and have recently discovered you failed to register as a sexual offender for your arrest in Chicago. You are going to need to go down to the Trooper headquarters in person and

271

register with them."

"I was unconditionally released, Glen," Lawson said angrily.

"That is a fact, Mike. You were released unconditionally from your prison term. However Illinois state law and Alaska state Law say that because of your conviction, no matter how long you were incarcerated or if you served your time, you must still register as a sex offender. It's the law."

I relished it every time I said the words "register" and "sex offender" to Lawson, thinking back to his ex-wife Renée telling me his biggest fear was anyone finding out he was a convicted sex offender.

For the first time, I heard Lawson's voice crack as he could only manage to stutter out, "Okay, why, well, maybe I'll call my attorney."

It was time to wrap up my phone call with him so I figured I'd end things on a high note.

"You can do that Mike, but you have seven days to get over to the Department of Public Safety and register or I will seek a warrant for your arrest. Bye-bye, Mike."

"Bye," Lawson said.

It should have been no surprise to Lawson when exactly a week later he answered his front door and found two uniformed Anchorage Police Officers standing there.

"Mike Lawson?" one asked.

"Yes?" Lawson answered, trying to contain his anger.

"We're here to ask you about failing to register as a sex offender," the officer explained.

Lawson was seething. Klinkhart had sent cops to his house. Lawson looked back behind him. Bob had come out of a room upstairs to look down on the commotion.

"I already registered," Lawson said, his voice rising, "I went in and did it this morning."

Lawson lifted up both hands. Remnants of ink from the fingerprinting process were still clearly visible. This was despite having washed his hands multiple times after coming back from Trooper headquarters.

The officer looked closely at Lawson's hands. It certainly looked like he had recently been fingerprinted.

"Do you have any paperwork showing that you registered as a sex offender today?" the officer asked.

Lawson rolled his eyes and gritted his teeth as he turned to try and find the paperwork the lady at the registry department had given him. He located his jacket on the railing of his staircase. Lawson fumbled trying to get the papers out of his coat. He finally extricated the documents and hurriedly pushed the letters toward the officers. The first officer took the paperwork from Lawson and opened it up. He purposefully took his time reading the documents.

Finally, the officer folded the papers neatly and handed them back to Lawson.

"Thank you, Mr. Lawson," the officer said as he began to back away from the front door. "You have a nice day."

Lawson said nothing and shut his front door. He watched from a side window as the officers walked down his driveway and up the street. It wasn't until the cops were completely out of sight that Lawson turned to his brother Bob, who was still standing on the landing above the staircase.

"Fucking Klinkhart," Lawson said.

Bob said nothing. He simply turned and walked back into his bedroom and closed the door.

I rolled down my car window as Officer Ritala approached.

When he got close enough to my car, Ritala's normally stoic, cop face transformed into a big, bright smile.

"Creepy Mike is apparently a registered sex offender now," he said.

"Was he happy to see you?" I asked.

"He was really pretty pissed off," Ritala said.

I laughed. "That's perfect."

"Klink, why did you have us go talk to him? Don't get me wrong, I love messing with guys like him, but how come you didn't want the pleasure of fucking with him yourself?"

"He is going to blame me anyway," I explained. "The more uniforms he and his brother see, the better."

Ritala laughed, "Good luck, Klink. If you need me again, give me a call."

I rolled up my window and tried to savor the moment.

Chapter 36   An Unnamed Task Force

The members of the unnamed task force worked tirelessly for the next several months. The federal agents from the FBI, the IRS and the U.S. Secret Service spent their time going through years of business records for Mike and Bob Lawson. They went through all of the brothers' documents and civil filings including divorces, bankruptcies and lawsuits. The agents pulled the brothers' tax filings and bank loans. Nothing was off limits.

Meanwhile, Detective Huelskoetter and I spent the holiday season cranking up the pressure on the brothers. We discovered that in November, Lawson and his brother had moved from their South Anchorage house to a rental property in Eagle River, Alaska, about thirty minutes north. It appeared from our investigation that Lawson's money situation was getting worse. He failed to make the payments on their South Anchorage home. We had daily surveillance of their new place. We even installed remote cameras attached to light poles next door. The ATF conducted routine undercover drive-bys. Mike Lawson appeared to spend much of his time staying inside the Eagle River house doing god-knows-what. Just for fun, I made sure some of the undercover cars tailed Bob from time to time, just to make sure he knew I hadn't forgotten him.

Even Rebecca took a turn at surveillance. She was parked nearby in an undercover vehicle one morning when Lawson walked out of his house. As he crossed the street to get his mail he noticed the attractive dark-haired female in the blue pickup truck parked nearby. Lawson could not resist the opportunity to introduce himself to a pretty lady. He walked up to Agent Bobich who by now was quickly trying to hide her police radio while at the same time positioning her handgun just out of sight but close at hand.

"Good morning!" Lawson said with a smile as Rebecca rolled down the window.

"Hello," she replied.

"I'm Mike," he said. "Can I help you?"

"Ah, no, thanks," she said as she gripped her handgun. "I'm just looking for a property around here that's for sale."

"Oh, so you're lost?" Lawson said with a grin. "You can come in and use my phone if you like... don't worry, I won't hurt you. I'm a nice guy."

"No thanks, I think it's back there," Rebecca said quickly as she started the truck. Without another word, Lawson smiled and waved as she drove off.

By the end of the year my conversations with Linda Correira drifted away from the routine to more distinctly personal subjects. She and I would talk at great length about what was happening in our weekly lives. She would share the latest information on Bethany's sister, Havilah and her work in assisting the poor in Africa. She would confide that her sons, Brian and Jamin, were not coping well with Bethany's disappearance. Each of them was distant and seemed unable to understand or communicate what they were going through. In our conversations, Linda would talk about her faith, her hope and her undying commitment to her daughter. When our talks would end, she would always thank me for everything I was doing, even though she did not know exactly what that might be. She had faith in me, she had faith in Bethany and that was good enough for her.

I also found something was changing in myself as well. It seemed as if I wasn't getting any closer to actually finding Bethany, but Linda's faith was starting to rub off. I just wasn't sure how I was going to do it, but I knew I would find Bethany and I wasn't going to do it alone. After the Johnson brothers fiasco, I had sworn to never again trust anyone else with my cases. It made sense to me that no one could ever do it better than I could, so I just learned to do it all myself. Now I was finding confidence and faith in my own friends. I realized I needed my fellow officers and investigators as much as Bethany needed me.

It was the end of December. It was cold outside and there was a lot of snow on the ground. While everyone else was getting excited about trees, presents and Santa Claus, I was focused on moving my case forward, no matter what. It was only a couple of days before Christmas when I summoned the task force to a meeting in the Homicide Lounge. Everyone showed up early. Detectives from APD took up half of the room. The ATF, the FBI, the IRS and the U.S. Secret Service were all represented. Assistant U.S. Attorney Tom Bradley was there, as was my friend and legal confidant, Sharon Marshall.

And then there was Sarge. He sat in a corner with his back against the wall with his hands crossed and looking angry. Sensing everything was normal, I proceeded with the meeting. I began by going around the room and personally thanking each of the members of our loosely formed group. I informed everyone that in my last conversation with Linda she asked me to tell all of them how much her entire family appreciated all of their hard work. Despite my not being a particularly religious person, I felt it was important to tell the group she said she was praying for each of us. The room was silent. I paused briefly and then continued by saying I had done everything I could do. I was proud of the work I had done, but now it was up to the agents seated at this table to move this case forward. I asked Special Agent Colton Seale to speak next.

Colton opened his notebook and leaned forward. His glasses were perched on his nose and his hair looked as disheveled as ever. He cleared his throat and began to explain what the FBI had discovered. Over the past several weeks, they had amassed a mountain of paperwork by using federal subpoenas and search warrants. After analyzing all of the information they had discovered several items of interest. The agents had found that several years ago the brothers had obtained loans for their roofing business in the amount of $600,000. Items of collateral the brothers told the bank they had were now missing and had likely been sold off for cash. The brothers were asking for more loans and were denied due to their current poor financial statements. Additionally, further review of the Lawson's records showed that their accounts receivable were either inflated or completely fictitious.

277

"We obtained a copy of the loan paperwork that Mike Lawson signed," he said. "It appears that he left out an important detail..." Colton smiled and then continued, "On the loan application Lawson failed to list himself as a felon or a sex offender as required by law, which is a federal offense."

He explained that both brothers obtained insurance monies illegally by accepting insurance checks from clients meant for other contractors and then pocketing the money. In some cases the client's names were forged and deposited into the Lawson Roofing bank accounts without the victim's knowledge or approval. Colton smiled and looked over at Rebecca, seated next to me.

Special Agent Bobich told the group that searches of the Lawson residence found two handguns and some marijuana in Bob Lawson's bedroom. DNA testing by the State of Alaska Crime Lab revealed Mike Lawson's DNA on one of the guns. "Thus making Lawson a Felon in Possession," she said with a smile.

Next, Assistant U.S. Attorney Tom Bradley informed the group the federal government intended to charge each of the brothers with bank and wire fraud. The penalties for these crimes included up to fifteen years in prison for each of the brothers. "These charges we came up with are not based on poor witnesses or anything else the Lawsons' might try and wiggle out of... these cases are black and white... it is their signatures on the paperwork," Bradley explained. "They can't talk their way out of it."

I turned and picked up the stack of binders I had prepared earlier. I walked around the table and dropped one of the documents in front of each team member. When I got to the back of the room, I handed my last packet to Sarge. I winked at him as he took it from me.

"This is the plan," I said. "Everyone has a role to play. Read it and commit it to memory. We have everything riding on this. The arrest warrants will be ready in a few days. We are set to hit them on Thursday morning just as Bob is leaving the house." I paused. "Any questions?" I scanned the room and looked at all of the faces before me. These were the people who believed in Bethany. All of them had been working just as hard as I had. I trusted them, just as Linda and Billy trusted me.

"Oh and don't forget to wear your badges and fly your agency colors. I want the Lawson brothers to know who we are and what we are there for. Make it a show," I said proudly. There was an air of excitement as the agents and the attorneys stood and left the Homicide Lounge.

All I had left to do was to wait to see if Bob had a conscience.

Chapter 37   The Arrests

I parked my police car on the road overlooking Lawson's Eagle River home. The arrest teams were in place. The first team consisted of FBI and Secret Service agents assigned to arrest Bob, while the other team, made up of APD and ATF Agents, was to take Lawson into custody. Each group was decked out in their flat black tactical uniforms. The front and back of each officer's ballistic vest was emblazoned with each agency's logo. Every officer had his handgun in a drop-down black thigh holster and each agent carried his or her rifle of choice, usually a short barreled Remington 870 shotgun or an H&K MP5 submachine gun. Each of the teams moved into position just around the corner of the house and was awaiting the signal. My radio sounded a momentary click followed by a static buzz. It was Rebecca, my eyes and ears on the ground.

"The teams are in place. Standing by for okay," she said.

I looked at my watch. It was 9:25 A.M. I knew Bob's routine was consistent. He left for work on time every morning at 9:30 A.M. I watched through my binoculars, waiting for anything that would tell me Bob was coming out alone. A few minutes later I could see the front door open. A man exited and shut the door behind him. He was wearing a black coat, a baseball cap and he was carrying a coffee mug in his left hand. The hot steam from his coffee was easy to see in the cold of the morning. It was Bob. I pressed the button on the side of my radio.

"Initiate. Initiate. Initiate," I said into the microphone. As soon as I spoke the command, I could see the first team begin moving towards the house on foot. They were in a direct line to meet Bob at the corner of his white pickup truck. By the time Bob came around the corner of his house he was met by half a dozen handguns and shotguns.

"Police! Stop! Don't Move!" the scout in the front of the team yelled. Bob immediately stopped in his tracks. Instinctively he put his hands up. Two of the team members came up from behind him and pushed him facedown into the snow bank. Bob's coffee mug went flying into the yard, leaving what looked like brown blood spatter across the snow. As the first team was securing him, the second team was already moving towards the front door of the house. Four members took positions on each side of the door while a fifth officer approached with a large breeching ram. With a single swing of the metal ram, the door exploded inward, splinters of wood flying. Right on cue, the team entered one at a time with guns poised in a ready position as they entered the house looking for Mike.

"One suspect in custody," I heard on the radio. I looked back and saw a snow-covered Bob being escorted in handcuffs into a marked police car. The APD vehicle was purposefully set up near the scene just to transport him back into Anchorage. I watched as the agents placed the disheveled, snow covered man into the back seat of the car.

I turned my binoculars back to the house. I prayed Lawson was not going to take the chicken-shit way out and shoot himself or start a losing gun battle with trained professionals. I wanted him to face a more earthly justice. I held my breath.

"Team Two coming out with one," Rebecca radioed. A moment later I saw her coming out of the house with a sleepy and pissed off Mike Lawson. He was still wearing his pajama bottoms and a large, wrinkled t-shirt. He was barefoot as the officers walked him, in handcuffs, over the snow-covered road and into an unmarked ATF SUV.

I hope your feet freeze, Mike.

"Is everyone 10-2?" I asked over the radio.

"Everyone is okay and the residence is secure," Rebecca radioed back.

"Have the teams begin searching the house," I replied. A moment later I pressed the microphone key again.

"Great job everyone."

I threw my radio onto my front passenger seat, I put my car into drive and began the 30-minute ride back to Anchorage.

Part one down. Part two to go.

I had to walk through several layers of heavy security at the FBI headquarters in order to just get to the meeting room. Special Agent Colton Seale escorted me through the heavily fortified doors and into the main conference room. Inside Sharon Marshall was waiting for me, along with Assistant U.S. Attorney Tom Bradley and Mac Whisler from the Secret Service.

"Do you have the file?" I asked Colton. "Right here," he said, pointing to a thick white binder. On the front of the notebook he had plastered a photograph for each of the agencies involved in the case. In the middle of the page there was a photograph of Bethany, the same one that was on all of her missing posters. On the top of the binder it read, "Bethany Correira Task Force."

"Nice name," I said.

Colton and Mac both stood at attention, waiting for the order to leave. They had an important role to play and I had chosen these two special agents for a reason. I wanted them to be the first people Bob gets to see. I was way too familiar to him. I wanted him to feel lost, alone and without anyone he recognized. Additionally, I knew the image of the FBI and the Secret Service carried a lot more weight with people than my little local police badge. I looked at Sharon.

"Anything else before they go in?" I asked.

"Don't forget to read him his Miranda Rights," she said with her brow furrowed. I knew when Sharon made that face she was being serious. I looked back at Colton and Mac. They both nodded. I had confidence in them. I had to. I could not do this part myself. I shook their hands and wished them good luck. Colton picked up his one-of-a-kind notebook and they left through a side door.

I took off my jacket and sat down at the conference table. I put my hands together, took a deep breath and waited. No one said anything. The FBI did not have video or audio feeds in their interview rooms so we had no way of knowing what was happening. We could only wait. The clock in the conference room ticked loudly. Two minutes became five minutes and five minutes became ten.

"What is taking them so long?" I asked Sharon. She looked at me and said, "The longer they are in there, the better it is for us."

Another ten minutes passed before the door opened. In walked a woman, dressed in a dark suit. I didn't recognize her, but she definitely looked like an FBI Agent.

"Detective Klinkhart?" she asked.

I nodded "yes."

"Our people at the Lawson residence found this and thought you should see it." She handed me a single sheet of paper. I looked at the note. I immediately recognized Lawson's terrible handwriting. The letter appeared to have been written some time ago, but it was addressed to me.

To Detective Klinkhart:

I did nothing wrong now go and find the real person who had something to do with Bethany. You are trying to get to me through my brother. That is about as low as you could go. How dare you lie to my boss, my brother, but most of all to Bethany's parents?

How can you put your head on your pillow at night knowing that you staged a witch hunt on an innocent man? I know that in your eyes once a con, always a con. Did you ever think that one con may have changed?

Mike

I sighed, laughed a nervous laugh and slid the note into my binder.

"What was that?" Sharon asked. I was about to say "nothing" when the door opened again. It was Colton and Mac. Immediately I stood up. They didn't say a word. Colton looked at Sharon and then at me. Finally he said, "Bob wants to talk to his brother."

"We can't let them talk," Sharon snipped, "He will convince Bob to shut his mouth."

Tom Bradley agreed. I looked over at Colton hoping for something, anything that might help me understand. He explained Bob would not tell them why he wanted to speak with his brother. I rubbed my face. I had to think. You never let suspects talk to each other. That is the basic rule of police interrogation. You separate them in different rooms and you play each of them against the other. That's how it's done. Letting them talk to each other leads at best to collusion. At worst they both stop talking.

Goddamn it, we are so close.

Why does Bob want to talk to his brother?

Does he want to warn him?

Does he want to help him?

Why talk to Mike?

I had interviewed Bob a dozen times over the past year. Each time I talked with him, I gained a little more insight into the brothers' co-dependent lives. I learned from Bob how the two inseparable brothers relied on each other for everything. Clearly, Mike had an evil side to him. He was the more aggressive brother, the talker, while Bob was passive, but a hard worker.

Is Bob evil like his brother?

I didn't think so. I had to believe Bob had a conscience. If he didn't have a conscience, then whatever I did next wouldn't mean shit anyway. I had to have faith in something. I had to have hope.

"Let Bob talk to his brother," I said.

Sharon was about to say something and then she stopped. She could tell my mind was made up. Maybe she agreed with my decision or maybe she didn't, but all I cared about was finding Bethany. If I had to trust someone that I shouldn't trust, then so be it. If I was wrong, then it was going to be my fault and mine alone.

I grabbed the phone and called Rebecca over at the ATF building. I told her to set Lawson up with a telephone. I wrote down the phone number on a piece of paper. I ripped off the paper and handed it to Colton. He and Mac turned and left the room. I sat in my chair and waited. No one said a word. Finally Sharon asked, "What do you think, Glen?" I nodded my head.

"I think Bob wants to know that his brother will do the right thing," I said.

She looked at me and replied, "You think so?"

"Lawson won't ever do the right thing." I said, not answering her question. "And that's the problem. That's been the problem the entire time."

Just then Colton came racing back into the room.

"Bob wants to speak with his attorney," he said. Sharon picked up the phone and began frantically trying to reach Bob's lawyer. I asked Colton to sit down and tell me everything. He began by saying when they first entered the interview room they introduced themselves and told Bob they were with the FBI and the Secret Service. They read him his Miranda Rights and he agreed to waive those rights and to speak. Colton said he did just as we had planned. He explained to Bob the multiple federal charges against him. He went through each charge, one at a time, to show Bob just how fucked he was. Colton then explained the potential penalties and how both brothers were looking at

286

fifteen years in federal prison.

"How did Bob react?" I asked.

"He was scared shitless," he said. "He was shaking the entire time."

"Good. What about the call to his brother?"

"Bob called the number you gave us and they talked for about a minute. Bob tried to explain to his brother that things were really bad and we weren't going away. Afterward Bob didn't say much. I could not hear what Lawson was saying on the other end of the phone but he was yelling a lot. When his brother was done yelling, Bob told him he loved him and then he simply hung up on his brother."

I breathed a sigh of relief and I turned to Sharon.

"I already got a hold of Sidney," Sharon said. "She is on her way."

Attorney Sidney Billingslea is a great defense attorney. I have a lot of respect for Sid. She is smart and she defends her clients honorably. By that I mean she won't stoop to underhanded or unethical means, but she works hard for her clients. I tell all new officers who have a case against her that they'd better have their shit together, because she will. That being said, I was extremely happy when I heard Bob had hired her after our last conversation. I had confidence she would see the federal case against her client was solid and that we had him between a rock and a hard place. It took a while for Sidney to get to the FBI headquarters but when she did, two FBI agents escorted her directly into the conference room. She walked in with her usual commanding presence, threw her coat onto a chair and got right to the point.

"What do you have and what's in it for my client?" she asked. Telling a defense attorney everything you have right away is not usually the normal process, but this wasn't the normal process and this wasn't a normal case. I opened up my folder and went over each of the federal charges against her client. I then explained to her what we really wanted. We wanted Bob to tell us everything he knew about his brother and about Bethany's disappearance. The deal was simple: if Bob told us everything, he would be charged, but would not serve any time in prison. Sidney nodded. She was then escorted out of the room to speak with her client. I was again left to just sit in my chair. A few minutes later Sidney walked back into the room.

"Bob will tell you everything," she said.

Chapter 38   Bob Talks

Bob was seated in a folding metal chair. His baseball hat was low on his head. He was slouched over with his hands in his lap. His eyes were red and his skin was pale.

"Hi, Bob," I said.

"Hi," Bob replied. He didn't look up.

I sat down and turned on my audio recorder. I went through his Miranda Rights once again to make doubly sure I could use whatever he had to say in a court of law.

"Okay, Bob," I said. "Tell me what you know."

Bob, still looking down, began to speak.

"That morning I got a phone call. But you guys know about it... you got the cell phone records," Bob said.

Bob had clearly read the evidence I had given him months ago.

"Yes, we did," I said. "Go on."

Bob breathed in deeply and then exhaled, "Mike called and told me he shot somebody."

Bob began to cry. He wasn't shedding the crocodile tears I had seen so many times before from other suspects. This was something much more real, something from deep inside Bob.

Bob continued, "He said he shot a girl."

He paused and tried to stop himself from crying, but it didn't work.

"And he wanted me to help him... I told him... told him he was on his own."

I leaned down, closer to Bob. I wanted to look him in the eyes.

"Did Mike say where he took her?" I asked.

"Mike said that he was going to go up to Fairbanks but he didn't make it that far. He said he went past Talkeetna. He put her in a gravel pit out there, I don't know exactly where."

I stopped for a moment. Bob was finally talking. He wasn't being completely honest. I still believed Bob somehow helped his brother, but he was talking and as long as he was talking my chances of finding Bethany were getting better and better.

Between sobs, Bob said Lawson called him, woke him up and told him that he hated women. Lawson asked Bob to bring him some plastic garbage bags. "No fucking way!" Bob said he replied.

It was increasingly difficult to understand his words through the sobs.

I had one of the agents bring Bob some tissues and a glass of water. A few minutes later we began again. Bob continued to insist he did not help his brother. He said his brother, acting alone, had driven up to a gravel pit several hours north of Anchorage. He said Lawson had wrapped the body up in plastic. He described in detail how his brother had checked on gravel pits along the road, past Talkeetna and found that most were occupied. He described how Lawson needed to get rid of her because the smell of decomposition was beginning to permeate the inside of the SUV. Lawson drove to the next gravel pit a little farther up the road and pulled in. Lawson then backed his white SUV up a small hill and then dumped the body over a little knoll. Lawson told Bob everything upon his return to their house. Lawson told Bob he had considered burying Bethany at the Bayshore construction site but ruled that out as being too risky.

Later that night both of them went out drinking and partying at the Blues Central bar. Bob said Lawson was drinking and doing a lot of cocaine that night.

"What did Mike do with the gun?" I asked.

"I have no idea," he answered.

Bob then looked up at me and said, "I want to apologize for lying to you guys early on."

"It's okay, Bob," I answered. "I know why you did it. It doesn't bother me, okay?"

I reached out my hand to Bob. He looked up and shook my hand. His handshake was slow, steady and real.

"It's been hard to deal with," Bob admitted. Again I could see that Bob was struggling to keep himself composed.

"Bob, what about the arson?" I asked, "The fire in the duplex the day after?"

Bob said he did not know anything about the fire. I didn't believe him. I figured it was time to see if Bob was ready to tell me the truth.

"Bob," I said, "remember what your attorney, Sid, told you about our agreement?"

Bob nodded his head.

"This case is not just about the federal bank fraud charges. The ATF and I are looking into the arson, which is also possible evidence tampering... If you lit the match, you need to tell me."

Bob paused. Then he looked down again. "I lit the match."

I said nothing. I wanted to give Bob time to think. A moment later, without prompting, he continued. He said he and his brother drove up to M Street late that night. Bob put on a pair of old sweats and took an old water bottle filled with a mixture of oil and gasoline. Lawson dropped Bob off in front of the duplex. Bob went inside and poured the mixture around the apartment. He lit a match and threw it in. There was a large burst of flame. He turned and ran out the back of the duplex. Bob ran up the hill and met his brother at the top of the road. They both went to the bar and met up with friends for the night. Later, Bob left Lawson at the bar and took a cab home.

We went through that two-minute telephone call from Lawson to Bob on the morning of May 3rd. The more I listened the more I was convinced Bob was with his brother that day and that he helped his brother out, just as he had done so many times before.

"Did Mike say where he shot this girl?" I asked.

Bob replied, "I don't know... I asked well, where did you shoot her? And I think he said he shot her in the side somewhere with a pistol. He said there was a struggle."

I noted Bob's breathing was speeding up and his eyes were tearing up again.

I reached into my binder and pulled out one of the missing posters with a smiling Bethany Correira printed on it. I held it up in front of Bob's face so that he could see it clearly. I knew Bob knew what Bethany looked like. I just wanted Bob to get the full impact of what I was going to say next.

"Bob, I've been looking for Bethany for a long time now," I said as I moved closer to him.

"Bob, Bethany is dead, there isn't a goddamn thing you or I can do about it. I talk with her parents, Linda and Billy, nearly every day. I have come to know these people. These are good people, just like you and me. For the past nine months they have had no idea where their daughter is or what happened to her."

Bob was holding his breath and again tears were beginning to fall from his eyes.

"Bob, the next time I talk to the Correira family I want to be able to tell them the truth. It's all about the truth. I want to tell them that it was you who did the right thing and that you told the truth."

Bob was not making a sound, but the tears continued to roll down his face. It was now or never.

"Bob, I know that you helped your brother and that's okay," I said. "I just need to tell Bethany's mother the truth. They need closure. They need to find Bethany."

I waited. The silence was almost too much for me to bear. Bob closed his eyes again.

"I helped him," Bob admitted.

That was it. That was what I needed to hear.

"It's okay, Bob, he's your brother," I said trying to comfort him. "Can you take us there? Show us where she is?"

"I can try," Bob said.

For the next five hours, Bob took me through everything he could remember about that day, Saturday, May 3rd.

Bob said his brother had been really upset about his last wife, Patty, leaving him. He was mad about having to do her job and his job, too. He was drinking a lot and doing a lot of coke. Bob said he had gone to sleep late and was in bed when he recalled hearing the phone in the kitchen ring. He didn't answer it. He then heard his cell phone ring. He reached over and answered it.

It was Lawson. He sounded pissed off.

"I shot somebody!" Lawson yelled.

"What the fuck are you talking about?" Bob asked as he quickly gained consciousness.

"I hate women!" Lawson said. "I hate them all!"

"Where are you?" Bob asked.

"I'm at the duplex on M Street," Lawson said frantically. "I need you to get me some rolls of plastic, some garbage bags and some tape."

"What the fuck did you do, Mike?" Bob asked.

"It was an accident, I swear. I need your help!" Lawson pleaded. "Get over here now!"

"No fucking way Mike!" Bob replied

"But I need help!"

Bob hung up his phone, got dressed, grabbed his coat and went outside.

Bob thought to himself, "Here I go again, same old shit."

He removed some large plastic sheets from the woodpile on the side of the house. He tossed the plastic and some duct tape in the back of his pickup truck. Bob ran back into the house and took a couple of shots of bourbon to calm his nerves. Then he grabbed a raincoat, rain pants, gloves and his tool kit and threw them in the front seat of his truck. He drove to M Street.

When he arrived, Lawson's white SUV was in the front driveway. Bob entered from the front door. The lights were off. Bob could hear his brother inside, stomping around. Sure enough when he got into the empty lower apartment, Bob found his brother, sweating and pacing back and forth along the hallway. Bob knew his brother had a problem with cocaine. Lawson's agitated state, the sweating, the inability to sit still and his dilated pupils all told Bob that Lawson was high on cocaine again.

"What the fuck, Mike?" Bob asked.

"She's back there," was all Lawson said. He pointed to the back bedroom.

Bob looked into the bedroom. In a far corner there was the body of a young woman. She was lying face down. She was completely nude. Bob looked closer. There was a large amount of blood along the right side of the body and the carpet.

"Was she dead?" I asked.

"Absolutely," Bob answered.

I pulled out another photograph of Bethany and showed it to Bob. I think we all knew the answer to the next question, but it was more for the record than for anyone else.

"Bob, is this the girl that you saw dead in that back bedroom?"

Bob put his hands to his face. He didn't want to see the picture of Bethany anymore but he had to answer the question.

"Yes," he said holding back the tears.

Bob described seeing a bullet wound on Bethany's left side, in the middle of her rib cage. Bob recalled seeing some silver toe rings on Bethany's foot. No one else except the Correira family and I knew about Bethany's toe rings. Bob was telling the truth.

He also described an indent in the wall about five feet above the body. The shape of the hole was about the size of a bowling ball. There were strands of hair in the sheetrock. When pressed, Bob said his brother had told him that Bethany's head might have hit the wall during a "struggle."

Bob also recalled seeing some white colored beads on the floor. He told me about seeing some clothes: shorts, a shirt or some blue colored cloth maybe and some panties that were on the floor about ten feet from the body.

Bob said that he did not stay long in the bedroom. While Lawson continued to pace about, Bob set off to move his brother's car into the garage of the duplex. Once the car was backed in, he put on his work gloves and grabbed the plastic sheeting and tape from his pickup.

When he returned, Bob asked his brother where he put the gun. Lawson pointed to his brown soft leather briefcase. Bob peered over the top of the opening of the case and saw a handgun. Bob had never seen that particular gun before. He thought it looked like a 9mm semi-automatic.

Bob asked his brother about the location of any shell casings. Lawson told Bob he flushed two shell casings down the toilet.

According to Bob, it looked like one shot had been fired downward just outside of the back bedroom. The round hit the base of a floorboard. Bob said he saw the hole. Bob also saw blood on the carpet near the floorboard. Seeing that his brother had no injuries on him, he assumed Bethany had been shot and bled at least some before she was forced into the back bedroom.

The more we talked about the body, the more uncomfortable Bob became. Bob said he went back into the room and laid out the plastic. He and Lawson rolled the body up in the plastic. Bob threw the clothes and anything else he could see lying around into the plastic sheeting. They then secured it with the duct tape. Together they lifted up the body and carried it to the garage. They opened the rear hatch of the SUV and put her in the back.

Lawson got into the front seat and after Bob raised up the garage door, Lawson drove the SUV out of the garage and out onto M Street. Lawson turned south and drove back to their house.

Bob had enough foresight to sweep the floor of the garage where the Mercedes had been in order to remove any possible tire tracks. I quickly opened up my binder and pulled out the photographs taken at the duplex only days after the fire. Sure enough there it was. A photograph looking into the garage from the outside clearly showed that the left side of the two-car garage was clean.

Bob then drove home in his truck and grabbed a vacuum cleaner and some wall plaster. He returned and vacuumed the floor, making sure not to leave anything on the carpet, especially not the puka shells.

The crime scene guys had taken the vacuum bag from the Lawson residence. They had even taken the commercial vacuums from the auto detailing shop. We found nothing in the old bags.

Bob solved that mystery as well.

"When I was done at the duplex I got rid of the bags just in case you guys came and got them," he said. "I then put in new bags and vacuumed up around the house to refill them."

Bob was smarter than I'd thought. Both figuratively and literally, Bob really was the one who cleaned up after his brother.

"Burning down the place was Mike's idea," Bob said. "I thought it would look too suspicious to start a fire, so I tried first to clean up and repair things. Mike just wouldn't have it."

Of course it was Lawson's idea.

He needed to get rid of the evidence, especially his DNA.

Holding the arson over Bob's head was just icing on the cake.

Although he was emotional at times, Bob's body language and his words were appropriate. When he spoke, it was from his memory. You could see it in his eyes and in his mannerisms that he was trying his best to recall things as accurately as he could. He didn't remember every detail, but that's normal. The more Bob talked, the more I believed him. In some ways I felt sorry for Robert Lawson. He had been in his brother's shadow all his life. He worked hard and as far as I could find, other than making some bad life decisions, Bob had not been in much trouble except for a single DUI conviction some years ago.

Bob had a conscience, just as I'd hoped. The more I talked with him, the more I could see that the man sitting in front of me was basically a decent guy. That decency was what his brother played and preyed upon.

I pulled out the letter Lawson had written to me that the FBI had found at the house. Bob looked at it and nodded his head up and down.

"That sounds like Mike's suicide attempt."

"Suicide attempt?" I asked.

Bob replied, "Back in the fall, when you guys were really watching us, following us, even talking with me a lot, I came home one day and found Mike in the garage."

Bob said his brother was really paranoid, likely because of his cocaine habit and because the cops were harassing him all the time. Bob said he came into the house one day and found a note on the door to the garage. The note indicated that Lawson had a gun. When Bob went into the garage he found the Mercedes was running. Lawson was drunk and nearly passed out in the back of the car. Lawson was talking crazy saying that if the police came to get him he would shoot it out with the cops.

Bob picked up his inebriated brother and put him to bed.

"So you cleaned up for your brother again, huh?" I said.

Bob looked down.

"Do you think that was a real attempt at killing himself?" I asked.

"I dunno," Bob replied.

Realizing I was getting off track, I asked Bob to recall what he and his brother did after they left M Street. Bob thought for a moment and then said they both stayed at the house for a while. Lawson's Mercedes stayed in the garage with Bethany's body still in the back. The brothers discussed what to do with her. They talked about taking her body to the Bayshore construction site or maybe putting her under the shed in the backyard. Eventually Lawson said he had a friend with a quarry up in Fairbanks where they could dump the body. The plan was to travel up to Fairbanks, dump the body and return to burn down the duplex.

"So what changed?" I asked.

Bob said that as his brother drove them north towards Fairbanks, he began to worry. He worried about the SUV breaking down and he worried about being pulled over by the Alaska State Troopers. The longer they drove, the more Bob could smell the odor emanating from the back of the SUV.

Finally, after about an hour and a half of driving, Bob began talking to his brother about needing to find a place to "get rid of her." They began looking along the side of the highway for a pullout or a place where they could get off the road and out of sight. They first stopped at an old gravel turnout, but there was a camper parked nearby.

About a quarter of a mile up the road they pulled into another gravel pit. This one was empty. They drove along the outer edges of the gravel pit and found a narrow path up a slight hill. Lawson backed the SUV up the path which allowed for complete cover. Bob unloaded a couple of shovels from the back of the Mercedes. Bob described a worn old path leading to an old campfire, circled with rocks.

As Bob recalled his actions, he often stopped in mid-sentence. He was clearly reliving that day.

"I'm sorry," he said again.

"That's okay, Bob," I told him. "You are doing great."

Bob said he and his brother tried digging into the earth, but the ground was still frozen, even in early May. They gave up and returned to the Mercedes. With some effort they pulled Bethany's body out of the back of the SUV and together they carried it into the woods. They set the body on top of a small rise of dirt. Bob pulled out a razor blade and cut the plastic sheeting covering the body. Without a single word to each other they pulled up on the plastic and Bethany's body rolled out. The nude body tumbled down the small hill and stopped at the bottom of the incline. Bob shook the plastic to make sure everything was out of it. Then he and his brother used their hands to cover up the body with leaves and debris. Bob bundled up the sheeting and stuck the used plastic under the back seat of the Mercedes.

Bob said that he drove the rest of the way back to Anchorage. Neither of them said a word during the two-hour trip. Bob made sure they threw the plastic in a random dumpster. When they got home they each changed their clothes and shoes and later dumped those as well. Bob even took the time to wash the shovels. He then used them to dig in the back yard of their home to insure nothing was traceable.

"Bob, are you sure you've never helped hide a body before?" I said.

Bob wasn't sure if I was kidding or not. I wasn't.

"I've never done anything like this in my life and I hope to never again," he said emphatically.

"So it was later that night you two went back to burn down the duplex?" I asked.

"Yes," Bob said nodding his head.

Bob had already said he lit the fire, that there was a large flame and that it was burning when he ran out the back door around midnight. However, the first report of a fire at the location didn't arrive until 6 A.M. the following morning, when Christine Bennett reported seeing the flames blowing out the windows of the duplex. I was no arson expert, but six hours seemed to me a long time for a fire to burn without destroying the building. I also believed Bennett saw Lawson's white Mercedes on M Street that morning.

"Are you sure that the fire was going after you left it?" I asked.

"I didn't stick around, but I'm pretty sure it was burning," Bob said.

"Did you go back the next day to check?"

"No," he said.

I explained to Bob my confusion over the difference in time between his lighting the fire and the 911 call. Bob was adamant that he was asleep that morning. Bob could not however be sure where his brother was Sunday morning.

"So, Mike never told you he went back to M street?" I said.

"No, he never did," Bob replied.

"What if the fire you set went out?" I asked.

Bob paused and then replied, "It would be just like Mike to go back and check to make sure that thing was burning."

"And if he did restart the fire, why wouldn't he tell you about it?" I asked.

"I don't know," Bob said.

Bob didn't burn down the duplex after all. The fire Bob set went out. There was nothing in the room except for carpeting. The gasoline Bob said he spread was a good fire starter, but there may not have been enough fuel and oxygen to keep burning. Bob did not use Coleman campfire fuel. When asked, Bob said he knew nothing about it. How did that fuel can get into the garage of the duplex? Bob said that he didn't put it there.

Lawson never told Bob the fire went out. He let Bob continue to think he alone had burned down the building.

Bob was clearly exhausted. Despite having lunch and dinner and plenty of bathroom breaks, emotionally he was beat.

"Are you going to be okay?" I asked.

Bob looked at me and said, "Yes. I'm tired, but it feels good to get this off my chest and if my brother won't do the right thing, I guess I have to."

A minute later Bob added, "When I'm eulogized... all I want somebody to say is I stood up and did the right thing. I always tried to do the right thing."

I closed my binder and began to gather up the papers, the drawings and the various photographs I had spread all over the interview room. As I did I turned to a very weary Robert Lawson and said, "You did the right thing here, Bob."

"I know I did," he answered.

I shook Bob's hand and escorted him to one of the agents standing just outside so Bob could have a ride back to his house for some sleep.

As for me, I took my stuff and drove back to the office. I had to plan a trip. In the morning we were all going on a road trip up north to an unnamed gravel pit.

Chapter 39   A Drive Up North

It was not easy to hide a caravan of four SUVs driving north out of Anchorage with a dozen law enforcement officers and Bob Lawson inside. It was January and it was another cold, snowy, day when we left town. We were going to need the four-wheel drive vehicles if we hoped to get close enough to the area where Bob described dumping Bethany's body.

Falling snow began to lift as we moved north. I sat in the back seat of the lead vehicle with Bob next to me. Most of the time Bob said little as the Alaska winter landscape rolled past. He was concentrating. He was working hard to remember. I could tell Bob was trying his best. It was emotional for him. Since our talk yesterday Bob looked better than I had seen him in a long time. I have had many people confess to me. Some of them, like Bob, had to have it coaxed out of them. They say that confession is good for the soul, but until now I really hadn't seen it so dramatically displayed in front of my eyes.

We drove north along the Parks Highway toward Fairbanks. Along the way we passed the turnoff to Talkeetna, Bethany's hometown. I had been so busy in the last 24 hours I failed to see the irony. All this time, Bethany hadn't been in Anchorage at all. She'd been so close to home. I began to wonder how I was going to tell Linda and Billy.

We were about two hours north of Anchorage when we approached a turnoff along the side of the road. We slowed down as Bob leaned forward.

"That's the first gravel pit we went into," Bob said.

"The one that had campers in it?" I asked.

Bob nodded yes, "Keep going. It's the next one."

About ten minutes later we approached another turnoff. The milepost sign read "Mile 129" of the Parks Highway.

"Is this it?" I asked.

Bob was now sitting up, scanning the side of the highway and trying to see through the trees.

"I think so," he said.

We pulled into the turnoff. The rest of the vehicles pulled in behind us. The snow was much deeper than I'd expected. The Alaska winter had been especially hard on this part of Southcentral Alaska. We were unable to drive into the gravel pit as winter winds had created a six-foot snowdrift across the entrance. As we exited the vehicles the freezing temperatures cut into our lungs, making it hard to breathe.

After meeting with the other agents, we gathered up our equipment, cameras, video recorders, backpacks and shovels and began to walk up and over the snow berm. We walked in a single-line formation with me in the lead, followed by Bob and then the rest of the investigators. We crested the top of the snow. The gravel pit had been untouched. The pit was really more like a large cleared area dug into the middle of the woods. The open area had no trees or brush, just a large area of snow the size of two football fields.

I motioned to Bob and he pointed me along the edge of the gravel pit towards the far corner of the snow-covered field.

The snow made walking difficult even though we had on snowshoes. The entire way Bob stopped every few feet. He moved his head from side to side trying to figure out where he was. At one point Bob turned himself completely around. Clearly Bob was trying to get his bearings and figure out where it was he and his brother drove. Bob kept apologizing for not being sure which way to go. The area was clearly very different in the middle of January then it had been in early May.

Repeatedly, Bob would indicate for us to go one direction. We would then walk that way for twenty to thirty feet and then stop. Then Bob would look around and then point us in a completely different direction. The entire time the snow and bitter cold were making my face sting and my nose run. Bob stopped again. He looked around again. His face was sullen and his head dropped.

"I'm sorry, Glen," Bob said. "I think we are in the right area, but I can't be sure. Things are too different. Maybe if we go back to the start I can try again."

We had already been out in the woods for nearly four hours. Bob was cold, I was cold and the rest of the team was cold. Clearly we were not going to find Bethany in this weather and deep snow. I was disappointed, but Bob was sure it was the right gravel pit. He just could not put us in the right spot. Even the cadaver dogs we brought with us were unable to help in such harsh conditions. We needed to come back after the snow melted. We needed to buy ourselves more time.

The long, cold trek back to the cars seemed even more difficult than when we came in, if only because I was frustrated. We were so very close, but spring wasn't for another four months

My mind raced with questions:

Bob was talking, but for how long?

And how long could we keep the location of Bethany's body a secret?

What if Lawson discovered his brother had rolled on him?

Even if he's in jail, could he get someone else to find Bethany before we do?

The drive back to Anchorage was even quieter than the drive up. We were nearing the city limits when Bob turned to me and said, "I'd like to meet the Correiras."

"Why is that?" I asked.

Bob looked at me squarely in the eyes and said, "I want to tell them I'm sorry."

Without hesitating I replied, "I can make that happen for you, Bob."

"I don't expect them to forgive me," Bob said as he looked away and out the car window.

"I think I know Billy and Linda and if you asked them... they will forgive you."

Bob said nothing else. I could make out a single tear moving down the side of his face.

I was exhausted by the time we got back to the police station. I threw my wet snowsuit and boots in the corner of my office. They landed with a thud. I sat my file folders and tape recorder on my desk. It had been a very long two days. I had only gotten a few hours of sleep between Bob's interviews and the trip to the gravel pit. The initial excitement of getting Bob to confess and confirm that Bethany was dead had been an emotional rollercoaster. I was glad to get out of my wet clothes. I was ready for a hot shower and some sleep.

I grabbed my car keys and I looked around one more time to make sure that I was not going to leave anything behind. I was nearly out the door when my phone rang.

I recognized the number on the caller ID.

"Hello, Linda," I said without waiting for the voice on the other end to speak.

"Hi, Glen," Linda Correira said. "How are you doing?"

I hesitated to answer. I had so much to say but I was not about to tell Linda what had just transpired. I couldn't tell her about Bob's confession. I dared not mention the trip up to mile 129 or the fact that only a few hours ago I had driven past the turnoff to Talkeetna. There was one secret though I knew I could no longer keep from Linda and her family.

"I'm doing great, Linda," I said hoping it sounded like I was telling the truth.

"Billy and I are in town. We are taking Havilah to the airport," Linda said.

Bethany's sister, Havilah, had come home from her work in South Africa to spend Christmas with the family. Now she was returning to continue her missionary work. Although I had only met Havilah a couple of times, I was struck by her quiet sense of confidence and her willingness to help others. Given how similar the two sisters were, I could easily see why Bethany and her sister were so close. Havilah was also very adamant in her deeply held belief that Bethany was alive.

"Would you mind stopping by the station?" I asked.

"Sure, Glen. We'll be there in about 20 minutes."

I hung up and dialed Sharon Marshall's cell phone. I wasn't going to call Sharon for permission. I just wanted her to know what I was about to do. In her usual supportive way, Sharon counseled me on the risks involved, but ultimately she agreed what was best for the case may not always be the best for the Correiras or for me. Sharon trusted me as much as I trusted the Correira family. I hung up the phone just as Rebecca walked into the office.

"Everyone has taken off, Klink," she said. Rebecca had her snow gear under her arm and her backpack slung over her shoulder. Despite being with me for most of the past two days and being just as sleep deprived as I was, Rebecca looked like she could go another 12 hours.

"Linda and Billy are coming in to talk," I said.

"What are you going to tell them?"

Being only partially honest, I replied, "I'm not sure yet."

Rebecca reached over and gave me a hug.

"Call if you need anything," she said.

Rebecca smiled and headed out the back door. I grabbed a box of tissues and headed the other way towards the front lobby.

It wasn't long before the Correiras arrived. I escorted Linda, Billy and Havilah into the conference room. They sat down along one side of the large table. I closed the door and set down the box of tissues. I walked to the other side and sat down facing them. Billy, Linda and Havilah looked at the box and then at me. I had my game face on. I had given lots of death notifications before and had learned to deliver the bad news quickly, succinctly and without any flowery words or other verbal garnish. Our police policies and rules of professionalism dictated it.

"I'm glad that you guys could stop by," I said.

"What's going on, Glen?" Linda asked. The friendly smile she had on her face when she came in was gone, replaced by a look of nervous concern.

"Over the past eight months or so I have told you things and asked you to keep it to yourselves," I said. "As you know I needed some things to not become public, simply for the good of the case."

Linda and Billy nodded their heads in agreement. The Correiras and I had created a special trust over time. Billy and Linda understood that trust. Havilah seemed a little unsure of just what I was getting at, but I continued.

"Before we go any farther, I need all of you to agree that what I'm about to tell you will not get out. If word of this leaks then the entire case may be lost and I may never be able to find the person responsible for Bethany's disappearance."

Linda, Billy and Havilah each assured me they understood.

"Linda and Billy, I promised you that when I knew for sure, when I had positive proof, I would tell you…"

I look directly into Linda Correira's eyes.

"Bethany is dead."

I stopped and I waited. I'd known this moment was going to come someday and that someday was today. I had just killed a family's hope. All I could do now was watch.

Billy was stone-faced. I looked at Linda and could see the tears coming down her face. She made no sound. I began to slide the tissue box over to Linda when I heard Havilah. She had gotten up from her chair and in one quick motion had thrown herself into the corner of the conference room. She began to cry out loud. Her moans and cries became louder and more intense as she slid herself down the wall and onto the floor and into a fetal position. Havilah's sobs became a scream. I could not understand anything Bethany's sister was saying, I could only hear that she was in pain. It was an uncontrollable and inconsolable pain.

I wanted to help her but I didn't. I wanted to go over to her and to hold her. I wanted everything to be all right but I sat just there and said nothing. That was my job.

Linda and Billy got up from the table and tried to help Havilah. Havilah pushed her mother away and slowly lifted herself up and back into her seat. Her face was red and stained with tears. Havilah refused to look at me. She just stared at the floor.

Linda was the first one to speak.

"Where is she, Glen?"

I took a deep breath and said, "I can't tell you, Linda."

Linda and Billy looked at me in disbelief.

"I need to balance what I tell you with what I need to do for the case," I said, "Telling you that Bethany is gone is a big risk, but one I felt I had to take. Saying anything more would be a mistake and I can't afford any more mistakes."

Billy extended his hand across the table. I reached over and I shook his hand.

"Thank you, Glen," Billy said. Billy did not look like a man who had just been informed that his daughter was dead. Like his handshake, Billy's voice was strong and unwavering.

"Please let us know when we can talk freely about this," he said.

"I will," was all I could muster.

Billy, Linda and Havilah rose from the table. I shook Billy's hand once more as he exited the room. Linda grabbed me and gave me a hug as she left. Havilah followed closely behind, still refusing to make eye contact with me. I escorted the family down the narrow hallway and to the lobby exit. I held the door for them. I watched as they walked across the lobby and out the front doors of the police station. I closed the door behind me and walked back to the homicide unit.

I wasn't sure of the time. It was late. No one else was around. The hallway was empty. Most of the lights were off. I walked into the homicide office. I looked around. It too was empty.

I walked over to my desk. I began looking for my keys. I needed to get the hell out of there. I couldn't find my keys. I started looking around the piles of Bethany reports littering my desk. Aggravated, I sat down in my chair.

"What the hell have I done?" I said out loud.

I closed my eyes and put my hands on my face. All I could see was Havilah curled up in corner, crying her eyes out. I did that. I caused that pain. I hurt for Havilah. I hurt for Bethany. I hurt for Dawn.

It started slowly, first one tear and then another. Bethany and Dawn were both dead. It all hit me at once: Twenty-one years of hurt, twenty-one years of guilt. I opened my eyes and could see nothing through the tears. The tears were followed by sobs. I could hear Havilah's sobs echoing in my ears... the cries I heard became stronger and louder. The sound became so loud that it was painful. I could hear the crying for Bethany. Soon I could hear the crying for Dawn. As the world began collapsing around me, I realized it was not Havilah that I heard sobbing uncontrollably. It was my voice, my sobs. I could not stop it. A few minutes later everything went black.

I awoke with my head on the top of my desk. My head hurt as much as my heart. I did not know how long I was out but sunlight was beginning to edge itself into the office. Soon the other detectives would be arriving. I couldn't let them see me in such rough shape. My eyes hurt and were crusted with dried tears. Despite the fog and the crud in my eyes I managed to find my keys, still sitting in my coat pocket where I had left them. I picked myself up and headed home for a quick shower knowing I had to be back in a few hours.

An aerial photograph of the gravel pit at Mile 129 of the Parks Highway in January. *Photo courtesy of the Anchorage Police Department.*

In the middle of winter, Bob Lawson leads the law enforcement team into the gravel pit. *Photo courtesy of the Anchorage Police Department.*

Chapter 40   Losing It

Lawson's white SUV was not at the house when we arrested him and Brother Bob. Using the GPS Bird Dog we installed, I located Lawson's white Mercedes hidden in a trailer park in Anchorage. The car was parked behind a beige colored, tin mobile home. As I walked up to the trailer I noticed the metal edging pulling away from the trailer's frame and the garbage interspersed with kids' toys spread along the front of the residence.

No one answered the front door when I knocked. I wasn't going to wait. I motioned to Detective Huelskoetter and he grabbed a camera and some gloves. I pulled out my cell phone and called dispatch for a tow truck. Huelskoetter began taking photos of the outside of the car. Based upon the amount of dust, dirt and snow on the car it had been there at least several weeks, if not months. One of the front windows was rolled down just enough that I could get my gloved hand into it and unlock the door from the inside. The interior of the vehicle was water damaged and beat up. The ashtray overflowed with old cigarette butts.

I reached over and opened up the glove box. There were various papers and a Mercedes user's guide. I lifted up the papers inside and that was when I saw it.

"Mark, you need to take a photo of this," I said.

Detective Huelskoetter came over to my side of the car with the camera. I pointed to the glove box. Mark focused the camera's lens. He had good lighting and was able to clearly see the object of my interest. In the back of the glove box was a large wad of hair. Human hair, cut into various lengths and tied together with a multicolored cloth. After Huelskoetter took his photos I dropped the hair into an evidence bag. We then waited for a tow truck to arrive and seize the Mercedes one last time.

It was going to be months before enough snow melted at the gravel pit. I had plenty of work to keep me busy. Besides trying to substantiate Bob's interviews I was working on simply trying to keep the fact that Bob had confessed to me a secret as long as I could.

I spent most of my days trying to get the federal and state prosecutors to speak with Bob's lawyer, Sidney Billingslea. I needed them to iron out an agreement for Bob to plead guilty to the federal charges. Bob was to receive parole and get no jail time in exchange for his cooperation. In addition, Bob was required to make recorded telephone calls to his brother, who was still in jail. Doing a telephone wire is not easy, especially when your suspect is in lockup. Prisoners are not allowed to receive telephone calls. That meant I had to get Lawson to call us. I devised a plan where we would plant an undercover telephone number with Lawson's sister in Minnesota. Bob was to call his sister, Sarah and tell her he needed to talk with Lawson. I knew from jail records that Lawson was in contact with Sarah and had called her on several occasions from jail. Bob was to let Sarah know he had gotten a construction job at a warehouse and there was a safe phone there that they could use.

I contacted the telephone company and arranged for the undercover telephone number. I had the line run to one of our conference rooms. I figured that Lawson might smell a rat but was confident that sooner or later he'd call. Lawson wanted to be in charge. Lawson wanted to control Bob. Lawson wanted to know what Bob knew. Therefore he would call. Eventually.

I was getting the wire room ready when my cell phone rang.

"Hello," I answered.

"Detective Klinkhart, this is Officer Janson, Robert Lawson's Parole Officer," the voice on the other end said.

"Have you seen Bob?" he asked.

"No, but I'm supposed to talk with him later today."

"He missed his meeting with me today," Janson said.

A chill went through me. Bob had never missed a meeting with his P.O.

"It's not like him," Janson said. "I just thought that you should know."

"Thanks," I replied as I grabbed my coat.

During the drive I repeatedly called Bob's cell phone. Every time it went straight to voicemail. Thirty minutes later, I arrived at Bob's apartment. His white pickup truck was parked in the driveway. The day was bright and cold, but I noticed there was no frost on the windows of the pickup. I put my hand on the hood of the engine. It was warm.

I approached the front entrance of the house. I pulled the screen door open and stood next to the main door. I listened intently for anything, a sound, a movement, anything that would tell me that Bob was inside and that he was alive. I heard nothing.

I turned the doorknob. It moved. I heard a click of the latch and I gently pushed the door open and away from me. The house was dark. I paused, wondering if I should call for backup. By now I was standing in an open doorway of a darkened room. I was backlit from the daylight outside. I was already an easy target for someone inside if they chose to shoot me. I reached to my side and instinctively grasped the handle of my Glock. I gripped the gun and cleared my holster in one quick motion. I stepped inside of the doorway and took a step to the left and out of the lighted entrance. I paused. My eyes needed time to adjust to the light. I could just make out that I was in the main living room. A television was to my left. I could just see a large dark colored couch on the other side of the room. There was something or someone, laying on the couch.

"Bob?" I asked.

The figure moved.

"Bob?" I asked again, this time louder and with an air of authority.

315

My eyes began to focus on the figure. It was clearly a person. I looked for the person's hands. Faces can't kill you, but hands can.

"Let me see your hands!" I shouted.

The figure raised his hands upward and towards me. As he did I focused on the front sights of my handgun and began to take the slack out of the trigger.

"Klink?" the voice said in a slurred speech.

It was then that I recognized Bob Lawson. Bob's hands were open wide and were still raised when I lowered my weapon. Bob began to lower his arms. As he did I noticed that both of his wrists were cut. Blood was running down his forearms.

"Bob, what the fuck did you do?" I said as I holstered my weapon. Bob rolled over. A pool of blood was on the floor near the couch.

"This is I-25," I shouted in the radio. "I need medics at my location!"

"Damn it Bob!" I said as I began to apply pressure to his wrists, "What the hell are you thinking?"

"I'm so sorry Mike... Please forgive me," he said deliriously.

I could not help but notice the stench of alcohol coming from Bob Lawson.

Chapter 41   The Phone Call

"Are we ready for tonight?" Detective Huelskoetter asked.

"The question is whether or not Bob is, I replied.

Bob had been out of the hospital for a few days and although he said he was ready to run the wire against his brother, it seemed like nothing was going as planned. Bob's suicide attempt nearly destroyed the case. I later found several postcards from Lawson in Bob's apartment postmarked from jail. Despite a no contact order from the judge, Lawson was still trying to control Bob. One of the notes reminded Bob that "brothers stick together" and that "blood is thicker than water."

Since his suicide attempt I had put Bob under 24-hour a day watch until further notice. The plan was to have Bob come to the police station and we would sit and wait for Lawson to call. There was no way to tell when the call might come. There were too many variables, too many unknowns.

My desk phone rang.

"What the hell now?" I thought as I picked it up.

"Detective Klinkhart, this is Rose in Dispatch," the voice said, "I have Rex Butler on the other line for you."

"This is not good," I said to myself as I asked Rose to pass the call through.

Rex and I had always gotten along over the years. Although we were always on opposing sides we seemed to have a mutual respect for each other. "Hello, Mr. Butler," I said into the phone as nicely as I could.

"Good day, Detective Klinkhart," Rex's smooth and deliberate voice echoed.

"To what do I owe the pleasure?"

"Well, as you know I represent Mike Lawson," Rex stated. "And we think that Mike has a story to tell."

"Go on," I said.

Rex went on to explain that he believed his client, Mike Lawson, was a patsy.

"So Mike is ready to confess?" I asked with as much disdain as I could muster.

"Mike says it was his brother Bob who killed Bethany," Rex replied. "He is prepared to run a wire against his brother Bob to prove it."

I could not believe what I was hearing.

Lawson wants to run a wire against Bob?

Does Lawson know about our wire?

Is this a preemptive strike?

Is this a trick by his attorney to derail the case?

"Rex, as you know I am always ready for the truth," I said. "If your client is interested in the truth then I will do whatever I can to help that. When does your client want to do this?"

"As soon as possible."

"I'll check with the District Attorney and I will get back with you."

"I await your call," Rex answered.

I hung up the phone and turned to Detective Huelskoetter.

"Now Lawson wants to run his own wire against Bob," I said.

Mark shook his head and laughed.

Bob showed up at the station right on time. I noticed his wrists were still bandaged as I shook his hand. I took some relief in the fact that Bob looked better than the last time I had seen him. He had cleaned himself up and had even showered. Bob's eyes were bright but his smile revealed his uneasiness.

"You nervous?" I asked.

Bob looked down.

"Very much so," he said.

"Did you give Sarah this phone number?" I asked.

Bob nodded his head yes.

"Do you think she will give the number to Mike?"

"I don't know," he replied.

As we sat around the conference table I explained to Bob how the telephone wire worked. I would be running the recording equipment listening to the entire conversation through a set of headphones. When his brother called, Bob was to say he was doing some construction work in a warehouse and that he thought the warehouse phone was a good way for them to talk. As I explained the process Bob became visibly more relaxed. He even began to help by working to improve the cover story.

"I'll say that we're doing sheetrock work and it needs to be done at night when everyone is out of the office," he said.

"That's good," I replied.

We began to construct a series of questions for Bob to ask his brother. After we had our whole plan laid out, we sat in the room and chatted about nothing in particular. Every so often one of us would look at the telephone placed on the desk between us. The phone sat there, silent.

I nearly jumped out of my chair when it finally rang. I looked at Bob. He too was surprised. I turned on the audio recorder. I knew that the jail records calls, but I wanted to make sure I had a good copy. It never hurts to have a backup.

By now the telephone had rung three times. I nodded to Bob.

Bob reached over, picked up the receiver and put it to his ear. As he did my nerves calmed and time slowed down. I pressed the sides of the headphones close against my head. A recorded voice came over the line.

"This call is from an inmate from the Anchorage Jail... To accept this call press one."

With that Bob reached over the phone and pressed a button. The automated attendant responded with a computerized beep. There was a pause.

"Hello," a voice said. It was unmistakably Mike Lawson.

"Hello?" Bob said back.

"Where you at?" Lawson asked, clearly suspicious.

Bob hesitated. "Yes, I'm sheet rocking at a warehouse downtown."

"Yeah... you're not at the cops are you?" Lawson asked. "And you're not wearing a wire are ya?"

I stopped and nervously looked at Bob. Bob didn't look at me, instead he responded calmly, "No... the guy here said I could take a call... I figured this was a safe place where we could talk without getting caught."

Lawson told Bob he didn't want to talk about the case. Lawson was clearly suspicious but he kept talking.

"I don't trust it...I just wanted to hear your voice, Bob."

"This shit is eating me up Mike." Bob's voice cracked as he pled for his brother to listen to him. "I've been drinking every night. They didn't just go away. This whole thing ain't going away Mike."

For a moment there was a pause.

"Yeah it is, Bob," Lawson said firmly. "Watch and see,"

Bob leaned back in his chair. He paused and tried again.

"I need to talk about it Mike. We never talked about it."

Lawson got indignant. "I don't wanna talk unless I could talk to you stark ass naked in a room where I could go and you're not wearin' a wire and nothin's bugged. That's the only way we could ever talk Bob."

Bob began to cry. Lawson was bullying his brother, just as he had for most of their lives.

Lawson continued, "Bob, I'm in prison. I am a sex offender. They are treated like fuckin' human shit here. You couldn't do ten to fifteen years' time. Try doing ten to fifteen days in my fuckin' shoes. You couldn't survive. You could not fuckin' survive." Mike began making sobbing sounds.

"I have to stay locked up in an eight-by-eight fuckin' cell. With no fuckin' cigarettes … I haven't had a cigarette in seven fuckin' weeks. Y'know... tell me about heat... I haven't had a visit. No one's fuckin' come to see me. Fuck the world, Bob!"

Lawson clearly knew how to push his brother's buttons. I watched the man sitting across the table from me. I looked for anything that would tell me if Bob was going to buy into his brother's guilt trip.

Bob would not look at me. He gripped the phone firmly in his hand and leaned forward as he spoke.

"I'm gonna say something Mike and you can either hang up on me or not..." He paused and then he asked the one question I had instructed him to ask his brother.

"You said it was an accident, right?"

Lawson became defensive. "Stop it... stop it right there, Bob."

Bob wouldn't let up.

"I'm just trying to understand Mike," Bob pleaded. It was clear Bob wasn't acting. This was something he truly wanted from his brother. I watched as a stream of tears began to roll down Bob's worn and weathered face.

Sensing that things weren't working Lawson reverted back to a demanding tone with his brother.

"Don't you get it, Bob?" he said. "They've got you to testify against me."

Lawson began to yell, "You're their star pupil! You showed them what the cat buried in the kitty litter... you showed them everything!"

Those words echoed in my head.

What the cat buried in the kitty litter... the gravel pit.

That son of a bitch.

"Well, I'm takin' everything to fuckin' trial, Bob! I'm playin' the courtroom. I'm gonna string this out for 20 fuckin' years!"

Lawson continued, "I want you to listen..."

For the first time, Bob cut off his brother in mid-sentence.

"Now you listen to me, Mike. If you did that on purpose that's a whole different story." I looked at Bob. His jaw clenched tightly. He had heard his brother's words and he was clearly angry. "If something happened and it was a goddamn accident... that's a whole different fucking story, Mike."

Bob was no longer speaking from the script I had given him. The voice on the other side of the line was quiet as Bob continued.

"If it was an accident Mike, you tell me that and I will go to bat for you."

Lawson paused before answering. I held my breath.

"You know it was an accident. I told you it was a fucking accident," Lawson admitted.

There it was. For nearly a year I had waited for Lawson to say what I had known since that first night I met him. He was there. She was there. Bob did not kill Bethany. Mike Lawson did. I knew it wasn't an accident, but that didn't matter at the moment. What mattered were Lawson's words. His words. Not Bob's words, Lawson's own words. Lawson's words had gotten him out of trouble for years. This time his words were going to be his undoing.

Lawson realized what he had just said. He tried to keep his words to his brother secret. "We were mum's the fucking word Bob... put us in the grave... I was taking her to my grave."

Suddenly I remembered there was something else I needed from Lawson. I grabbed my notepad and began to scratch out a message for Bob. I managed to quickly spell out a note, "WHY NO CLOTHES?" I held it up in front of Bob. He looked up and nodded his head.

"Mike, can I ask you one more question?"

"WHAT?" Lawson answered, clearly annoyed.

"Why no clothes?"

"No running," Lawson answered.

Bob and I looked at each other.

"What?" Bob said.

"No running," Lawson repeated.

"No running?" Bob was confused.

Lawson sighed, "To get away... runaway."

"Ohhhh," Bob said.

So that was going to be Lawson's defense I thought. Lawson had to somehow explain to his brother why Bethany's body was nude when Bob arrived on M Street. I shook my head. It was bullshit. Clothes or no clothes, Bethany would have done everything she could have to get away from Lawson. She was tougher than most boys. She was certainly tougher than Mike Lawson. That is why he had to shove her head into the wall. That's why he had to shoot her. Having no clothes on would not have stopped her from running out of that duplex if she could have.

"Why are you doing this to me, Bob?" Lawson pleaded to his brother. "I swear to God I will hate you for the rest of your life if this is all being recorded... If you are doing this for the police..."

Bob interrupted his brother once again.

"I love you, Mike," Bob said.

Lawson acted like he didn't hear his brother's words.

"Are you doing this for the police?" Lawson demanded.

"No I am not!" Bob said angrily.

"Swear on mom's grave you aren't doing this for the police," Lawson said.

"I swear," Bob answered.

"Swear on everything," Lawson asked. "Swear that you're not workin' with the police."

"I'm not, Mike, I swear," Bob said as he broke down crying.

Lawson ignored Bob's tears and began asking his brother to bring him some more money in jail. Bob wiped the tears away from his face with the back of his hand and said, "All right, I'll get ya some money."

Lawson now told Bob, "I love ya."

Bob responded "I love you, too," as he hung up the phone.

I reached over and pressed the stop button on the recorder. The red light flashed off.

Bob looked exhausted. I sat there in silence and let him have a few moments to get himself together before I began to gather my equipment.

Finally Bob stood up and began to walk toward the door. As he reached for the handle I asked him to hold on for a moment. Bob stopped. He stood at the door with his back to me.

"Bob, can I ask you a question?"

Without waiting for permission I continued, "What you did tonight, did you do it for the police or did you do it for yourself?"

Bob hung his head down. Still unable to look at me, Bob replied, "I did it for Bethany."

Robert Lawson reached for the doorknob and opened the conference room door. Without another word he walked out.

Chapter 42   Walking In Her Shoes

Spring could not come fast enough. The plan was to have teams of detectives and agents ready to go up to the gravel pit as soon as the snow had melted enough to search. Finding volunteers wasn't a problem. Agent Colton Seale and his FBI teams were ready. Rebecca and the rest of the ATF had pledged their help as well. I had Officer Daily and his crime scene team ready to go. Everything was set. All I needed was the right time. Every day I looked at the weather reports for the area. I even had planes fly over the gravel pit once a week to update me on the snow level.

Given my workload I tried to stay in touch with Bob as best I could. Unlike his brother, whose bail was set so high Lawson could not get out of jail, Bob was still free under our agreement and as long as he stayed out of trouble he would remain on the street. Keeping the brothers separated was still the best thing for the case and it was important for Bob to be away from his brother's control. I didn't want Lawson trying to contact Bob, continuing to affect him, control him. Bob needed to feel free to make his own decisions and to find his own way without his brother.

One morning in late April, Captain Holloway summoned me to his office. Holloway had been giving me plenty of space to work the case and all he wanted in return was the occasional update. He would ask for just enough information to assure the Chief and the Mayor's Office that we were making real progress. I always appreciated his running interference for me, so I didn't mind going up to his office to brief him from time to time. But that morning I could sense when he asked me to shut the door and to sit down I wasn't there for a simple briefing.

"Klink, the Troopers want to go now," Holloway said.

"We can't, sir. My spotter tells me there is still five feet of snow in that gravel pit."

"The Troopers don't want to wait," he said. "They feel we are

327

dragging this on. They want to start searching."

"They can't do that," I argued.

"They can and they will. It's their land, their jurisdiction." Holloway looked at me. I could see he agreed with me but he was clearly getting pressure from above.

"Captain, they are not going into my crime scene." I said. "We will go up there when I say so and not before. This is my case." I could hear my voice getting louder as I spoke. "If I screw it up, I will take the fall for it. If not, I will give the Troopers all the credit, but they are not going to fuck this up just because it looks bad for them. We need to be patient. There is too much riding on this."

I had never talked to a commanding officer that way. I looked at Holloway and waited for him to speak.

"You've got a week," he said. "That's the best I can do."

I got up from the chair and began to leave.

"Klink, you are doing a good job."

"Thanks, Cap."

As I walked back into my unit, I spied Detective Huelskoetter sitting at his desk.

"Mark, can you bring your truck into work next Monday?" I asked.

Mark looked up from his case files.

"Sure, why"

"We're going on a road trip."

The week passed quickly and along with it came blessed sunshine. I left my suit and tie at home and showed up to work in my jeans and a black polo shirt. My plan was to have only the two of us go back up to 'Mile 129' with just enough gear to take a look around, but not so much as to draw attention to ourselves.

While Mark was gassing up the truck and packing gear for the trip, I took a few minutes to pay a visit to M Street.

The sun was coming up as I pulled my car into the driveway. The driveway was all that remained of the duplex where Bethany was killed. Greg Branch Construction had bulldozed the building months before. A large portion of the debris was gone, but pieces of wood, metal and brick lay in small piles around the grounds. As I walked up I could see a large cement foundation that outlined where the duplex once stood.

Upon the concrete floor I began to pace out my steps.

"5, 10, 15, 20," I whispered to myself.

I stopped. This was where Lawson confronted Bethany. This is where he tricked Bethany into believing she would be showing apartments. She met him here, in this old duplex. It was quiet and it was secluded, just as he had planned. I could see Lawson using his verbal charms trying to convince Bethany he was a great guy. He might have even offered her some cocaine, which he had likely been using all night long. She, of course, would have nothing of it and would have refused his advances, perhaps politely at first, but it wouldn't have taken long before she would have told Lawson off. Lawson would not have taken kindly to this. In fact, he would have been infuriated. He wouldn't take that kind of shit from anyone, especially a woman. Bethany would have tried to leave. Lawson would not have allowed that because he took it as yet another rejection from yet another woman.

I stood on the spot where Lawson pulled the 9mm handgun. That must have thrown Bethany but only for a moment. She was raised in Alaska and around guns. There was likely a struggle, perhaps for the gun itself. Lawson pulled the trigger and the gun went off with a loud bang. The bullet hit Bethany in the shoulder before striking the trim on the wall outside of the bedroom.

At that point Bethany must have been stunned, wounded, but not completely out of it. She likely tried to collect herself, mind reeling, maybe looking for an opportunity to grab the gun or make a dash for the back door.

At gunpoint, Lawson forced Bethany into the back bedroom, the one in the farthest corner of the duplex.

I paced my steps off again... 5, 10, 15, stop. I turned around as I stood in what was once the back bedroom. There was nothing here anymore but I closed my eyes so I could see the empty bedroom. Dank, dark colors and a single light bulb made the room a perfect place to take her. No one would hear anything. No one would see anything.

Just as he had done to others before, Lawson ordered Bethany to remove her clothes. At first she hesitated. Lawson's sweet charming voice was all the way gone. He was now revealing his anger, his evil, his true self.

Bethany removed her shoes and her pants. Lawson demanded that Bethany take off the rest of her clothes. I saw it happening this way: gun or no gun, Bethany had to make a stand. The young lady who grew up in a cabin in Talkeetna, the girl who played hockey on the boys' teams and who could do one-arm pull-ups suddenly went on the attack. She surprised Lawson. They fought. Lawson was losing. Bethany was going to get away unless he did something to stop her. Lawson grabbed Bethany by her hair and threw her into the wall as hard as he could. The impact of Bethany's head hitting the sheetrock left a large crater in the middle of the wall. The puka shell necklace around her neck snapped in two sending tiny little white beads into the air. Bethany collapsed, unconscious, in the corner of the room.

Lawson was determined to take what he came for. He pulled the rest of Bethany's clothes from her limp body and unzipped his pants. As he entered her he set the gun on the floor next to him. Bethany began to stir.

"Get the fuck off of me!" Bethany yelled as she again began to struggle. For a moment she saw the gun on the carpet next to Lawson. Stretching out her arm she reached for it.

"Fucking bitch!" Lawson screamed.

He grabbed the handle of the gun and shoved it into Bethany's side. He pressed the trigger and the gun made a loud thud as the bullet and the gasses from the chamber of the barrel exploded into Bethany's side. Bethany's body went limp and fell onto the carpet. Blood began to trickle from the open wound on her side.

"Why the fuck did you make me do that?" Lawson yelled at her motionless body. He lifted himself slowly up off his knees, the gun still in his right hand.

Lawson was sweating profusely. His heart was pounding and he was out of breath. He never expected her to put up such a fight. He stood there in the dimly lit room. He noticed the small brass shell casing on the floor. Hurriedly he picked it up. He walked out of the room and began to look for the other shell casing. Once he found it he walked down the hallway and into the bathroom. He tossed the two shell casings into the toilet bowl and pressed the handle. He watched the brass pieces spin around and disappear into the sewer. Lawson reached into his pocket and pulled out his cell phone. He dialed the number from memory and pressed the send key.

I opened my eyes. The morning sun felt warm against my face. I looked at the empty space around me that was once the duplex. I looked up at the blue sky and again felt the morning sun.

"Bethany, it's time to come home," I said aloud.

I waited. Where the morning air had been still, a slight wind rose up across the empty lot and gathered around me. I felt the breeze rise and begin to move across my face.

As quickly as the breeze came up, it disappeared.

Chapter 43   The Gravel Pit

Mark and I didn't say much on the way up the Parks Highway. I began to imagine Bob and Lawson driving their white SUV along this same road, passing the same spruce trees and turnoffs, the two of them driving in silence, with Bethany's body wrapped in plastic in the back. I could see Bob becoming more and more nervous as they drove north. He would have been looking for places to stop, while Lawson was focused on getting as far north as he could, likely Fairbanks, some six hours away. The farther north they got the more insistent Bob would get that they needed to stop and dump the body.

It took a couple hours for Mark and me to reach the gravel pit. The farther north we traveled, the more the snow had melted. The spring sun over the weekend and the longer days had blessedly sped up the process.

Mark and I remained quiet as he slowed the truck down and signaled the turn into the road of the gravel pit. I leaned forward, looking for anything I recognized. It had been four months since we had been here with Bob. As the truck turned off the road I noticed we were not driving on snow. There was dirt beneath our wheels. As we made a wide turn into the entrance of the gravel pit, a single, small drift of remaining snow blocked access to the road. I don't know which I was happier with, the all-but-melted snow or the fact that what snow remained was pristine.

"No one else has been through here, Mark," I said as we drove over the small snow berm.

As we pulled inside the gravel pit I could see how big it really was. The gravel pit wasn't very deep, but its area appeared much longer and wider than it had looked in the wintertime. It looked like a moonscape. Small pools of snowmelt dotted the uneven, rocky terrain.

We drove along the north end of the pit toward the area Bob had described. I looked for the small break in the trees. As we got farther along the edge of the bumpy road I could see to our left a small turnout, no bigger than the width of a car.

"Hold up, Mark."

Detective Huelskoetter pressed the brakes and the truck slowed to a stop. The turnout was there. The trees had budded and the small leaves created a narrow pathway. What we could not see in the dark depths of winter was now clearly visible in the light of spring.

Mark and I got out of the pickup and met each other at the front of the truck. The path led up a hill and disappeared into the trees. It was narrow, but big enough that Bob and Lawson could have easily backed their vehicle up the rise so that no one would have been able to see them, even from the gravel pit.

"You ready?" Mark asked.

"I've been ready," I said as I stepped forward and onto the path.

I walked slowly, taking in everything. We headed up the rise and the path wandered to the left. As we moved forward and around the bend, I stopped. The path widened into a small clearing. In the middle of the small clearing there was a ring of rocks that were circled together around old burned pieces of wood and melted cans, just as Bob had described months ago.

I walked past the fire pit and followed the path. I had only taken a couple of steps when I looked down. The naturally flat ground along the path was interrupted by a clearly unnatural indent. A square shaped area of earth had been cut into the middle of the path. The hole was only four or five inches deep and a couple of feet wide. One would hardly notice the indent in the ground unless you were looking for it. I bent down and felt the earth along the leading edge of the indent with my hand. The frozen ground chilled my fingers. The edge was clearly created with a tool, likely a shovel of some sort. There was no doubt in my mind that this was where Bob and Lawson tried in vain to dig at the frozen ground, attempting to make a grave for Bethany.

I stood up and looked at Mark. He said nothing. I turned and looked past the discarded grave. Several yards away at the end of the path was a rise in the earth. The other side of the rise was where they put her.

My steps made a soft crunching noise as my shoes pressed against the ground. As I got closer I began to see over the rise. I stopped at the top and looked down.

Where the snow had melted old leaves and twigs covered the forest floor. I scanned the area looking for Bethany. My eyes moved side to side, looking for anything out of place. Suddenly a patch of blue caught my eye. There, near a birch tree, was a flash of blue among the leaves. I slowly stepped over the rise and walked around the outside of the area in order to try to preserve the crime scene. As I got closer I could see the blue item was cloth or material of some sort. I pulled a pair of rubber gloves from the inside of my coat. I called out to Mark, who was still standing on the top of the rise, to run and get some bags and the digital camera. I knelt down next to the item and began to push the leaves away, trying to see what it was. Upon closer inspection I saw it was a blue and black fleece jacket with a zipper on the front. I could tell it was inside out as the tag was on the outside of the garment. I read the label. It said, "Woman's Size: Small."

Mark returned to the top of the rise wearing gloves and carrying the camera. I instructed him to take some photos of the area first and then of the fleece jacket. Once he had taken some photos I reached down and picked up the small, leaf-covered jacket and placed it into an evidence bag.

I handed the bag to Mark and began examining the forest floor again, this time concentrating on the area on the other side of the rise where Bob said they rolled the body.

Why is there no body?

Did Lawson come back and move it?

That's not Lawson. Too much work for a guy like him.

As I carefully pushed snow from around the forest floor, I began to make out a black material. It was still half frozen in the ground. I pushed more snow and leaves away. As I did I began to recognize the material as it took shape. It was a bra. I was about to discard my last handful of debris when I saw them. In amongst the snow, the rotting leaves and sitting in the palm of my hand were several little white puka shells. So I could get a better look, I began to gently pull the debris away from the shells. It was then I began to notice the strands of human hair.

An hour later Mark and I were back at the truck tagging and bagging each of the items we had recovered. Mark photographed each item and placed them in their own individual bags. I carefully secured each of the bags with evidence tape to preserve them and maintain the chain of evidence. In order to insure that a bag was not tampered with I wrote my name, my badge number and the date the item was found on the top of each new piece of tape. With a black permanent marker on the first package I wrote my initials, "GEK." I then scribbled my badge number, "1345." As I began to write the date I realized I had no clue what the date was.

Mark will know.

"Mark, what is the date today?"

"May 3."

I stopped cold. It had been exactly one year to the day since Bethany had disappeared. One year since Lawson had killed her and his brother helped him dump her body here at this gravel pit. I had been looking for Bethany and her killer for exactly one year. I pulled the cap off of the pen and wrote the date, "May 3."

It was then I remembered something else that I had forgotten for so many years. May 3 was also Dawn's birthday.

The fire pit and the path leading up to the rise near the gravel pit on May 3rd. *Photo courtesy of the Anchorage Police Department.*

Chapter 44   Another Death Notice

Even with my office in total disarray, I didn't have to search for them. I knew right where they were. I pulled the brown manila envelope from the shelf behind my desk. I unclasped the back and reached inside. I pulled out Bethany's dental x-rays and held them up to the light. I wasn't sure exactly what it was I was looking for on the x-rays, but I knew that smile. I had been looking at posters of that smile every day for the past twelve months. I slipped the film back into the envelope and grabbed up the white box on my desk as I headed out the door.

It had been less than 48-hours since I had been up to the gravel pit. I had returned to Anchorage specifically for this one chore. It wasn't easy leaving everyone else up at Mile 129. The forensic teams from APD, the FBI and the ATF had all arrived soon after my phone call on May 3.

Over twenty of the best men and women in Alaska law enforcement had volunteered to come up to the site and help. The work was not easy, nor was it glamorous. The remaining snow, mud, dirt and bugs made the tedious work even more difficult.

They combed over the site inch by inch. The search for Bethany's remains had been enlarged to nearly a square mile of forested wilderness. Each square foot of terrain was walked by searchers for hours. I was notified as soon as the skull and jawbone were discovered. They were found approximately 300 yards from where Bob and Lawson dumped the body. A four-legged predator this time, likely a brown bear, had moved the body shortly after it was left at the base of the rise. What the bear didn't consume, other smaller animal predation managed to spread over a wide area of the forest floor.

Everyone put in hours upon hours of tireless work throughout the day and into the night. No one wanted to leave, especially me, but I had to have the proof the bones we were recovering were indeed Bethany's.

Kristin Denning at the crime lab had already informed me the hairs I had found at the site were consistent with the hairs from the brush in Bethany's apartment. Having that information was good, but I needed more before I told the Correiras about Mile 129. That was why I was now on my way to the Office of the Medical Examiner. Soon I would have the final confirmation of what I already knew.

I was confident. So confident in fact I grabbed my cell phone and dialed the number. The phone rang twice before Linda Correira answered.

"Hello?" Linda said.

"Hi, Linda, it's Glen," I said.

"Hi, Glen, how are you?" Linda said in a cheery voice.

"I'm doing okay, but I have a favor to ask of you."

"Sure," she said with a slight hesitation in her voice.

"Please get your family together," I said. "I will be coming up to see you in a few hours."

I found myself speaking in my monotone, official detective voice. I hated that, but it was the only way I could keep my emotions under control.

It was late afternoon when Detective Huelskoetter and I pulled into their Talkeetna driveway. To call the Correira home a log cabin would simply not do it justice. Linda and Billy had built their house by hand from large logs made from Alaskan timber. The large golden logs of the home shone in the late afternoon sun. We parked next to Billy's workshop on the other side of the driveway. As we walked across the road to the house I heard the distinctive blare of a trumpeter swan swimming out on the lake near the edge of the Correiras' yard. The swan seemed to be calling out our arrival as we walked up the steps to the front door of the residence.

Linda Correira greeted us. She wore a red sweater and blue jeans. I tried to smile as she extended her arms. I gave her a great big hug.

She led Mark and me into the house. We walked down the hall and into the open living area. The kitchen was to our left. I could smell the coffee even before I saw the pot sitting on the stove.

"Would either of you like some coffee?" Linda asked.

Both Mark and I said thank you, but we would pass. My stomach was in knots. The entire drive up I had tried to think about what I was going to say and how I was going to say it. Linda ushered us in to the living room. The entire Correira family was there: Billy, Havilah, Jamin, Brian, along with Butch and Sandy. Havilah gave me a hug as I walked in. I shook Billy's hand and I turned to sit down. Everyone was seated facing me. I sat forward in the rocking chair. It creaked as I balanced myself.

"Linda, Billy," I began. "Several months ago I told you the news that Bethany was dead."

I looked up trying to see if there was any reaction from anyone. It was silent and all eyes were on me.

"I told you that information because we had evidence of her death. I also asked you to keep that information private."

I could feel my throat begin to tighten as I continued.

"I promised you from the first day that we met that if I had any news, good or bad, I would tell you in person. That is why I am here."

I directed my gaze and my words towards Linda and Billy, who were seated in front of me and then I said it.

"We have found Bethany's body," I said.

Linda and Billy looked at me. For Linda and Billy this was, in a sense, their second death notification. I did not have anything else to say.

Billy spoke first.

"Thank you, Glen," he said in his soft but strong voice. I could see Billy spoke from his heart.

"Yes, thank you, Glen," Linda said.

The rest of the family began to speak. Their words of thanks spilled over each other's voice, almost in unison.

"I wanted you to know before anyone else did. I believe we owe you all that," I said.

I explained to the Correiras how we'd had solid information about the location of Bethany's body for several months but we were not able to reach the place until the snow melted. I wanted to tell them about Bob Lawson, about what Mike Lawson did to Bethany, about the brothers. But I couldn't. Not yet. Bethany's killer had yet to be charged for her death.

Choosing my words carefully, I explained that dozens of law enforcement officers were working to recover their daughter and that none of us would stop until we were satisfied that we had done everything that we could.

I wasn't sure who finally asked the question, but it came.

"Where did you find her?"

"The recovery site is just north of here at Mile 129," I said, being careful to not use the words "dump site."

"There is a gravel pit along the Parks Highway," I said, "That's where we found her."

The room fell silent. They were all trying to process what I had just said.

Bethany's brother, Jamin, spoke first.

"Why there?"

"I believe that it wasn't planned," I said. "I have reason to believe that the person responsible for her death randomly chose the location."

That was my official answer. That was a fact. In this case however I knew Linda and Billy were close in their spiritual beliefs and there was no denying there was something more here than anything I could fully begin to understand or to appreciate. I decided I needed to speak to my own thoughts in the hope it might comfort them.

"There is another way to look at it," I explained. "I have known for some time Bethany had to be somewhere north of Anchorage. I know the plan by the person or the persons responsible, was to take Bethany's body as far north as Fairbanks. The fact that she was brought north, the fact that they deviated from the original plan and the fact she was brought here, so close to her home, is a sign to me. No matter how you look at it, I believe Bethany came home."

It was now, for the first time since my arrival, that I could see the tears begin to flow. I began biting my own lip in an attempt to stop myself from following the rest of the group.

It was Jamin who again found his own voice and asked, "Can we go see where she is?"

I nodded. The sun was still up and would be for a few more hours. I wasn't planning to take another trip that night up to the gravel pit, but there was no question now that we would be going.

"We will take anyone up there who wants to go," I offered as I pulled out my cell phone to call the crime scene team and let them know of our impending arrival.

As we pulled into the turnout and rode along the dirt road that led into the gravel pit I realized just how big our recovery operation had become. There were now four large recreational vehicles parked near the entrance that led to the campfire and the recovery site. Half a dozen pickup trucks, most of them personal vehicles belonging to various members of the crime scene teams and several campers were all aligned along the corner of the pit. It created a barrier of sorts and allowed the teams to go into and out of the area with some level of protection from prying eyes. As I had asked, there were no police logos or other features visible that might give someone who stumbled upon the pit a clue as to our purpose.

As we pulled closer, I could see members of the search teams stop whatever they were doing. Each of them began to walk forward from wherever they had been working. Other agents and officers began coming down from the path as we approached.

Mark pulled the car up to the edge of the circle of campers and RVs. As we came to a stop more than thirty police officers, special agents and medical examiner personnel began to form a single file line. The row of people began in the middle of the camp and led all the way up the pathway to the recovery site. Each person stood at formal attention, feet together, heads up and arms down at their sides.

Linda, Havilah and Jamin got out first. I motioned for them to go ahead of me. I didn't move. I simply stood there. This moment was not for me. This was about the Correiras. It was about these hard-working men and women. It was about Bethany and what she meant to each of them. I watched as my fellow officers stood in a formal procession, at guard, in their coveralls, their dirty shirts and work boots. Each of them stood in the gravel pit and saluted the family.

I watched as Linda Correira slowly took her time hugging and speaking to each person in line. I could not hear what she was saying but I watched each of the faces of my fellow officers. There were tears on both sides of the line as the family slowly moved up the formation.

When the family reached the end of the procession, Rebecca and Officer Daily escorted Linda, Havilah and Jamin up the path towards the site. I watched as the group disappeared into the forest. I got back into the car, I closed my eyes and I tried to rest until it was time to take them back home.

Bethany's Puka shell Necklace as found by the Crime Scene Team at the forest recovery site at mile 129 of the Parks Highway. *Photo courtesy of the Anchorage Police Department.*

Chapter 45   You Have The Right To Remain Silent

The building itself is a huge, gray cement structure. The fact it has no windows gives a clue as to the purpose of its high out-stretched walls. I had been to the Anchorage Jail many times before in my career, but never to arrest someone already incarcerated within the confines of its walls.

I pulled my police car up to the front gate, rolled down the window and pressed the blue intercom button. It buzzed in a loud audible tone.

"Yes?" the voice on the other end of the speaker said.

"Detective Klinkhart to see a prisoner."

I heard the buzz again. Two large metal doors on the side of the building slowly parted in front of my vehicle. With a loud clunk the doors fully extended, giving me room to drive my car into the prison's garage bay. I pulled forward and into the bay. The doors closed behind me with a loud thud. I got out of the car and was met by one of the jailers.

"Good morning, Detective. How can we help you?"

"I need to see a prisoner," I said. "And we will need a quiet place to talk."

I handed a form to the young officer.

"Can do, sir," he replied. "It will be just a minute."

He took the form and spoke into the microphone on his lapel. I stood in the middle the large command center and waited. Soon I heard from behind me, the familiar buzz of a prison door being unlocked and a metal door opening. A few moments later Mike Lawson walked around the corner, escorted by a jailer. Lawson had only been in jail for a few months but had packed more weight on his already large frame. Wearing bright yellow jail clothes he immediately stopped when he saw me. I could see a moment of confusion on his face.

"Hi, Mike," I said. "How are you?"

"Okay, I guess," he replied.

"They treating you good here?" I asked, faking concern.

"Uh-huh," he said. His hair was greasy and his face unshaven.

"Well, Mike, I've got some bad news for you," I said.

"What's it about?" Lawson asked

"It's about Bethany," I said coldly.

Lawson's face turned white. For a man who always seemed to have something to say, this time he said nothing.

I turned to the young jailer and asked if they had a room for us to talk. He nodded and led Lawson and me out of the area and through a locked door. Four doors were aligned along the walls of the hallway. The jailer opened one of the doors with a key and motioned with his hand for us to enter. I let Lawson go in first and then I followed. The gray colored brick room was empty except for a table and two white plastic chairs. Lawson sat down in one of the chairs and leaned forward. The jailer shut and locked the door behind us as I sat down. I opened up my folder and pulled out several documents I had prepared just for this meeting.

Before Lawson could say anything, I began to read from my Miranda rights form.

"You have the right to remain silent," I read. "Do you understand that right?"

"Yes, sir," Lawson responded.

As I continued to read Lawson each of his rights, he responded with the same, quietly respectful, "yes, sir."

I didn't care whether Lawson waived his rights or not, I just wanted to get to the reason why I was sitting across from Bethany's killer.

"And do you understand each of these rights as I have explained them to you?" I finished.

"Yes, sir."

I put away the Miranda card and got right to the point.

"Mike, this is about Bethany Correira. I am here to inform you that you are being charged with Bethany's murder."

Lawson looked at me. His face was devoid of emotion. He simply replied, "Okay."

"Specifically, let me tell you the charges and then you can respond if you like," I said.

Lawson nodded as I began to read off the list.

"Count one, Murder in the First Degree," I paused to let it sink in.

"Count two, Murder in the Second Degree," I said as I continued. "Count three Kidnapping, count four Conspiracy to Commit Murder in the First Degree."

By now Lawson was leaning so far forward trying to hear everything I said, that I thought he might actually fall out of his chair. I kept going.

"Count five, Arson in the Second Degree; Count six, Misconduct Involving Weapons in the Third Degree and finally Count seven, Tampering with Physical Evidence."

I took the copy of the official charging documents that I had just read from and I turned it around and slid it under Lawson's face

I had been planning this moment for days. I knew if I hit Lawson just right he might say something I could use. I reached over to my right side pocket and felt my digital recorder to make sure it was still in position. My plan now was to simply wait and let the silence speak for me.

Sure enough, Lawson started to talk.

"I wanna tell the whole truth about this," he said.

"Okay, I'd like to hear it," I replied.

Lawson explained to me that he wanted to stay in the federal corrections system. He said it was because the Feds had better doctors, but Lawson and I both knew he would be better treated in the federal system as the killer of Bethany Correira. Alaskan inmates in the State Correctional System would make the rest of his life miserable if he was found guilty under state charges.

"I might be able to make that happen Mike, but I can't make you any promises you understand that?"

Lawson nodded and as he did he began to pretend to cry. It started slowly and then built into an all-out bad acting sob. I sat there and watched. Nothing about it seemed genuine.

"It was just an accident, Glen, god damn it anyways!" Lawson said through his alligator tears.

"It was an accident?" I asked, just to make sure I got it on the recording again.

"It was an accident," Lawson repeated.

"I'm a father, Glen, I don't want to put the Correira family through this," Lawson cried.

Despite years of learning to keep a poker face on when interviewing criminals, I found it very difficult not to jump over the small table and begin beating Lawson for uttering such empty words, for daring to use their name.

Lawson continued to make his case for getting consideration in the federal system rather than dealing with the State of Alaska. The more he pled the more I wanted to end the conversation.

Lawson then made one more attempt to plead for leniency. "And I will tell the whole truth and I will save my brother from having to testify," he said.

"You would do that for Bob?" I asked. Clearly Lawson still had no idea Bob had run the wire against him just a few months ago.

"He's my brother," Lawson said.

That was enough of Mike Lawson for one morning. I gathered up my folder and left Lawson with a copy of his charging documents. He would be arraigned in court that afternoon.

"Okay, Mike, I will see what I can do," I said as I got up.

Lawson stayed seated with the documents rolled up in his hands. I knocked on the metal door. The jailer appeared in the window. The metal latch of the lock clicked as he used his key to let me out.

"Goodbye, Mike."

"Yeah," Lawson responded as the door slammed shut.

Chapter 46　Telling Evan

"Where the hell are you going?" Sarge yelled.

"I've got something I need to take care of," I said as I grabbed my coat.

"Don't forget the press conference!" Sarge screamed as I walked out the door.

The door closed on the words *'press conference'*. How the hell could I forget about the press conference? In a few hours the whole world would know the secret I had known for months. Bethany was dead, murdered. I had charged Mike Lawson with her murder and everyone was going to want to know about it, but right now I had a much more important message to deliver.

As I drove along the highway I knew my fellow officers were still up in the woods trying to find the last remaining pieces of Bethany's body. Bone fragments lay in a white body bag on the forest floor. It looked like a macabre jigsaw puzzle.

Before I left the gravel pit, I told everyone there to do me two favors. First, I asked everyone not to leave until we were all completely sure we had found all of Bethany's body that we could. Secondly, I asked that everyone try to find any of the jewelry Bethany had on her when she disappeared.

The drive to the large, new elementary school downtown was a short one. For the last year I had passed the school almost every day driving between the station and M Street. My search for Bethany didn't leave me time to ever stop by and visit Evan's kindergarten class. In fact, other than that first day of school, I hadn't been there but once all year. The one time I was at the school I ended up making a dozen phone calls trying to follow up leads and missed most of his class Christmas presentation. The thought of missing Evan's entire first year of school hurt. I was at times angry at myself, my job and every so often I found myself feeling angry at Bethany. I had missed so much because of her.

Field trips, projects, crafts and the rest of Evan's school experiences all became stories I had to hear about second hand. I had put a murdered girl before my own son.

I pulled into the school lot and parked my car. I walked past the office and began looking for Evan's classroom. After making a couple wrong turns I found Ms. Paula's room and opened the door. Instead of a class full of loud and energetic five-year olds, the room was empty, except for Ms. Paula, who was standing near the back of the classroom.

"Good Morning, Detective," she said turning around to greet me.

Ms. Paula looked every bit a prim-and-proper kindergarten teacher with her round glasses, gray hair and blue-checkered dress. With her broad smile and energetic personality I could see why Evan loved being in her class.

"I'm looking for Evan," I told her.

"He's out on the playground for recess," she explained.

Ms. Paula looked at me and her smile quickly disappeared. "Is everything all right?" she asked.

"Everything is fine," I told her. "I just need to let Evan know I found Bethany Correira."

Ms. Paula stared at me hoping for some sign of good news. I looked down and shook my head. She directed me to the back door of the classroom that led onto the school courtyard. I opened the door and walked across the yard towards the playground. As I did I scanned the faces of the other children who were running, laughing and playing. I wondered for a moment what Bethany was like when she was five. At that age kids show so much promise and so much innocence. They don't know about the dark side of life. They don't yet know of the real monsters that are out there. It was just then I spotted him. Evan had always been a little shorter than the rest of his peers, but there was no mistaking that bright, blond head of hair and his big smile.

"Hey, Evan!" I called. He turned and quickly ran over to me.

"Hi, Dad. Whatcha doing?" he asked.

I leaned down towards him. "I need to tell you something, Buddy." I paused, cleared my throat and said nervously, "I found Bethany."

I wasn't quite sure what was going to happen next.

Evan turned his head and thought for a moment.

"Where did you find her, Dad?"

"She was in the woods," I replied.

"Where is she?" he asked.

"I took her home to her mom and dad," I told him.

"Was she cold?"

"Not anymore, Buddy."

Evan smiled.

"Good job, Dad. Can I go play?"

"Absolutely partner, but I need a hug first."

Evan reached over and pulled his small arms around me. He squeezed tight and smiled. He turned around and ran back into a sea of kindergartners. Fighting back tears, I stood up and turned around. I didn't want anyone to see me cry. As I turned I looked over and saw Ms. Paula watching me from the classroom window. I waved to her. She forced a smile and waved back. I turned down the sidewalk and headed towards my car.

As I continued down the path, I began hoping all of the media back at the police station were going to be easier to deal with than my own five year old son.

This news was big, really big. Everyone was talking about our finding Bethany and the arrest of Mike Lawson. There were calls from all of the local newspaper and television stations. National news was covering the story, as well. I had prepared a speech for the press conference, however I wasn't allowed to speak. Instead the head of the local FBI, the Alaska State Troopers, the ATF and my police chief each took to the podium to give their side of the story. I stood in the back at attention with my hands clasped behind me. I had never seen so many reporters, camera crews and citizens attending a press conference. The number of people present became so large we had to have it out on the front steps of police headquarters.

The media asked their normal boring and unimportant questions and the police administrators did a fine job of answering them in their own politically correct way. I stayed in my place and waited for it all to be over. Finally the speeches and the questions stopped and I was allowed to take off my tie and get back to my office.

I threw my sport coat and tie on the chair next to my desk. Out of the corner of my eye I spied one of Bethany's missing posters among the various papers on my desk. I must have moved that poster a dozen times or more. I always meant to find a place for it, but never did.

I reached over and picked up the poster. I began to move it over to the edge of my desk. I held it over the trash can. My hand would not open. I still could not let it go.

Crime Scene Teams from the Anchorage Police Department, the ATF, the FBI, the Secret Service and the State of Alaska Medical Examiner's Office at the entrance to the body recovery site. *Photo courtesy of the Anchorage Police Department.*

Evidence markers at the body recovery site near Mile 129 of the Parks Highway. *Photo courtesy of the Anchorage Police Department.*

Chapter 47   I'm Sorry Mike

I was in a rare slumber when the phone rang. I rolled over in bed and looked at the time. The clock displayed 3 A.M. I reached over and grabbed the ringing phone.

"Hello?" I mumbled.

"Detective Klinkhart?"

A half-awake "Yeah" was all I could muster.

"This is Kara in dispatch. I have an Alaska State Trooper on the other line. He says he needs to speak with you."

"Okay, Kara, put him through."

I heard a click and then a background of static.

"Klinkhart," I said into the phone. I rolled over on my back. I knew no matter how insignificant the information the Trooper had for me, I was not going back to sleep.

"Detective Klinkhart, This is Trooper Stanski with AST," he said. From the static and background noise I could tell the Trooper was on a cell phone. "My corporal asked me to call you," he said. "I just came from a residence out in Wasilla and was told to call you and let you know we just found a Robert Lawson dead out here."

I bolted upright.

"What the hell are you talking about?" I asked.

"We were called out to a residence here a couple of hours ago," he explained. "We got a call from Lawson's roommate that he returned to the residence after work and found Robert Lawson dead. Lawson was identified by his roommate and by photo ID."

"How did he kill himself?" I asked. I still did not fully comprehend the information the officer was telling me, but I kept asking questions hoping there would be something at some point that would make sense to me.

"He was found in the garage." Trooper Stanski explained. "Lawson's truck was running inside. Lawson was declared dead at the scene."

"Had the body been there long" I asked.

"A couple of hours."

"Is the death consistent with carbon monoxide poisoning?" I asked.

As I listened I could tell the trooper was clearly well versed in the signs of suicide by CO poisoning. The trooper explained the readings in the garage were 999 parts per million, as high as their instruments could read.

The trooper further described Bob's body, including his positioning, his vomiting and the pinkish color of his skin. Trooper Lewis said he checked for a pulse and found none. The body was warm but there was lividity in the hands, back and legs. Trooper Stanski believed the numerous beer cans and liquor bottles were a strong indication Bob had been drinking prior to his death.

"Is there a suicide note?"

By now I was in my closet. I began pulling out a suit coat and pants. There was no doubt I was going into work today.

"Yes, sir, I will fax it to you once I get back to the Palmer Detachment."

I hung up the phone. I stood in the closet and stared at the floor.

"Fuck," I said out loud. "Fuck, fuck, fuck."

The room of the jail was as cold as it was stark. I had already called Sharon at the DA's office about Bob's suicide. After I told her the news there was a moment of silence before she echoed my sentiment.

"Fuck," she said.

She of all people knew Bob's death was a bad thing for us and a good thing for his brother. Without Bob we couldn't use any of the hours and hours of interviews I had with him. A jury would never hear what he saw that day in May on M Street. Sharon and I talked as best we could about what we could do. Neither of us had any great ideas. Sharon assured me we were going to go forward with our case against Lawson. She tried to make me feel better. It didn't help.

How could he have done this?

When I finally got to the police station an hour later, Bob's suicide note was in the fax machine. It was addressed to me.

"Glen, I will not testify against my brother," Bob wrote. He said he loved Mike and felt great remorse over what he did to help his brother. Bob asked someone to feed his cats for him. The handwriting on the note was difficult to read as Bob clearly wrote it hastily and with a lot of alcohol behind his words.

To My Family,

I am so sorry. I miss my brother so much. Life has become unbearable. I can't endure the pain any longer. It hurts so terribly bad. I helped do one of the most terrible things imaginable and I can't live with that. Please take the money in my wallet and my final wages and give it to Mike.

I could not read any more. I set the note down and I went out into the cold night. I got into my car and drove downtown.

When I heard the electronic buzzer, I looked up. The heavy metal door opened and in walked Mike Lawson. He glared at me.

"I'm not talking to that motherfucker," Lawson said to the jailer behind him.

"Lawson, sit your ass down and listen to what he has to tell you," the jailer barked back at Lawson. Lawson hesitated and then defiantly walked over to the table and sat down in the plastic chair across from me. I had come to do the right thing, maybe not for Lawson, but for Bob.

"Don't say anything, Mike," I began.

Lawson tried to stare me down. I felt nothing for him but a mutual sense of contempt.

"Mike, your brother committed suicide," I said very calmly and officially. "He is dead."

Lawson just stared at me. His look of contempt changed to a simple blank stare.

I'm not sure why but for some reason I added, "I'm sorry, Mike."

Lawson just stared at me blankly. I stood up and motioned to the jailer. He pressed the button and opened the door. Without looking back, I closed the steel door behind me leaving Lawson in the jail interview room all by himself.

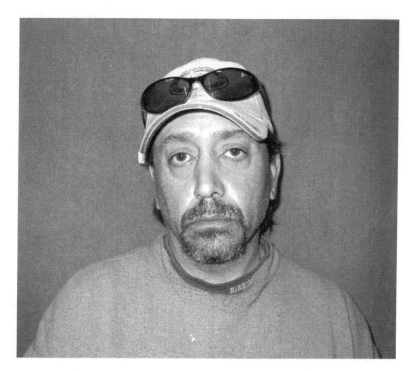

Robert "Bob" Lawson *Photo courtesy of the Anchorage Police Department.*

Chapter 48   A Parole Hearing

"This hearing is now in session," were the first words I could understand coming out of the conference room loud speaker. The room wasn't very large. There was only enough space for a table and a couple of chairs. My mom and dad sat next to each other, holding hands. I had my binder, the letter I had carefully written and a pad of paper for taking notes. I didn't want to miss anything.

It had been over a year since I had told Lawson of Bob's death. His murder trial was scheduled but was still months away. I was just getting back into the swing of things at work when I received word of this pending hearing. I was forced to deal with this before I could concentrate on Mike Lawson again.

The voice on the speakerphone said, "Members of the Parole Board, today we are here to review the application of parole for Alan Chase Jr."

I jotted down the date and time. We weren't able to be physically present at the hearing for Dawn's killer. He was now incarcerated in Arizona and the flight down was too expensive, so we listened in over long distance. Several months ago I had been sent a letter saying he was due for his first parole hearing. I could not believe after only twenty five years Alan Chase Jr. was being allowed to try to convince the parole board he should be released.

As soon as the letter arrived I knew I needed to do anything I could to keep him in prison. I went to my parents with the letter. When I spoke with my mother and father they surprised me by saying they were thinking about supporting the release of the man who had killed their daughter. Part of me was angry at the thought, but I listened as my mother explained they wanted to know what Alan Chase had done with his life since being in jail. She said they had hoped and she had prayed he was able to do something, anything, positive while incarcerated. If that was the case, then my parents said they were both prepared to support his release. I was not so forgiving. I pulled some strings and learned Chase had not been a model prisoner. He had been in several fights and had multiple other violations. He had done nothing to better himself. I was particularly pissed off that he had only begun to take some classes a few months before his parole hearing. I explained to my parents his behavior was not one of a person who was truly remorseful. I was sure he was doing whatever he could to manipulate the system to his own advantage.

When I informed my parents of the results of my investigation, they reluctantly agreed to not support his release. I volunteered to write a letter to the parole board on behalf of our family:

To the Parole Board,

In the past 25 years of incarceration Alan Chase Jr. has ignored the Judge's original order for him to use his time in prison to fix his problems and to give himself a chance to be released. Alan Chase's own prison record clearly shows he did nothing to repair what every mental health expert said were serious psychological problems. It was only last year, as he neared his eligibility for parole, that he began taking menial courses to increase his parole chances. Instead of doing what was expected of him Chase's prison record clearly shows he has continued his anti-social behavior.

Chase's own written request for parole lacks any substantial reasoning for his release and he fails to acknowledge the full extent of his crimes against my sister and my family. After 25 years he still hides behind his story of "blacking out" when it comes to what he did to Dawn. The fact that years later he still cannot admit what he did was his fault, tells me he is still a danger to others. When he was sentenced, the Judge gave him something Chase never gave my sister, a chance. Alan Chase wasted the life of Dawn. Alan Chase has wasted the last 25 years of his incarceration and in so doing, it is my firm belief Alan Chase has wasted his chance ever to be paroled back into society again.

Sincerely, Glen Klinkhart

The head of the parole board had clearly read my letter. Each of the three board members asked Chase to defend his application for parole. I listened to the words on other end of the phone. Chase's voice was not that of a teenager anymore, but that of a middle-aged man. He was clearly taken by surprise by the parole board's insistence that he answer many of the questions I brought up in my letter. Chase was curt and defensive with the board's questioning. It was obvious he expected them to believe he had changed and deserved to be let out. Things were not going his way and the more apparent that became to him, the angrier his voice became. Chase shouted at one of the parole board members who wanted to know why he had only begun taking classes recently. Chase did not want to answer the question. The board insisted that he answer the question. In frustration Chase told the board to "go to hell."

The head of the board responded, "Mr. Chase, the board will find you are not going to receive consideration for parole. In fact, not only are you not going to be paroled, you are not to return to the Parole Board for at least eight more years."

There was no answer from the inmate. The board shuffled their paperwork and was preparing to move to the next applicant when Chase spoke up.

"Fine," Chase said. "If you let me out, I'd probably do it again."

I reached over the table to the speakerphone sitting between myself and my parents. I pressed the disconnect button and the telephone line fell silent.

Chapter 49   The Trial Begins

The trial of Michael Lawson for the murder of Bethany Correira began on a sunny Monday morning. I stood on the third floor of the Nesbitt Courthouse waiting for Sharon and the Correiras to show up. Havilah was back from another humanitarian trip in Africa and I was expecting to see her for the first time in over a year. It had been a long year of waiting for all of us. Lawson had tried to make good on his vow to string out his case for 20 years, but Sharon was finally able to stop him. Eventually Lawson had only two choices. Plead guilty to murder or go to trial. He chose to go to trial.

I watched the elevator doors open and close. National TV news crews from ABC and NBC arrived along with camera crews from all three Anchorage television stations and newspaper reporters from all over the state.

The doors of the elevator opened once again. I looked up and saw Sharon pulling a handcart full of white cardboard boxes. Each box was filled with a year's worth of Bethany's case files. Linda and Billy Correira exited the elevator behind her. They were casually dressed. Linda held in her hand two white flowers. They looked like orchids. Billy had a backpack slung over his shoulder. It was a gray North Face pack. I recognized the backpack and the multitude of patches sewn on the outside of it. Havilah walked off the elevator behind her parents. There was no mistaking Havilah. She and Bethany shared some of the same features, including a thin but muscular frame. Havilah looked taller than when I last saw her. Her hair was longer. I walked over to the Correiras. Linda smiled and gave me a hug. Billy shook my hand and I stepped over to Havilah. Havilah smiled and gave me a hug.

"Welcome back," I said.

"I'm happy to be here," she said.

"Hav, can I talk to you a minute, in private?" I asked.

Havilah turned her head inquisitively and said, "Sure."

I excused us from the rest of the group and led Havilah down the other end of the hallway away from the media. I sat down on a bench and motioned for her to sit down next to me. I reached into my briefcase and pulled out the package. It was about the size of a book and it was wrapped in a purple paper. I didn't have time to find a bow or any ribbon, but I didn't think Havilah would mind. I held the gift in my hands.

"Havilah," I said, "I owe you an apology."

Havilah looked at me and smiled.

"When you and your parents came to the police station and I told you Bethany was dead, it was very hard on you."

Havilah looked down, as if she were embarrassed.

"I can't stop thinking about how much I hurt you that night. How much I hurt you and your family and I want to say I am truly sorry."

I handed her the small package. She took it and she placed it in her lap. Her hands rested on top of the gift.

Havilah paused and then said, "Glen you don't need to apologize."

She looked up at me and said, "I need to thank you."

"I didn't want to believe Bethany was gone. I never wanted to believe it," she said. "When you told me Beth was dead, it was the truth. I knew it was truth because of you, Glen. If anyone else had told me Beth was dead I would have never, ever believed them. But it was you who told me and so I knew it was the truth and that it was real. You wouldn't have told me unless it was true and I am thankful to you for that."

I brushed the tears away from my face and said, "That means a lot to me Havilah. Thank you... now open up your damn gift."

She smiled and pulled at the purple paper. As she did it revealed a frame, a black picture frame. She turned the frame over to reveal the photograph I had placed in it the night before. It was from my very first night on M Street when I seized Bethany's camera from her apartment. I had poured over the dozens of photographs Bethany had taken during the last few months of her life. There wasn't much I could use for my investigation, but there was one picture in particular that caught my eye. It was that image I now gave to Havilah.

"Do you remember that photo?" I asked her.

"It was at the airport as I was getting on the plane to Africa," she said. Havilah gently touched the glass in the frame, moving her hand over the two faces looking back at her. Two sisters, each holding the other close, smiling at the camera and saying goodbye.

"This was the last time I ever saw her," Havilah said. "Thank you, Glen." She gave me a hug.

We stood and walked back towards the crowd that had gathered in front of the courtroom.

"It's show time," I said.

Havilah (left) and Bethany (right) Correira in their last photo taken together. *Photo courtesy of the Correira Family.*

Chapter 50   Bethany And Me

It didn't take long for Judge Suddock's courtroom to fill up. Every seat was taken and the aisles were all occupied by the media. I was glad to have my own seat at the prosecution table next to Sharon.

Mike Lawson entered the courtroom, still in handcuffs. Lawson was always a large man, but clearly he had been eating a lot while in prison and awaiting trial. He had put on weight and was close to 300 pounds. His face was rounder and he filled out the gray suit his new attorney, Mike Moberly, had gotten him. Lawson was un-handcuffed by the officers and he plopped down at the defense table next to his attorney.

Judge Suddock entered. Everyone stood. Judge Suddock's white beard stood out in contrast against his black robes.

Sharon rose to begin her opening statement. She pushed her glasses up and seated them firmly on her face. Sharon wore a gray suit and walked with a purpose as she approached the microphone situated in front of the jury.

She had been practicing her opening statement for days and I was excited to hear it. In all of the years Sharon and I had worked together, I had never seen her so nervous. The microphone made a low rumbling noise as she lowered it closer to her short frame. She cleared her throat and began to speak.

"Ladies and Gentleman of the Jury, this case is about a girl named Bethany Correira," she said, as she held up a photograph of Bethany.

"Bethany was a 21-year old girl who moved to Anchorage from Talkeetna to go to college. She moved into an apartment down off of M Street in Bootleggers Cove."

Sharon moved away from the podium and the microphone. She raised her voice so the jury could still hear her.

"Bethany Correira got exactly four days in that apartment," she said as she walked over to the defense table.

Sharon raised her hand and pointed right at Lawson and continued, "Because on May 3rd, Michael Lawson, the manager of these apartments, murdered Bethany Correira."

She explained to the jury some of the evidence we were going to present and all of the charges leveled at Lawson.

After Sharon was done she walked over to the table and sat down. I leaned over and whispered, "Good job." Sharon simply nodded.

Mike Moberly walked over to the podium. His suit was pressed and his beard neatly trimmed. Moberly paused and said he was going to make a short statement to the jury. Moberly adjusted the microphone and looked at the twelve men and women before him.

"Ladies and Gentlemen of the Jury," he said. "This case is just what my client told the police that it was, an accident. We believe that this case is not a case about murder, it is about an accident. We believe that the evidence presented to you will bear that out."

Moberly did not need to say much more. He didn't have to. He was planting his defense theory with the jury. Moberly thanked them for their time and he returned to his place next to his client.

The judge decided to take a break. Everyone in the courtroom rose as a sign of respect for the jury. The jury filed out of the courtroom as we waited patiently for them to exit. We then waited for the judge himself to leave. The rest of the courtroom slowly filed out and into the hallway.

I waited until everyone had left the court before walking out to stretch my legs. The sun had gone behind the clouds. I saw Linda and Billy at the end of the hallway, standing away from the crowd. They were trying to avoid contact with the media.

As I approached, Linda smiled and Billy extended his hand.

"So what did you think?" I asked.

"I thought Sharon did a great job," Linda praised.

Billy, in his usual quiet manner, nodded his head in approval. I told them that at least we knew where Lawson and his attorney were going with their defense.

"You do know it wasn't an accident? Right?" I asked.

Linda tried to assure me as she touched my shoulder, "We know that."

Nervously I wanted to change the subject. I noticed the backpack on Billy's shoulder.

"Is that Bethany's backpack from her apartment?" I asked.

Billy suddenly became animated, more animated then I had seen him in a long time. He smiled and said, "Yes it is. Bethany traveled everywhere with it. It was her favorite pack."

He stopped and looked at his wife for a moment. They shared a look and she nodded. I could tell there was more to the story.

Billy looked around before asking, "Do you want to know a secret?" he asked with a devilish grin on his face.

"Bethany was always a character and she would have appreciated all of this," he said, "so we thought it would be perfect if she came to court with us."

Billy grinned. I was shocked to think Bethany's ashes were actually in the backpack on Billy's shoulder. The shock quickly disappeared and was replaced with a sense that having Bethany's remains in the courtroom was nothing short of wonderful. Inappropriate, but wonderful.

"Nobody can know about this," I said and then added, "including Sharon."

They both smiled and nodded okay.

"I love that she is here with us," I said and then added, "Can she sit up front with me?"

"Absolutely," Billy said as he removed the backpack and handed it to me. I took the fabric backpack and set it gently and respectfully on my shoulder. It didn't feel heavy at all.

People began to file back into the courtroom. Linda and Billy walked in front of me as Bethany and I took our seats at the prosecution table next to Sharon.

My big moment came two weeks into the trial. We had already put on lots of witnesses, including Bethany's boyfriend, Ray and the newspaper carrier who reported the fire the day after Bethany's disappearance. ATF Special Agent Lance Hart testified about his investigation of the fire at the M Street duplex and his finding that it was arson. What he wasn't allowed to tell the jury was that Bob admitted to starting the fire for his brother and that Lawson never told Bob he went back and restarted the fire.

Nothing that Bob told me or other investigators was allowed into evidence. But his recorded phone conversation with his brother was. My job on the witness stand was to simply play the wire between Bob and Mike Lawson. I set up my computer and the audio track recorded from the night Lawson called us.

When the jury was again seated and it was my turn to testify, I patted Bethany and the backpack sitting in the chair next to me. I took my place in the witness stand and waited. Lawson and his attorney were seated at the defense table. Lawson looked nervous. Even from across the room I could see he was scribbling nonsense with a pen on his yellow notepad. I waited for Sharon to begin.

Sharon started by asking me about how the audiotape that I had for the jury came into being. I described the process of how Lawson's brother, Robert, agreed to take a call from the jail and how I went about prepping Bob to ask questions to try to get Lawson to talk about Bethany. Sharon then asked me to play the audio recording for the jury.

The lights of the courtroom dimmed. The projection screen to my left was brought down and I pressed a key on my laptop. Everyone was quiet as the audio presentation began. All of the jurors turned in their seats to watch. Subtitles appeared on the screen as the audio played throughout the courtroom.

I had heard this thirty two minute conversation hundreds of times before. I could almost repeat it word for word. I had heard it in my sleep. I didn't need to listen to it again. I was watching the jury as Bob and Lawson's voices echoed throughout the courtroom.

While I listened I reached into my front pocket. I could feel the worn necklace and the cross in between my fingers. Dawn's cross necklace, the one I'd found in my sister's burned-out bedroom so many years ago, felt smooth as it warmed with my touch. I'd recently come across it amongst some boxes of old things. I thought it might be nice to have with me, so I kept it in my pocket every day during the trial.

I sat quietly as the jury heard Lawson speak to his brother about Bethany and how he described putting her in the kitty litter. They heard how Lawson said he was taking the secret of murdering Bethany to his grave. As those words echoed in the courtroom I glanced over at Mike Lawson. He was clearly trying to get the jury members to look at him. Lawson was trying to force some sort of emotion at hearing his dead brother's voice again. He began to wipe nonexistent tears from his face with a tissue. I watched as he was becoming more and more frustrated that none of the jurors was watching him or his emotional act. After a few minutes he realized I was staring at him. Lawson glared back at me with disgust and threw his wasted tissue paper on the table in front of him.

I sat quietly for the rest of the audio wire. When the sound ended the lights in the courtroom came up. No one spoke. Finally Judge Suddock called for a break. I rose along with the rest of the gallery and waited for the jury to leave. The door closed behind them with a soft click. Mike Lawson was still trying to stare me down as I left from the witness stand. I glared right back at him. I kept my eyes locked on his round ugly mug until he finally broke eye contact and looked down at the table in front of him. I was done.

Michael "Mike" Lawson at Anchorage Police Department
Headquarters. *Photo courtesy of the Anchorage Police Department.*

Chapter 51   Goodbyes

All of us were there. Linda, Billy, Havilah, Butch, Sandy, Rebecca Bobich, Detective Huelskoetter, Sharon and I all met at the Snow City Café a few blocks from the courthouse. We had been together for over four years. Each of us was connected in so many ways and on so many levels and yet this was the first time all of us had sat down in one place. We were there to celebrate not just the guilty verdict but the 99 year prison sentence that Judge Suddock had imposed on Mike Lawson.

At the table there was no talk about the trial or even the sentencing. It was more like a family gathering, a Thanksgiving. Everyone was sharing what their kids were doing, what their plans for the rest of the summer were and who was going where. There were laughs and smiles all around.

As the meal was nearing its end, I reached into my bag and pulled out a small wooden box. I had built the box myself from wood I found in my garage. I lifted the box up and over the table. I handed it to Linda Correira.

"What is this?" she asked.

"This belonged to Bethany," I said, "and now it belongs to you."

Linda held the box in front of her. Billy snuggled closer to her in order to get a good look. She slowly opened up the top of the box. Inside there were several smaller velvet containers. Linda pulled out the first box and looked at it. She opened it up. Inside were several bright and shiny silver rings. Linda looked at me with disbelief.

"Bethany's toe rings," I said.

One after the other she opened up each of the remaining boxes. Every box contained a different piece of jewelry we had recovered from the gravel pit. Like Bethany, her jewelry had been scattered in the woods. Bethany's golden MC ring was there as was her watch. Through days of searching and painstakingly hard work a small miracle had occurred. All of her jewelry was recovered. Even the tiny toe rings that Bethany wore on her foot were discovered by the searchers looking for her remains.

I had personally taken all the jewelry, still in evidence bags, to my friend and jeweler, Josh Jennett. Josh stayed up all night to clean and delicately repair each of Bethany's personal belongings. He even managed to get her watch, which had been exposed to the six feet of snow and a year out in the elements, to work again. He put each of the items in its own special box. Josh called me the next day to tell me they were ready. No matter how hard I tried, he refused to let me pay him for his time. He just smiled and said it was the least he could do.

Linda Correira wiped her eyes and looked at me from across the table.

"Thank you, Glen," she said.

"You're welcome," I said, "It was a team effort."

No one seemed eager to leave but eventually it became clear we all had to go. We grabbed our coats and headed for the door. Everyone hugged and said their goodbyes. Linda told me she loved me. I said I loved her too. I held the door for Sharon. As we got back onto the street, Sharon turned and hugged me. I held her hug for just a few moments longer than usual.

"Is everything okay?" she asked.

"I'm good," I said as I let go of my friend. As everyone else walked down the street, I turned around and began walking in the other direction. I heard Sharon's voice from behind me.

"Where are you going?" she asked.

"I'm going for a walk," was all I said.

I walked down L Street and turned right onto 4th Avenue. The sun was still up and I could see the ocean water along the coastal trail as I walked down the hill. I had spent my entire life in this town and yet never spent any time in Bootleggers Cove until Bethany. I walked down the alley and turned onto M Street. Soon I was standing in front of what was left of Bethany's apartment. The gray two story apartment building was boarded up. Several pallets of cement blocks were stacked near the old driveway entrance indicating that a new townhouse development would soon sit on the spot where Bethany was killed.

I walked up the broken driveway and stood in the middle of the empty piles of dirt. Across the inlet the sun was beginning to go down behind Mount Susitna making the sky turn a golden hue.

Standing there alone, I looked up at the sky once more.

"Bethany," I said out loud, "Are you there?"

I waited. The air was still. I was standing in the middle of a neighborhood of people and yet I heard nothing. There was no wind. No breeze. There was nothing.

"Dawn, are you there?" I asked.

I could hear only my own words in my ears. I waited. I waited some more. There was nothing. Nothing at all. I don't know how long I stood there in the silence before I stopped looking up at the sky. I smiled briefly as I turned down the driveway and walked away from M Street one last time.

Epilogue   What Is Love?

What Is Love? by Bethany Correira

It is difficult to have a single definition of love that fits all of its varying feelings. A typical dictionary definition might try and define love as "a deep and tender feeling of affection for or attachment to a person or persons."

For me, Love is too big for words in a dictionary and too varied for science to measure and test. I feel that love can often be a contradiction; a state of being that simultaneously evokes exhilaration, despair and joy. What is it about love that produces such an extreme and varied reaction? Shakespeare said, "Love is a spirit all compact of fire." Some have died for love.

The feeling of love is irreplaceable and untouchable. There is no other feeling or emotion that can compare to it. Love can touch a person's life forever and leave an impression never to be forgotten.

Discovered on a camera in her apartment, is the last photograph taken of Bethany Correira. *Photo courtesy of the Correira Family.*

Made in the USA
San Bernardino, CA
11 March 2015